Seven Movements
One Song

For Minette —
Tell your story;
Sing your song!

Carolyn North
Berkeley
May, 1992

Seven Movements
One Song

Memoir As Metaphor

by
Carolyn North

North Star Editions, Regent Press
Berkeley, California

Cover photograph of author by Martha Cook
Cover design by Carolyn North and Sara Glaser
Book design by Carolyn North and Georgianna Greenwood
Lotus design by Georgianna Greenwood
Word Processing assistance - Herb Strauss, Laurie Silverman, Jan Thomas, Jack Tessman
Proofreading - Naomi Rose, Jeanne Pimentel, Duncan Campbell
All errors are the author's
ISBN# 0-916147-17-7

North Star Editions : Regent Press, Printers, 1991

This book is printed on recycled paper.

*This book is dedicated
to everyone,
living and dead,
who appears in it.*

*Especially, it is for Herb,
companion of thirty years
and MORE.*

"For what is a human being
but the root and flower,
the image and substance
of the universe itself?"

Frank Waters **Masked Gods**

CONTENTS

Preface 11
Introduction 13

1. AIR UPON THE GROUND
Root Chakra - *Adrenal Glands*
21

2. DUO D'AMORE
Sacral Chakra - *Gonads*
43

3. KINDERLIED
Solar Plexus Chakra - *Pancreas*
87

4. HARMONIC CLUSTERS
Heart Chakra - *Thymus Gland*
133

5. GOSPEL SONG
Throat Chakra - *Thyroid Gland*
195

6. MEDITATION AND VARIATIONS
Brow Chakra - *Pituitary Gland*
235

7. FINALE
Crown Chakra - *Pineal Gland*
307

PREFACE

This book began in 1984 as a research project with Jill Kuykendall, who was my Anatomy teacher at the time.

We were interested in the correspondences between the endocrine glands and the Chakra system - an ancient Vedic system of energy centers which sits at approximately the same levels as the glands in the body. Jill delved into the scientific literature while I read esoteric texts, and we met weekly in my studio to create an experiential method of using our own bodies in motion to glean subjective information on the glands and their energy centers.

For three years we worked this way, amassing notebooks of data before starting to organize the material into a scholarly book on the subject. But the movement work seemed to nudge us in the direction of multi-dimensional awareness rather than objective scholarship. Dancing, we evoked dreamlike images, bodily sensations and synesthetic perceptions of the subject and our information came in the form of pictures, of stories.

Gradually we realized that our book would have to reflect this intuitive perception of things, for it was there, where all the dimensions of the continuum spread out like an interconnected web of events, that our subject really lay.

And so SEVEN MOVEMENTS, ONE SONG was born. The stories are my stories but the research we did together is embodied in every plot line, symbol, image and sentence of the book. What we learned is hidden in the weave of the stories.

Don't look for the details, however. We urge you to be intuitively receptive to the quality of energy implicit in each Endocrine-Chakra pair, rather than to search out the information. If this book has succeeded in its purpose, these stories will be like resonators which strike chords in the appropriate parts of your body, your heart and your memory.

May the reminiscences warm your hearts!

During the years our research was in progress, Jill and I talked to scientists, healers, and esotericists who gave generously of their time and knowledge on subjects ranging from the structure of DNA to the physiological effects of meditation on the body. We thank them all - and mention none, for fear of forgetting one.

Many friends, including my husband and children, have read the manuscript in all its stages, offering invaluable insights and gut reactions. Some have read it twice, many have laughed and cried, and most have insisted upon deeper and deeper levels of honesty from me. I have heard you all; look and see where I've followed your advice.

More friends, now, are assisting in the production of the book, offering their artistry and skill for its manifestation. Thank you, thank you, thank you.

So this book is not just mine, it comes from a community of friends and family. To this gifted company I bow with admiration and gratitude.

Carolyn North
Berkeley, California
March 9, 1991

INTRODUCTION

In SEVEN MOVEMENTS, ONE SONG, the seven fundamental forces of the Universe are explored metaphorically through seven stories from the life of a woman of our time.

According to the sacred texts of many of the world's ancient traditions, the Universe is composed of seven streams of fundamental force which emanate from the Source of All Things, the 'Godhead.' As these seven streams combine and recombine with each other through time and space, evolving from matter into form; plants; animals and finally human beings, they ultimately become the created world as we know it. The One has differentiated into the Many, and the Many has blossomed gorgeously into the Ten Thousand Things. It is in this world that we have our life and being.

Like the seven colors of a rainbow, each of these streams of force has a different quality, a different mood or color. The differences are subtle, but definite. The quality of 'red' is not the same as the quality of 'yellow'; blue and green evoke quite distinctive moods. However, we recognize red, yellow, blue and green as colors.

The seven discreet forces together compose a spectrum; out of the context of the whole none would exist. Their qualities, in brief, are:

1. The will to be embodied in physical form;
2. The force of mutual attraction;
3. The propensity to shift and change;
4. The urge to bond into groupings;
5. The need to connect and communicate;
6. The urge to perceive and understand;
7. The yearning for re-union with the Source.

As these forces - called *Powers of the World* by the Sioux people - are subtle in nature, they do not lend themselves easily to either observation or description. Even though they are the basis for all existence, they are not clearly extractable from the busy weave of life in the world. Language, which primarily describes the visible world, falls short.

"In the archaic universe," explains the philosopher Giorgio de Santillana in his book *Hamlet's Mill*, "all things were signs and signatures of each other... to be divined subtly. This was the philosophy of the Pythagoreans and presides over all classical language, but not," he adds, "over contemporary language."

However, even in the archaic world the language used to describe the subtle, nonmaterial aspects of existence was the language of story, of myth. Through stories the truth could be pointed toward, felt, understood intuitively. Stories were not meant to impart literal truth, but rather to provide a direction in which to listen and perceive the truth.

Myths, according to Joseph Campbell, are stories which are transparent to something deeper, something universal. They are reflections of the ultimate design of the universe; clothed in metaphor, a story makes the truth of the world accessible to human understanding.

Every ancient culture in the world has its body of stories in which gods, animals and people, in their interactions, reflect the deeper truths of existence. And interestingly enough, in most of these traditions, the universe is seen as seven-fold in nature.

"The principles of Truth are Seven," begins a Hermetic dictum so ancient its origins are lost in the mists of time. "Those who understand this possess the magic Key before whose touch all the doors of the Temple fly open."

Metaphors and symbols for the seven streams of fundamental force abound in the ethnographic literature.

Mount Meru, in Hindu and Buddhist cosmography, is surrounded by seven oceans, each separated by seven intervening circles of golden mountains; a ladder of seven steps is climbed by initiates of the Mithraic mysteries; the shamans of Siberia have seven notches in their 'axis mundi' and Toltec initiates pass through a seven-chambered cavern. Mesopotamian pyramids are seven-storied; the city of Nineveh was surrounded by seven walls and in Revelations, at the end of the New Testament, we hear of seven stars, seven churches, seven lamps, seven angels... The list is endless.

While this notion of a seven-fold universe is not current in our culture, echoes of it still persist: our week has seven days, there are seven colors in the spectrum, seven notes in the musical scale, seven is considered a lucky number, and when we are happy we say we are in seventh heaven.

Amongst traditional Hindus, the seven basic forces are said to enter the body via a system of energy vortices at the level of each of the major nerve plexii. Joseph Campbell, in *The Inner Reaches of Outer Space*, refers to these seven areas as

"...bioenergetic stations ranged in ascending order along an invisible spinal nerve or channel..."

These wheels of energy, called Chakras, were perceived by the Hindus as swirling lotuses through which the seven streams of universal force were funnelled into the body to be assimilated into the physical, three-dimensional world. Indeed, according to them, without the transformative function of these seven bioenergetic stations, the human body of flesh, bone and blood would not exist.

The first, and slowest in vibration, entered the body in the area of the base of the spine - the Root Chakra - and carried the quality of physical embodiment, the will to be alive in a body.

The second, of a somewhat faster vibration, entered at the sacral level - the Sacral Chakra - and carried with it the force of attraction.

The third, still faster, came in at the solar plexus level - the Solar Plexus Chakra - and was the force of transformation and change.

The fourth, faster yet, was at the level of the heart - the Heart Chakra - and brought the bonding energy, the urge to cluster in groups.

The fifth, still faster, came in at the throat level - the Throat Chakra - and carried the connecting, communicative energy.

The sixth, whirling quite fast, brought the force that impelled understanding and perception to the brow region - the Brow Chakra.

And the seventh, vibrating fast as light, entered at the crown of the head - the Crown Chakra - and resonated with ultimate, transcendent reality.

Thus the human being - body, mind and spirit - was seen by the Hindus to reflect the natural order of the Universe and to recapitulate its evolution from the material and mental planes through to the spiritual. And every human life was a process of growing in awareness as one whirling center of energy after another, through the ordinary experiences of human existence, opened to its full potential.

In SEVEN MOVEMENTS, ONE SONG, each story reflects the quality of energy of one of the seven basic forces, starting with the issue of physical embodiment (survival, anchoring to the earth) and progressing, following the Hindu order from the base of the spine to the crown of the head, to the awakening to a transcendent, spiritual reality.

Taken together in the order of the Chakras, these seven stories can be read as a contemporary, seven-part myth outlining the stages of the evolution of consciousness.

Everyone has such stories. The issues of survival, attraction, transformation, and so forth are universal. The very structure of the universe is implicit in human existence.

Is there anyone who has not, at one time or another, been in mortal danger; fallen passionately in love; asserted personal power; been part of a family; expressed a deep conviction and been heard; thirsted to understand what was going on; gotten a glimpse of a larger reality? These are the ultimate forces at play in our lives and they belong to all of us, all of the time.

In the normal course of things these forces mix and mingle and may not be readily apparent to us, but there are inevitably periods in each of our lives when one issue or another stands out memorably, as if it were spotlighted. We have come close to death; we have fallen madly in love... These times tend to be fraught with struggle or deep emotion and their resolutions are like epiphanies. Something opens up and we see in a way we have not seen before. A new stage of consciousness has been reached and we are ready, willy-nilly, to take the next step in the evolution of our personal consciousness.

Using seven such 'epiphanies' from my own life as metaphors for the seven fundamental streams of energy, I have taken the liberty of fictionalizing at will and calling myself by another name to suggest that stories like these belong to everyone.

All of us hold within us the ultimate design of the Universe and your stories, like mine, reflect it perfectly.

1

AIR UPON THE GROUND
Root Chakra - Adrenal glands

The will to be embodied in physical form;
the survival instinct;
anchoring to the earth;
identification with the natural world.

A shrill yelp of pain roused me from a dream:

I have discovered another room in my house. It's right off the kitchen - how could I have missed it? A room for dancing; long, with a polished floor and a roof open to the sky. Yellow light pours in and the floor is smooth to my feet. I twirl round and round and the air swirls like wind around me, flowing in eddies about my arms, my legs, my face...

The yelps persisted, more urgent now. Reluctantly, I let the dream go, the dance giving way to the massed stars of the Southern Hemisphere sky and the muted shushes of surf against the shore. My cove was briny with guano and seaweed. Sealions snuffled and sneezed in their sleep and a pup bleated for food, mewling until its mother rolled over to give it her teat.

I rolled over too, jabbing my hip as I reached for my flashlight. A shooting star flared across the sky, sped and burned out in the night. The air was pungent with wet sand and sealion shit; the sea, in the darkness, was indistinguishable from sky. Yawning, I rubbed my eyes - awake now.

Another pained howl from the other side of the cove ended in a bubbly whimper. Pushing my sleeping bag down I slid out, jammed my feet into sneakers and followed my flashlight beam through the sleeping sealions to the source of the racket - a female in labor.

She lay high on the beach, out of reach of the tides. Shielded by salt-bushes in shallow sand at the edge of the lava, she heaved and shivered, scratching for traction with her flippers in the sand. Her slit bulged rhythmically, oozing blood and mucous with each contraction. Excited, I squatted down beside her.

The other sealions slept on, nuzzling each other, coughing and scratching at pesky flies. The waves burst in spurts on the curving shore; otherwise, all was still.

With the next contraction, the sealion gave a choking groan. Her body rippled like a visible shudder and then she lay back, blinking out huge saltwater tears. Remembering my own childbirths my belly gave a sympathetic lurch.

"I know," I whispered to her, training my light at her opening.

She gasped, bucked hard and heaved. Her slit spread and released a steaming spurt which attracted a buzzing swarm of sandflies. I brushed them away. Her perineum swelled and she grunted, bore down hard and then lay panting before the next big push. Digging in her flippers, she lifted her upper body and pressed the baby forward until its head began to show at the opening.

"You're doing fine," I heard myself say, my voice strange in my ears. It was a week since I'd spoken a word to anyone. "Here it comes!" I shouted into the night air.

For a moment, the baby's head slipped out of sight, but with the next push it shot forward. One more heave and it crowned, and emerged into the world, dropping onto the sand in its sac, cord and all. The placenta dribbled out last.

The mother rolled right over. Gripping the sac with her muzzle, she nipped it away from the pup, swallowing down the whole mess of afterbirth, famished. Then tenderly nuzzling her babe, she licked it clean and steered its tiny mouse-head to her teat.

I sat back on my heels and watched. My flashlight hung useless from my hand as the dawn began to flush the sky beyond the volcano with mauve light. Across the lava fields, the massive cone of Fernandina Volcano separated itself from the darkness, deep purple softening to gray and mist. On the beach, just yards away, the tide moved in, waves glistening with white foam as they broke, churned and slid ceaselessly back into the sea. By my side, the new creature took its first breaths and suckled wetly at its mother's teats; she, arching back her rubbery neck, held it protectively with her flipper and gave in voluptuously to the ecstasy of its sucking.

I had to tell someone.

"Hey!" I yelled to the harem's current bull who patrolled back and forth along the breakers. "Hey! You've got a new baby!"

I tracked him with my flashlight, but he nosed under and reappeared further on, blinking. Barking hoarsely, he gargled on seawater and dove under again.

"Hey! It's a boy!" He thought I was too ridiculous to take seriously. "Or maybe it's a girl!" I teased. He barked menacingly and did a swift turn towards me. I pretended to retreat. He barked again; I stepped back again. This was typical of our relationship; we were, both of us, bluffers.

When I had arrived a week earlier, we had had to come to an understanding, the bull and I. The fisherman who had brought me here warned me about the machismo of the male sealions.

"He will make a big noise," he had said, "but if you obey his rules he won't bother you, Marta. When he lets you know what he wants, then you must pretend to be afraid - like this." He jumped back in mock fright, waving his arms in the air. I laughed. "Truly," he said. "That makes him feel good…"

Still, he had been very reluctant to leave me alone on Fernandina, so far from the other members of my party. But a solo stay on a uninhabited island had been the whole purpose of my trip to the Galàpagos and I was determined to do it.

"A woman alone..." he had muttered.

"It's just for two and a half weeks," I assured him. "What can happen?"

"The sun at the equator, it can make you crazy."

"I'll wear my hat."

"And you go every, every afternoon into this lava cave, Marta, you hear?"

"I promise."

"And you stay on the coast - no walking inland, no matter what!"

"Cross my heart."

"But Marta, you'll have nobody to talk to!" This he couldn't understand.

"I can hardly wait," I replied.

When his boat was a mere dot on the horizon and I stood alone on the shore, I singled out the bull, noted where he was in the water, and set about choosing a site for my camp. In a soft hollow of sand in the center of the beach I lay out my tarp and battened it down with four gerry cans of water. I watched him for a reaction, but he paid me no mind. I dragged over my backpack and retreated to the salt bushes to pee. He was upon me in moments, blubber a-quiver and eyes outlined in red. I ran like mad to the safety of the lava behind the beach, my knees like water and my heart pounding in my chest, acting very afraid indeed. His fishy breath and his meaning were impressively clear. With a disdainful grunt he lumbered back towards the water, waiting at the surf to see what I would do.

It was a while before I ventured back onto the sand, and only after a full afternoon of negotiation did we reach a compromise about where I could set up my camp. Soft beach sand was out of the question, he let me know, but a bumpy bit of beach half in the rocks at the back of the cove, he would tolerate. The bed was a hard one, to be sure, but after we made our contract we became something like friends. That is, he bluffed, I ran; I teased, he snorted. We thought each other outrageous, but basically harmless.

"Your baby is beautiful!" I shouted at him, tickling his whiskers with the beam of my flashlight. But he ducked underwater, ignoring me, and skimmed beneath the waves, a cloud of evanescent bubbles streaming greenly behind him.

Through the graying mist of dawn, the coastline emerged out of the uniform dark of night. The rocky cape- a broad arm of basalt flung out into the crashing sea- took form as the air softened with the coming light. The winds awoke and swept in from the ocean, carrying hints of running fish. Birds stirred in cliff-face rookeries and the sun spread a mantle of mauve upon the flanks of the volcano. On Fernandina Island in the Pacific Ocean, it was morning.

High on the beach, the new mother nursed her babe and scratched idly at her pelt with her flipper. Sniffing the air, she sneezed wetly and gazed down at the wrinkled bit of brown fur burrowing at her teat. All around them the other sealions in the colony snuffled and coughed, rolling over lazily or waddling down to the water's edge for a swim. By the time the rising sun had cleared the volcano's rim, all the shoreline animals were out for their morning feed.

Seabirds darkened the sky with their wings - gulls and boobies and frigates and shearwaters. Pelicans divebombed into the surf, Sally Lightfoot crabs scuttled red and quick over black rock and sea-going iguanas flopped into the surging waves. The water teemed with fish, and every diver was out to get them: tropical penguins, flightless cormorants, dolphins, skates, sharks. This is what the world must have looked like before people came onto the scene - an ocean soupy with life, the land crammed with creatures and a sky thick with birds. The show had a cast of billions, and included every variation possible on the themes of form, movement and color. Charles Darwin was right to observe that not a niche went unfilled, that adaptations to every environment were rampant. I stood on a rock by the sea and I marvelled.

By the third day, I followed the same schedule as the animals; I ate in the cool of the morning and evening, took some rest in the shade during the heat of the day, and otherwise hung out to watch what was going on.

Early mornings, I fished, dropping a rope and bent nail into deep water and hauling my catch, still shuddering, onto the rocks of the cape. Early evenings I watched for seaturtles lumbering up the beach to spawn. They paid no attention to me, no matter how close I got. And when the sun went down I stretched out on my back and gazed up at a sky filled with galaxies and stars until my eyes, weighty, closed.

The sun, the next morning, rose into a cloudless sky and reflected off the black lava fields in waves of heat. I tied up my boots, put on my straw hat and sunglasses, packed a canteen of water and some biscuits and strolled across the cove to visit the mother and pup before setting out on my day's explorations on the other side of the cape.

The baby nursed noisily and the mother stretched her neck all the way back, whuffling with satisfaction. Blinking her liquid black eyes at me, she belched loudly and curled protectively over her little one.

"He's a beauty," I told her. She huffed and wriggled the baby closer to her side. He lost the teat and squealed plaintively, causing her to eye me with distress.

"I won't hurt him," I promised, taking a backwards step to reassure her. But I tripped over a spur of lava and fell down, clumsy in all my paraphernalia. I felt like an out-of-town guest at a party where everyone else has known each other for years. In my boots and hat and long sleeves, I was the interloper; here the natives wore sleek pelts and streamlined flippers. This was their turf; I was just an awkward tourist.

Roused by the action on the beach, the bull came roaring out of the water and charged me, as he did every morning. I ran, as expected. He whumphed at me, teeth bared and breath steaming, and I whumphed back. Humping back down to the surf, he glanced around one last time and barked menacingly.

"Whoof yourself," I retorted, picking my way over jumbled rocks to the other side of the cape.

Already, the day was hot. The wind blew in steadily from the sea and the sun heated sand and rocks to glaring cinders. On the reefs, crabs scuttled and fish darted into dark crevices in the tidepools; hermit crabs in borrowed shells climbed laboriously up tidepool walls only to slip and drift down again to the bottom. At the debris-line of the tides, the hum and buzz of sandflies merged with the slap and spill of the surf.

I bent down and scooped seawater into my hands, rubbing it onto my face. The salt stung where my sunburn had peeled and I scrubbed quickly, letting the wind dry me. Another bull - the reigning male of the colony on this side of the cape - dragged himself out of the water, bloodshot eyes intent upon the beach. I got ready to run, but he humped right past me, nudging a female who basked on the sand. She reared away from him, humph-ing indignantly; he selected another one dozing close by.

"Hu-oooo!" she bellowed, slithering out from under him as he attempted to mount. Undeterred, he shimmied over to another who was more receptive. At the touch of his flipper she rolled over and received his whole weight on top of her. They coupled without further ado, the surf washing over them in rhythmic spurts. With each wave she was all but submerged; with each thrust, he groaned like thunder. At the edge of the sea, they bubbled and gasped, bubbled and gasped...

In the following days, the pup became the center of my attention. Like a doting Auntie I marvelled at his every milky yawn, his every tinny squeal. I snapped his picture daily and brought his mother offerings of fish scraps; I watched his first swimming lesson near the tidepools, enchanted by how his nostrils flared with each wash of the waves. I loved the way his miniature flippers flailed in the swirl of surf and how his mother lifted him with her muzzle to ride the bigger swells. They had captured my heart altogether, this Madonna and Child of the Beach.

She taught him to follow her, his little body toddling in her wake like a wind-up toy. When she went too fast, he tended to nosedive into the sand and lie there panting. Waiting for him to rest, she would start him up again and look back to see how he was doing. When he flopped and gave up, he would gaze at her with winsome eyes and mew piteously to be fed.

Day by day, they entered more into the normal round of life of the colony. They fed, basked and slept in the center of the beach amongst the others, all but indistinguishable from the rest of the mothers and pups in the cozy bedlam of sealions.

For one anxious night, I worried that I might soon not be able to tell them from the others, so I spent the next day in camp and followed them discreetly on their rounds. I got to know my pup's particular way of sneezing, scratching, waddling. His black marble eyes were etched on my brain; his own unique way of twisting his head became indelibly imprinted. By the end of the day I was so bonded with him I felt I could recognize him anywhere.

I returned to the cove from the other side of the cape after a day of whalewatching. The sun was losing its shape in a blaze of gold on the horizon and the sea was lit, and molten. In the distance the volcano, the color of honey, looked more like an immense pudding dripping with treacle than a mountain streaked with lava.

The pup was growing daily. I scanned the beach for him, seeing him at play with his mother on a sand shelf not far from my camp. She guided him up the incline with her flipper, catching him when he slipped head over heels to the bottom. Swiftly picking him up with her muzzle, she placed him again on the slope and guided him as he scrambled up the soft sand.

This was not playing. I sank down on the sand and watched intently. She was teaching - or testing - and he wasn't learning very well. The pup dug in his hind flippers and pulled hard. Wriggling, he gained a few inches, lost hold and slumped again to the bottom. His mother let him go, and gazed out to sea. My fingers tensed around my camera.

"You can do it!" I whispered, my jaw clenched. The mother twitched her whiskers and blinked moistly. The daytime winds lowered with the coming of dusk, and the light faded rapidly. She picked him up again in her jaws and placed him on the incline, guiding him up with her flipper. As he approached the top, she let go. He scrambled to reach the top, but he was not strong enough. Disconsolately, he slid down the slope and landed in a sorry brown heap at the bottom.

The sun, in a flash of light, went under. Venus appeared, and held the horizon. Moments later, higher in the sky, Jupiter came out. Night crept in, star by star, until all was held together by the glistening darkness. In shadowy silhouette, the mother lifted the pup by the scruff of his neck and deposited him at the top of the sand shelf, out of reach of the tides. Motionless for a moment, she looked down at him and then, with swift decision, turned away and humped down the beach to the surf.

I waited with him for her to return, but she didn't come that night, nor did I see her the next morning. When I tried to locate her, I realized that while I had memorized the pup, I had not learned to distinguish his mother from the other females.

For two days I tried to feed him myself. I smeared my fingers with evaporated milk and I minced up bits of my fish, but he would take neither. He lay passively on the sandy ledge, his pelt drying rapidly into brown fuzz. His eyes remained moist, but his little nose was dry and crusted. I hovered nervously, washing him down with seawater every hour, not knowing the right thing to do.

On the third day, after sprinkling him with water, I hesitantly stroked his fur and he didn't resist. Carefully picking him up, I cradled him in my arms, a feather-light bundle of tiny bones encased in loose fur. His little heartbeat thumped right against my chest, and his breath rasped in and out of his miniature nostrils. I stroked his head, brushing away the sandflies that clustered about his rheumy eyes.

I couldn't leave him to die as his mother had. Those were sealion rules, perhaps - the survival of the strongest.

But I wasn't a sealion! My rules were human rules and that meant I had to try and save him. I didn't know how - or even if I should - but I had to try anyway. I carried him down to the water and lowered him in. For a moment he seemed to respond, his flippers moving in a swimming motion. My heart leapt. But then he went inert again and lay floating in my palm. I doused him with water again and again, trying to encourage him back to strength, but it didn't work. This was Nature's way of protecting a species, wasn't it? I was nothing but an ignorant meddler. His colony, his mother, even the pup himself had accepted his fate without a murmur. I had to accept it too.

Resolved, I brought him back to the sandy shelf, lay him down tenderly, explained my reasons for leaving him there, and marched back to my camp. Gathering up my daytime gear, I started out for the other side of the cape to watch pelicans.

But it was no good. I was stupid and distracted. I had forgotten my fieldglasses; I tripped and soaked my boots in a tidepool. Morose, I stared at the debris on the beach: seaweed, shells, jumbled bones all buzzing with flies. A lava lizard, perched on a rib-bone tangled in seaweed, waited with beady eyes and snapped up sandflies. Flicking him off, I picked up the bone. It was smooth, bleached and curved; probably a seabird's. From the matted tideline pile of debris I extricated other bones: a scapula, a pelvis, some vertebrae.

I placed them in correct skeletal order: ribs beneath scapula, pelvis at the base of the spine. It hardly mattered which species they originated from. Getting down on my hands and knees, I rummaged through the debris to complete my skeleton, finding more ribs, a skull, limb-bones, vertebrae. My creature was part bird, part lizard and part sealion, and she-he-them had once lived right here on this beach. They had breathed this air, felt this sun. And now they were reduced to bones, pitted, bleached and bunched up in a matted pile of debris on the sand, soon to crumble, grain by grain, back into the earth.

I rubbed at a crumbly piece of bone until it was reduced to chalk. Once part of a living animal, it was now nothing but a lump of chalk dissolving in the equatorial sun. Who was to know or care?

My mouth was dry. The sun blazed overhead near the zenith and the wind drummed in steadily from the sea. I got up stiffly, sticking the lump of bone in my pocket, and went back to my camp to find some shade, dreading what I would find on top of the sandy shelf.

The volcano, in the heat of the day, lurked like a poised beast. The lava beds shimmered with heat, shrouding the air with haze. I felt the stirrings of pre-menstrual cramps and wanted to cry. But I was alone on an island in the middle of the Pacific Ocean, where I had dreamed of being for ten years. I couldn't cry!

The pup lay listless on the shelf, swatting languidly at flies. I doused him with seawater and then retreated to the shade of the lava cave. Crawling in, I bumped my head on a rock and wanted to scream, but there was nobody to scream at. I could hardly go pick a fight with a sealion. I curled up on the dank floor, cradling my head with one arm and willing myself to sleep. But sleep wouldn't come.

A crab in full moult clung to a shadowy corner of the lava tube. When I touched her soft body with a cautious finger, she waved her eyestalks in alarm.

"It's all right," I whispered. "I'm in hiding too."

I felt haunted by the image of the pup shrivelling in the sun, and my belly ached with my coming menses. Ill at ease, I squirmed onto my side and the crab delicately moved deeper into the shadows.

What was to stop me from bringing the pup into the shade with me? He didn't have to suffer any more than was necessary. I sat up with resolve and crawled towards the opening, banging my head on a rock. Damn!

Holding onto my head, I curled up until the pain passed. Of course I couldn't; it would only prolong his agony.

Yes, I'd do it anyway. It would at least make *me* feel better. I got onto my knees and crawled carefully out of the cave backwards. The sun was blistering. I crawled back in again.

There was no way...

But I had to...

No...

Yes...

I fell, finally, into a jittery doze, my mouth dry as powder. I dreamed immediately.

I have left my adopted child to go on a trip. I call home to learn that he is ill, and not expected to live. With my heart in my mouth, I race home, overcome with grief and guilt.

"We'll play the whole thing again from the beginning!" I announce, knowing this is a dream. "This time I'll be right here the whole time."

We start over. The child is well again; this time I do not go away. He falls ill. But I nurse him this time. I watch over him; I give him medicine.

But his illness follows the same course. No matter what I do, he keeps getting sicker. Soon he is at the edge of death, just as the first time. Despite me.

I woke up, sobbing.

The cave closed in like a cell. The mucky floor, softened by my sweat, clung to my skin like slime. In the shadows the soft crab picked ceaselessly at the dripping walls, bringing one spongy claw and then the other to her unprotected mouth.

I spent the whole afternoon with the pup, washing him down continuously and brushing sandflies from his eyes. I brought him sardines from a can, but of course he wouldn't eat. Ten times I walked away from him, determined to let Nature take its course, and ten times I came back.

The day, at long last, came to an end in a blazing sunset over the sea. The moon, at the same time, rose huge and yellow over the volcano. For awhile their light hung in the sky together and then the moon held sway, sending moonshadows across the sand.

I gave the pup one last visit before crawling into my sleeping bag without supper. One by one, and then in hordes, the stars came out and the night sky took over. I felt effaced by the enormity of it all, alone in the dark on a beach in the middle of the ocean with only a dying baby sealion for company.

Crazed by the full moon, the bull barked himself hoarse while the tide, creeping up the beach, covered more and more of the soft sand. The whole colony of sealions pressed towards the lava, surrounding me on all sides with their whuffling, blubbery bodies.

What in the world was I doing here? I had thought that a solitary stay on an uninhabited island would teach me profound truths about myself, but all it did was make me desperate. Instead of wisdom, I had found loneliness. Why had I left my husband and children for this? All I wanted was my own kind who I could love and talk to and be heard by. I had come here for solitude, for communing with the natural world, not for desperation. This wasn't what I had in mind at all! I stared up at the sky, feeling its indifference and wondering how many days I still had to go before the fisherman came to get me.

I awoke the next morning with an aching belly and swollen eyes. The sun was already scorching. Dully, I prodded my feet into sneakers and shuffled across the beach to check on the pup.

When I reached the far end of the cove, I realized I must have walked right past him. I wasn't paying attention. More mindful, I retraced my footsteps, but still I couldn't find him. Stopping, I took a deep breath and tried to clear the cobwebs from my head. The shelf should be - *right here* - but here there was only tideline debris.

Again, very slowly, I walked the same ground. The bull, weak with barking, made a halfhearted show of bluff. I ignored him. The shelf was not there. The contours of the beach had changed completely with the high tide. Nothing was the same. Of course, dummy, that's what tides do!

Oh my God - my pup!

I went numb. A groan rose into my throat but never emerged as sound. I stared blankly out to sea; it curled in wave after wave towards the land, just as it always did. Everything was exactly as it had been before. Everything was inexorably changed.

Feeling returned, and with it, action. Enraged, I went berserk. There was blood behind my eyes. Wildly grabbing off a sneaker, I slammed it hard onto the lava. I picked up rocks and hurled them until they smashed into pieces. I flung my notebook, the cooking pot, dried sealion shit - yelling curses. Then I sank onto the sand and wept hard.

Still sobbing, I set out to find the pup's body, searching through heaps of rotting seaweed, pushing lounging sealions apart, splashing into tidepools. He had to be somewhere - unless the sea had already claimed him for itself.

I found him at last wedged between two sea boulders, a sodden bit of brown flotsam. The next high tide would have swept his shrunken bit of fur and bones out to sea. Even now, he had withered to almost nothing.

But I knew him immediately, and lifting him I cradled his lifeless body against my chest. The flies found him right away and I covered him with my arms, hiding him, this child of my heart. The surf spurted at my feet and the wind, gathering strength, rocked me. And him. I waded in up to my knees, holding him close and when a perfect, unbroken swell reached us, translucent and green, I whispered farewell, lowered him into the water and let the ocean take him.

I slogged out of the waves, disconsolate. In the distance, the volcano was etched clearly against the sky as if it were just beyond the nearest lava flow. Close enough to walk to. The rim was vivid, free of clouds. Not more than an hour away.

I had to move, walk swiftly. I was too cooped up on the coast and hadn't explored inland at all. The fisherman had said not to go into the lava fields, but I knew my way around by now. What could be so dangerous?

Changing quickly into shorts, I laced up my boots, grabbed hat and sunglasses and avoided looking in the direction of the sea. I picked up my backpack, then decided against it. I'd walk lighter without it, and furthermore, without food or water I'd be forced to turn back before the sun got too high in the sky. Out on the lava, there would be no shade at all.

Jumping onto the rocks behind my camp, I started out for the volcano without looking back. Negotiating a stretch of loose piles of sharp lava took all my concentration, but once on the harder, platey surface of the pahoe-hoe flow, I caught my stride. After the confines of the cape, this loose-limbed loping felt exhilarating. Beneath my feet the black crust crunched deliciously, and in my ears the winds drummed a changing beat. Unfastening my barrette, I shook out my hair until it whipped about my face. Strong and free I felt better, and I quickened my pace.

I leaped onto a pressure ridge, skipping from one broken slab of lava to another, and scrambled down the other side. Frozen lava swirled like the skin of a giant pudding, and tiny craters dotted the lava field like popped bubbles. Except for the thrumming of the wind, nothing moved, and except for an occasional insect blown there by the wind, nothing on these barren wastes lived.

Perhaps it was time to turn around. The volcano was still very far away, and the sun's glare already felt painful. But I had hardly gotten started, and there was an interesting outcrop of rock ahead of me. A spatter cone. I would just go that far, perhaps climb it, and then turn around.

But it took longer to reach than I expected, and once there, I had to mount its side and peer into the crater. Dry rock and silence.

From the top, the sea glinted in the distance, a strip of blue ribbon; on the other side the volcano loomed like a brooding monster guarding its territory.

I had to turn back. My throat was already dry. But just past the spatter cone, something strange - an anomaly in the landscape - stood out. It was reddish, and right there. It wouldn't take me long. I'd never get this way again. I could still make it back to the coast before noon.

The lava fields dipped into troughs and rose into pressure ridges; the reddish place was farther away than I thought. Slowing down, I trudged up and down the ridges, and climbing another rise, it was suddenly right there beside me, searing in the sun.

As if I had been punched in the stomach, I came to an abrupt halt and fell down. I lay on the burning rocks, gasping for breath, right next to the rusting hunk of broken metal. Menacingly familiar. Nose cone smashed into the lava; tail fins twisted, pitted. A bomb. From the war. Target practice. Whose? Didn't matter.

The last remaining drops of moisture left my body. Like the bomb, I also could become a dry husk. They would never find me. I would decompose slowly; my bones would bleach. Finally crumble. Grain by grain, back into the earth. I closed my eyes.

For how long I lay there, I don't know. Through clouds of unknowing, an insistent voice pounded at my brain.

"Get up!" I had no strength to budge.

"Up!" I ignored it.

"UP!" The sun sucked harder.

"GET THE HELL UP!" I barely heard it.

"GET BACK TO THE COAST! UP! UP! UP!" It pounded with the beat of the winds. UP! UP! UP!

By some force that wasn't me, I was dragged stiffly to a stand and teetered, at the edge of consciousness, unsteadily down the ridge, headed towards the sea. Every step was burning agony. My feet were blocks of fire. Wobbly, I put down one foot, then the other.

Had the winds not been at my back, I doubt that I would have made it. I gave up a dozen times, but the persistent voice kept screaming in my cells. I walked a treadmill of glaring lava which rose up to meet me each time I lagged.

"STAY UP!" it insisted. I pushed on, across beds of fire, my mind a blank, my body senseless.

When I stumbled off the platey pahoe-hoe lava into the shifting piles of sharp lava, I fell. I lay there, inert. My legs bled from jagged cuts and my back was bruised. I began again to drift.

"UP!" the voice shrieked. I ignored it.

But it had a hysterical persistence. A surge of saving energy brought me to my feet and sent me scrambling forward, at a desperate run, towards the cape. Once again I slipped, but I got up and lurched on. Within sight of my camp I fell again, but stayed on my knees and crawled the rest of the way home.

Collapsed, I lay on my tarp gasping for breath until I could fumble for my canteen. I drank it dry. Then I fell into a short, hard sleep.

Awakening, I drank more water and unearthed a bar of chocolate. The sun had melted it to mush. As my strength returned, I grabbed a can of sardines and one of pineapple and crawled into the lava tube for shade. There I ate, and then slept.

I came out only when the sun began to set over the ocean. I was cut and bruised from my misadventure, but intact. When the moon rose, I bandaged my wounds, ate a package of biscuits and two more bars of chocolate. Then I stopped feeling shaky.

A cramping in my belly announced the onset of menstruation and I squatted to relieve the tension.

The moon held sway in the sky, lighting land and sea alike. The volcano, far away loomed like an immense shadow, inscrutable in the dark. The sealions, settling down for the night, coughed and sneezed and snuffled and the rookeries were covered with seabirds tucking their feathers in close.

The tide was out. I wandered down to the exposed reefs, letting the surf lick my bare toes. The pup would be well out to sea by now. Fingers of foam spurted, popped and disappeared into wet sand. A pathway of moonlight on the waves reached me, and passed right on through.

My womb cramped again, releasing a hot gush of blood. I wiped it away with seawater and rinsed my hand in a tidepool. The water ruffled, then cleared.

The moon, reflected, jiggled into fragments and then reformed into a round ball of light. I bent over to see more closely, and imposed upon the moon, saw also myself.

I smiled in surprise. And the face smiled back.

AIR UPON THE GROUND

     Up the shallow tidepool wall a hermit crab climbed slowly towards the moonlight.
        Reaching the top
              it let go
                    floated in the water

                    and drifted
                      gently

                            back down
                            to the
                                bottom.

2

DUO D'AMORE

Sacral Chakra - Gonads

*Sexuality;
the force of mutual attraction;
magnetism;
the longing for union.*

He caught my eye the moment he boarded the train at Bologna - perhaps because he carried a cello case, but I rather think it was something unusual in his manner that attracted me. He was, in fact, an ordinary-looking Italian - dark and slender, with a prominent nose and a shock of black hair - but it was his air of being comfortable in his own skin, of being both intense and at ease at the same time, that got my attention. The other musicians with him scrambled for seats as they got on, but he simply stepped in, lowered his cello to his feet and reached for the hanging strap by the door in one graceful motion.

"Franco!" they called, squeezing to make room for him as the train lurched into motion. His smile towards them made me inadvertently smile back and I was tempted to reach into my backpack for my flute so he would know I played music too. Instead, I looked out the window. He leaned into the strap, swaying with the train's rhythm as it gathered speed, and then walked his cello over to his companions' seats. By the time we had cleared the outskirts of Bologna, I couldn't take my eyes off him.

From across the aisle, I listened to his voice, understanding nothing. I pretended to read, but was aware only of his back, hoping at each stop that he would stay on the train. One by one his companions got off until he and I were the only people left at that end of the car. He looked over at me frankly, and then turned to gaze out the window, his cello between his knees.

We journeyed deeper into the countryside of Emilia toward Ravenna. Unzipping my backpack, I casually let the flute case stick out as I rummaged for a map, but he didn't look up. If he noticed he made no sign, and I studied the map to find the Youth Hostel at the edge of the city. Three stops later we reached Ravenna, and when the conductor announced it we both stood up and shouldered our packs.

"You were looking for something on the map?" he asked me on the platform in careful Italian. I nodded and fumbled with my map, suddenly too shy to speak. Unfolding it, I pointed to the Youth Hostel.
"That's right across from my house," he declared with a smile. "Come with me and I'll show you how to get there." I followed him to the street where lines had begun forming for the trams, now so timid I could hardly smile, much less speak. My shyness almost made me wish he would go off and leave me.
"You don't speak much Italian, do you?" he asked, enunciating carefully.
"*Poco*," I admitted in a small voice. "I can speak some French, but..." To my meager French I added some of my even more meager Italian, making a patois of rather low order. He grinned and replied, mixing up the languages as I had done,
"*Comprendo parfaitement*. I understand you perfectly. Let's talk."

By the time the tram reached the center of Ravenna I knew that his name was Franco Falluci, that he had just matriculated from the Bologna Conservatory of Music and that he was a member of the Bologna Symphony Orchestra. In the Fall he planned to audition for the Maggio Musicale in Florence, but during the summer he was practicing at his home in Ravenna and commuting to Bologna for concerts.
When we got off the tram at the edge of the city he knew that I was an American, that I was infatuated with the medieval churches of Europe and that I was a beginning flute player. What he did not know was that I had fled from a crazy household in

Brooklyn, had saved up money from babysitting and birthdays to get here despite my father's maneuvers to stop me, and that my backpack held nothing but a pair of jeans, a skirt, a sweater, almost no money, three books on medieval iconography and my flute.

We stood on the street corner talking as the day darkened into dusk. Passing us on their way home from work, neighborhood people greeted Franco and gazed with frank curiosity at me. When the streetlights came on, he pointed across the narrow street to a balconied building with a Youth Hostel triangle on the door.

"Marta," he said formally, pronouncing my name the Italian way, "that's the hostel, but I'd like to invite you to stay at my house instead." He indicated the building just opposite.

I blushed furiously.

"My parents' house," he amended, seeing my confusion. "And my sisters..." he added, smiling. I was too embarrassed to smile. "Truly, you can come."

"But you don't even know me," I protested. "I am a stranger..."

"You are a *compagna della musica*," he corrected me. His voice mellowed into a tease. "Furthermore, I forgot to tell you the Hostel is always full by this time of day. I guess you'll have to say *Oui.*" Picking up his cello, he turned towards his doorway, gesturing for me to follow. My heart, pounding, followed him right up to the house, but my feet remained rooted to the sidewalk. I couldn't imagine going home with someone I liked so much.

"Maybe the hostel isn't full tonight," I murmured. "Couldn't we see?" His face fell, but he parked his cello in the foyer of his house and accompanied me across the street. There was, in fact, a single place left in the girls' dormitory. Unreasonably, I felt disappointed.

"For this night only," the matron announced. "Tomorrow we are full up."

"*Domani*...," Franco mused.

Tomorrow, I thought, I'll find another room. I can't stay

with him. He's too attractive. If only I weren't so shy. If only he wasn't so...

I was very confused.

"*Ecco,*" he said, his dark eyes intense upon me, "I'll leave you now..."

"*Grazie* - for everything," I said, reaching reluctantly for my pack. It was too late to change my mind. He'd think I was crazy.

"Sleep well," he said, not turning to leave. We both stood unmoving, looking down at the floor. The matron broke it up.

"I'll show you to the girls' dormitory," she said, giving me a gentle push in the right direction. He reached out to shake my hand and when my fingers met his, the warmth and pressure hit me like a shock.

Before bed, I stepped out onto the dormitory balcony to brush out my hair. The stars were bright down to the rooftops, and the moon, heralded by a yellow blush of light, appeared above the dark hills in the distance. The neighborhood smelled of hot oil and frying garlic, and from every curtained window came the homey warmth of lamplight.

I undid my long braid and slowly ran the brush through my hair. It crinkled with static and I smoothed it down after each stroke, watching the moon rise higher in the sky. I brushed one side, then the other, noticing that someone else was also out taking the evening air. Just opposite, on a darkened balcony, Franco stood and watched the moon, one hip casually thrust against the railing. My breath tightened, and I brushed like mad.

Pretending to be oblivious of his presence, I bent over and let my hair spill over my head. He shifted his weight and even from across the street I could hear his sigh. I brushed upside down and then straightened, letting my hair cascade back onto my shoulders, smoothing it behind my ears.

I had his full attention.

Separating my hair into three hanks I began another braid,

glancing across at him when he turned back to the moon. When I moved, he looked; when he shifted, I looked, peeking through my hair at his profile. Cat and mouse, we took turns peering at each other in the dark.

Beneath my shirt I was naked. I felt every place the cotton touched my body and heard the thud of every beat of my heart. Could he hear it too?

For a moment I felt the familiar urge to look over my shoulder to see if my father were hovering, watching. But I was in Italy, an ocean away from my family and the humiliations of my childhood. I was an anonymous traveller standing upon a balcony in a city he had probably never heard of, brushing out my hair in the dark, watched by an attractive stranger across the street. And my shirt could fall softly against my skin, and I could enjoy the touch and not be afraid.

Luxuriously, I swept my hair back, undid the braid I had started, and pulled the brush through it again. Stealing a glance at the remarkable profile of my new friend, I sighed loudly enough for him to hear. He also sighed. An invisible wire held us there, each facing out and leaning against the balcony railing, as aware of each other as if we were standing next to each other. It was I who finally broke the connection, languorously strolling back into the dormitory, one arm trailing seductively behind me. Climbing into the top bunk of the bed assigned to me, I lay and stared into the darkness, smiling.

I slept hardly at all, and by morning my boldness had deserted me. I left the hostel at first dawn before anybody was awake, and took off. Even the churches had not yet rung the bells for morning prayers; even the cafes had not yet pulled up their shutters.

I had to not be there in case Franco came calling for me. Why? Because I was scared - scared he might come, and scared he might not come. What if he didn't? Then I would die. What if he did?

I had no choice but to leave.

For two hours I wandered distractedly. At every corner I looked for him, terrified I would see him and praying he would be there. Would I even recognize him in the daylight? People emerged from their houses and boarded the trams; cafes pulled up their shutters and the aroma of *espresso* drifted into the streets; children came out into the *piazzas* to play.

I knew I had made a terrible mistake, that I should go back to the Youth Hostel and wait for him. I could even knock at his door. No, that was too forward. But it was rude to leave - he'd be hurt. I had no sense. By this time, I wasn't even sure I could find my way back. Confused, I stood by the fountain in a cobblestoned square and fumbled through my pack for my map, my head too scrambled to think. That was when he found me.

"Where did you go?" he asked in a hurt whisper, his arms lifted to his sides. I had no breath to answer. "I came to the hostel at eight o'clock - only eight o'clock! - and they said you weren't there." His voice cracked, and he plunked himself down at the edge of the fountain, shaking his head. I wanted to cry.

"I was so shy..." I finally stammered out in French, not knowing how to apologize in any language. Tears brimmed in his eyes; they brimmed in mine, too.

"It's for my parents - not me. I told them I met an *Americana* on the train, and they said to bring her for lunch. An American *signorina* who plays music."

"It was *stupido*..." I faltered.

"It's for them - if you don't want to be with me, you don't have to. But it's for them - they were so pleased - an *Americana* who plays music..."

"Please. That's not how I feel. I just got so - shy. I ran away. I am so stupid..."

"I am too..." he admitted, grinning sheepishly. We both took in big breaths. "But my parents, they are still waiting. Will you come?"

I nodded gravely, relieved more than scared. We both began to speak at once, and we both stopped. Then we both giggled nervously. He stood.

"*Andiamo?*" he said. I fell in step with him, not knowing what to say.

"I am not dressed very well to meet your parents," I mumbled at last. He took in my jeans and sweater.

"You look very beautiful," he said earnestly. We both looked elsewhere, embarrassed. Then he smiled shyly, and I did too.

"I'm sorry I made so much trouble," I told him again.

"Oh," he sighed, "I don't mind having a morning constitutional." He grinned and we both laughed, turning into another square which led out onto the central boulevard. The distance I had covered since dawn was considerable. It was a wonder he had found me at all.

His parents greeted me with a warm embrace, beaming welcome. From the moment they met me at the door, I was enveloped in the family's excitable concern. Mamma, a large woman smelling delectably of onions and laundry soap, pressed me immediately to her tomato-smeared apron and hugged hard. Babbo, who was a rounded, balding version of Franco, smiled delightedly and pulled me into the light where he could see me better. I knew now from where Franco had gotten those intense, shining black eyes, his angelic smile. In rapid Italian they commented on my face, my hair, my shoes.

"She does look like the painting," they observed, judging my eyes, the way I stood. I could not be sure I understood what they were saying. Franco leaned against the door, amused.

"American girls are very independent to travel alone," Babbo said.

"But look at her," Mamma interrupted, "She doesn't look loose - she's *simpatica, bellina*..."

"She understands every word you're saying," warned Franco. "She can't speak so well yet, but she catches everything..."

"*Intelligente*..." murmured Babbo with shake of his head.

"This is what we are like," Franco told me in our own patois, with a fond smile at his parents. I vowed to myself never to let him know how different it was in my own family. "Mamma, let her sit down - she's been walking all morning." He made a wry face at me, and they both turned on him, demanding,

"So what took so long to bring her here? 'I'll just go over to the *'ostello'* to get her,' he says, and we wait and wait - but where is Franco? Where is the American *signorina*. ?"

"Oh," I cried, fumbling in my terrible Italian, "It wasn't his fault. Mine. I did it. He had to find me - I went far..."

Shortly, everyone was talking at once: Franco to explain, Babbo not believing his story, me interceding to defend him and Mamma insisting it was time to come to the table. By the time we sat down to eat, I was laughing as much as they were.

"See, you got me into trouble," Franco chided me at the kitchen table. His two sisters, home for lunch, sat on either side of me.

"Please pardon me," I said again to all of them, "I was *stupido*." There was great laughter while Franco leaned over and whispered to me what the word meant in their local dialect. I blushed, but they all smiled warmly at the joke.

"Let her eat," Mamma scolded, pushing my plate closer to me. "You like *macaroni*?"

"*Molto*," I replied with enthusiasm. "*Es delicioso!*" Four beaming faces watched me swallow.

"See - she's learning Italian already," declared Babbo through a mouthful of bread. "So intelligent..."

"If she speaks French to me and I translate it for you into Italian, then she can learn how to speak," Franco proposed. "You'll see, she'll be speaking in a few days."

"What a good idea," I exclaimed. "I just have to listen to what I've just said!"

"*Esattamente*," declared Franco with a smile. His sisters gazed at him awestruck. Was there anyone as brilliant as their brother? Was there anything as amazing as a girl who played the flute, from America?

By the end of the afternoon it was clear that Franco was right. It was an excellent way to learn. After listening closely to his translations, I picked up enough vocabulary to communicate quite a bit on my own. Which was a good thing because by evening I was offered a bed in the girls' room and invited to stay for as long as I liked. With my heart in my mouth, I moved in.

In the mornings, Franco practiced for his auditions and I sallied forth to explore the city of Ravenna and its mosaic-filled churches. My plan for the year was to wander through the old cities of Europe and immerse myself in its medieval cathedrals, following the path wherever it led me and stopping in each place for as long as I was held there. I wished to wake up in places I had never seen before; to hear languages my ears didn't recognize; to swim in the blue water of strange rivers and to practice my flute beneath trees in green meadows. I wanted to not think of Brooklyn at all, and more, to fall madly in love with someone who had never even heard of it. In short, as I came of age far away from home, I wished to cleanse myself of the grime of my childhood and breathe in new air.

Few tourists came so early in the day, and I walked down hushed naves beneath mosaics that sparkled with the changing light. Sunrise and sunset were my favorite times of the day for viewing the art, and in the early afternoon before meeting Franco at the house, I meandered through the street markets and the old harbor.

"I love it here, Franco," I exclaimed one evening just at dusk as we stood beneath the cupola of the small mausoleum of

Galla Placidia. The rounded vault gleamed with blue mosaic speckled with stars. The four Evangelists appeared to be swimming in sky, gazing down at us in evanescent benediction. "I think this is my favorite in all of Ravenna."

"It is gorgeous," he agreed, stepping into a slant of late sun which glinted off blue, then green, then white bits of glass. "Of course, you haven't seen Sant' Apollinare in Classe yet. That'll be your favorite, I think. Listen to this..." He sang a note into the vault, which echoed off the curved walls of the chamber." Like the acoustics?"

"I love them," I replied fervently. I loved everything in this city, everything!

"Funny, but I rarely come here," he remarked. "I guess it's too close to home."

"So it's a good thing you have a tourist to show it to, right?" I teased. For a moment he regarded me thoughtfully. Then sauntering over to the sculpted sarcophagus he sat down on the edge and watched me in the deepening light. A slow smile started on his face.

"*Si*," he admitted after a long pause, "it is *estremamente bene*."

I had thought to spend only a few days in Ravenna, but already I had been there a week. Each day I thanked the family for their hospitality and announced I would leave the next morning, and each day they assured me I was welcome to stay. After the seventh day I no longer bothered to give my polite speech, and they no longer bothered to give theirs. Instead, there were knowing smiles all around.

I was treated, by now, like another daughter. I helped in the kitchen, did laundry with Mamma, met the girls' friends. They showed me off to the neighbors, proud of how quickly I picked up Italian, proud that I studied music like their Franco.

He, however, remained discreet. He would not practice the cello while I was in the house, much to the chagrin of his parents who longed to show him off to me. He would not touch me, either in the house or out, and paid no attention to the teases of his sisters. It was they, in fact, and not he who proposed marriage.

"In San Vitale you'll have a beautiful gown and a long white veil," they bribed, tittering behind their hands.

But Franco kept his own counsel, coming no closer to me than the soft contact of the hairs on our arms. We talked, as we walked through the streets of Ravenna, about everything. His sisters kept watch but we gave them nothing to see. We were as innocent as cousins, however restless we became in the night.

On my ninth day there, Franco had to return to Bologna for a night and a day. I could hardly bear the thought.

"I'll come too," I offered.

"No," he said sadly. "I'll be in rehearsal every minute. It's just a day - please stay. When I come home we'll go to Sant' Apollinare in Classe, in the country. I've borrowed a bike for you."

By then, I would have done whatever he wanted. Smitten with his every gesture, his voice, his smile, the way he walked, his smell - my range of vision was filled with him.

"O.K.," I agreed shakily, anticipating his departure with exquisite agony. "As long as it's only for one day."

The day he was gone, it rained. The skies dripped like angels in tears. I felt the same - gray, cold and sniffly. Bundling up in borrowed sweaters and a pair of Franco's wool socks, I left the house after breakfast with my flute and went to the tomb of Galla Placidia.

Nobody else was there. The blue mosaic of the cupola looked dense, like the overcast sky, and the marble floor felt cold. I sang a note, as Franco had done, and it echoed through the vault, throbbing. Throbbing. I could still hear his voice, see his hands, the way his black hair curled at the nape of his neck...

Shivering, I stamped my feet against the marble floor to

bring back the circulation, and unpacked my flute. The day grew darker; the dome reverberated with the drumming rain and the eaves dripped mournfully outside. My fingers were cold and I warmed them with my breath, doing the same with the mouthpiece of the flute.

As I blew the cold silver into life, I imagined Franco in the orchestra pit of the theater, his cello between his knees. One hand would embrace the instrument, one hand rest lightly on the strings. The conductor would raise his baton and Franco would lean into his bow and draw it firmly across the strings which would tremble, sing...

My body swayed, feeling his arms, feeling his bow. I drew in a shuddering breath, lifted the flute to my lips and sounded a note. It was wavery and thin. Concentrating, I listened in my mind for the correct pitch, relaxed my lips and belly and brought out a rich, full tone. It hovered in the air, ringing off the next note, and the next. Accompanied by myself, I played through the whole range of the flute, starting with scales and proceeding to arpeggios. By the time I got to chromatics, the resonant domed chamber made the notes sound like music.

The next morning bloomed rainwashed and clear. I was waiting at the station an hour before Franco's train arrived, and by the time it chugged into Ravenna I could hardly breathe.

He jumped off the train before it fully stopped, and we met with a rush of gladness. Walking home, we held hands and he told me about the performance. The first cellist had been ill, and Franco had taken his place. I told him about practicing in Galla Placidia while it rained. We talked about the changing weather, my day with the family in Ravenna, his day in Bologna, but our attention was actually on the warmth of our clasped hands. It was not easy to focus on words.

An hour later we left the city on bicycles, weaving around

parked cars, careening across cobblestoned streets and bumping across the railroad tracks until we were pedalling out on open country roads, side by side. Fields on either side of the road spread out green and fresh after the rain, and the air in our faces smelled of wildflowers.

"*Buon giorno,*" he greeted me, reaching out to touch my arm.

"*Buon giorno,*" I returned, seeing myself reflected in his sunglasses. For a moment we grasped hands, still moving forward until my front wheel wobbled towards his and we let go, laughing. He spurted ahead of me and I followed behind, content to watch his strong back and legs. We rode through countryside pastoral and green. The breeze was filled with brightness and flowers - and us two. We sped down hills and cycled through villages, waving at children and singing lustily.

"Look!" he shouted, pointing at gulls winging in from the Adriatic Sea. Then he slowed down, hollering words which the wind snatched away before I could hear them. We stopped at a village market to buy bread and cheese, and found a basket of chicks for sale, all peeping plaintively. I picked one up and Franco's hand brushed my neck. We gazed at the fuzzy bit of life and smiled tenderly before we put it down and continued on.

Franco cycled ahead of me, his rhythm easy, his weight tilting effortlessly from one side to the other as if he were pedalling to music. I tried to match his rhythm, leaning right and then left and then right, my legs warm, my hair windblown and my face full of sun. There I was on an unknown road, on a bicycle I'd never ridden before, going towards an unknown destination with a man whose existence I had not even guessed at only ten days earlier. And I was in the only place in the world I wished to be at that moment.

We stopped for lunch at a culvert between two fields of ripening corn. On the warm, moist grass we lay down amidst chirrupping crickets and snapping insects. Above our heads birds darted from tree to tree, singing. We lay on our backs, perfectly still.

A lazy cloud floated across the sun, chilling the air for a moment before drifting on. We both murmured, moving ever so slightly closer together. When the sun emerged, full of heat, we did not shift back.

We shared our bread, fruit and cheese saying little but gazing insatiably at each other. Taking sips from the same bottle of wine, we took care not to touch. I memorized his eyebrows, the swirl of his ears. He grinned at nothing, plucked grasses from the earth, tucked a wildflower behind my ear.

"*Andiamo,*" he said at last in a husky voice. "Let's go to Sant' Apollinare in Classe."

The little town of Classe has remained on the coast of the Adriatic, but its basilica sits inland, all by itself in the center of green fields. Once it was in the town, on the coast, but when the sea retreated the church was left stranded, like a beached ship, brooding and incongruous out in the countryside with its huge *campanile* and massive portals.

The land was flat, fertile and empty. In the heat and glare of midday we got off our bikes and felt the stillness throb around us. Once there were waves lapping at the base of the church. Right where I stood, in fact, the tides had slid forward and back, water and land meeting again and again and again. In the cricket-clicking field I could feel the old rhythms of surf. Franco lifted his finger to my cheek and stroked softly.

"Your thoughts?" he murmured. I leaned imperceptibly into his finger.

"About the sea that once was here," I whispered back. With a catch of his breath, he tucked a loose strand of hair behind my ear. In his sunglasses I saw his hand and my cheek reflected together. We stood, unmoving, caught in a bubble of sun and we shivered as if we were cold.

After the dry glare outside, the interior of the basilica was like a wash of cool, sweet water. For a few minutes I couldn't see in the dimness, but then it took shape before me, long and broad and completed by a curved apse resplendent with mosaics. I felt drawn forward by the altar, by the arched columns leading towards it, by the welcoming figure of Saint Apollinare standing in open-armed benediction beneath the Cross. Etched in a million bits of colored glass and surrounded by his flock of pastel sheep, he smiled me towards him. Hypnotically, I started down the nave.

"Not yet," said Franco, restraining me. "Get used to the light first." I waited by his side until he took a step. The arches, rising and falling, determined our pace. When I became impatient and hurried, Franco held me back with a soft pressure on my arm, as if to tell me that we must not arrive too soon at the altar or we would lose the effect of the moment. Franco knew this church well.

Angels of colored-glass bits flew upon walls impregnated with candlewax and incense, and our footsteps echoed upon ancient stones which resonated with our very breaths. The pulse of the pillars pulled us forward; the pulse in our clasped hands beat in tandem. The apse spread gently, admitting us into its precinct and when we reached the altar steps we sank to our knees, as if in prayer.

Actually, we were both too shaky to remain upright. I felt giddy. For a long while we knelt, heads bowed, our hearts thumping and our hands glued together. Neither of us dared make a move. Then I pulled away.

"Look!" I exclaimed, pointing at the mosaic angels with a finger that still tingled from his touch. The angel-faces were disconcertingly familiar. "They look just like you." Franco rubbed his nose and gazed up at the cherubim, chuckling.

"All the angels in Emilia have big noses," he claimed.

"Not only your nose - your smile, too." I gazed back and forth from him to the angels. "You could have been an angel, Franco."

"But I'm not..." he joked, regarding me with a lewd grin.

"I'm not so sure..." I countered.

"Anyone could tell you're not from around here," he teased, touching his finger to the tip of my nose and bringing it ever so slowly down to my lips.

Every rustle we made reverberated off the old walls. Our whispers were returned to us, our laughs repeated. I hummed experimentally, and the church echoed my sound.

"You should hear what it does to the cello," Franco declared.

"Have you played here a lot?" I leaned my head back and stared up into a firmament of glowing color. A wave of vertigo took me over, and for a moment my head wouldn't stop spinning. Crumpling clumsily onto the altar steps, I bent over my knees and waited for the dizziness to pass.

"Marta, *va bene*?" cried Franco, kneeling beside me and gathering me into his arms. The vault echoed his voice. I leaned against him, still woozy, my face very close to his. His dark eyes burned into mine and our lips touched as he crushed me to him. Then we hastily pulled apart, flustered, and held our pose like the angels on the walls. The moment passed, and we both sat up.

"Marta," he said when he found his voice again, "Please, I want to know everything about you - your people, your country, your family. Where have you come from, how did you get here?"

I had dreaded this. Why couldn't my past stay buried? How could I explain to this provincial artist from a simple, loving family about a Russian-Jewish refugee childhood filled with ghosts and curses?

If he knew of the secrets I held of a psychotic father and enraged mother, of a Communist grandfather and bedridden grandmother, would he still want to know me?

"What was it like to grow up in America?" he prompted.

"Well, my family," I sighed, "only became American one generation ago. They came from Russia after the *pogroms*." He looked puzzled; *pogroms* were not in his vocabulary. "We are Jews,"

I added. Such a configuration was new to him. "Hebrews," I clarified. He was still mystified.

"Do you speak Russian?" he asked. I shook my head. I told him about the waves of immigrants who came to New York in the early part of the century - Jews from Eastern Europe, the Irish, the Italians. He was fascinated.

"And the Italians live there as Americans?"

"Of course."

"And what language do they speak?"

"English, mostly." He nodded, trying to imagine it. I shifted the subject from my family to his.

"What about your family - have they been in Ravenna for hundreds of years?"

"Oh, no," he mused. "I suppose we're refugees, too - from the hills of Emilia, though. We've only been in Ravenna eight years. Before that, we lived in a little village - Cusercoli - where my mother is from, and grandparents, forever, I think."

"Why did you leave?"

"It was for my schooling, mainly. But really, we are peasants at heart. It was just that this little boy had music pouring out of him, and in the village I was making everyone crazy. In Cusercoli, the only music is from a crank-up gramophone in the bar, and I would wind it up all the time." He laughed. "Babbo is the same about music - he could have been a wonderful singer, you know - and when he saw I had it too, he was determined to give me a chance."

"So the whole family moved to Ravenna?"

"To the big city, yes. When I was thirteen. Babbo found work there and we three kids went to school. From the first time I heard the cello, I knew it was my life." He stared thoughtfully into the basilica.

"I haven't heard you play yet," I reminded him softly. "I would like to."

"I haven't heard you, either," he countered, "and I would like to, also."

"I'll play for you, if you play for me," I offered. "But I'm only a beginner, and you'll probably be bored."

"I will play for you tonight," he sighed, as if he had waited all this time for me to ask. "If you will play for me tonight." We both gazed into the empty church, and then at each other.

"*D'accordo*," I agreed, adding, "But you have to go first."

Mamma and I stayed in the kitchen after supper to dice onions and garlic for the next day's sauce. The girls had gone to the apartment below to visit their friends and Babbo stationed himself in a chair in the corner of Franco's room. Franco had taken out his cello and was starting to tune it.

"Go!" urged Mamma, pointing towards the bedroom. "I'll finish up here." Her cheeks were flushed; for two weeks she had anticipated this moment. She all but pushed me out of the kitchen.

Babbo, stripped down to undershirt and suspenders, had planted his feet firmly on the floor, his eyes bright with anticipation. Mamma poked her head into the room and they glanced at each other with unconcealed delight. Their Franco was finally going to play for me.

"Sit, sit," she urged, smoothing a place for me on Franco's bed. I took off my shoes and found a spot by his pillow. The concentrated smell of him reached me like perfume, and I leaned against the wall, breathless. Franco, tuning, had not looked up when I entered the room and he continued plucking each string, listening closely for the pitches. Then he tightened the hairs on his bow, let the cello rest against his body, and sat back.

Babbo settled himself by the corner and sat very still in a kitchen chair. There was not a sound from the kitchen. I tucked one leg under me, and waited. One small light glowed by the bed and Babbo was lost in shadows. Only Franco seemed lit. Eyes closed, he focussed his attention, leaned forward slowly and at the right moment lifted his bowing arm.

The cello stood loosely between his knees and with his free

hand he teased the strings, opening his eyes gently as he drew the bow lightly across one string.

The sound that emerged sounded human, like a sigh. It resonated through my whole body, starting in my chest and spreading until it flooded my head like vertigo. This could hardly be coming out of an instrument of wood and glue - this was Franco's voice itself.

The single note rose into a melody which seemed to pick me up and hold me suspended in air - except that my body, as if it had lost its bones, had slumped down on the bed, one hand sliding beneath his pillow. I clutched his pyjamas for traction and leaned my head on my arm. My knee, bent under me, wouldn't stop trembling.

Franco toyed with a tone, holding it and stroking every possible subtle nuance out of it. Maddeningly, delicately, he stayed with the same tone until he capriciously dropped to a low whisper which grew, gradually, into a roar. Lunging into a series of strong double-stops, he sang out the theme melody once, then twice and then let it hang, ringing, in the air.

My heart lunged with him. He played through the Largo again. Babbo sat hunched forward, his head marking time with the music; Mamma crept to the door to listen, a wooden spoon dangling from her onion-wet hand. The melody wound into a cadence, beseeching for something more, something swifter.

With a sharp intake of breath, Franco launched into the Allegro, skipping up and down the scale like water over rocks, like whirlpools swirling, like a flashflood in the desert. He swooped down into a phrase of persistent triplets, thumping out the beat. Leaping, he rose again to the top of his range and raced down again, a waterfall tumbling over a brink.

The hidden melody, concealed within its embellishments, revealed itself again. Franco sang it out, the music growing in intensity as it insisted upon response. He reached a high tone and held it there - suspended, resonant, pure.

My chest was not large enough to hold my heart. I held onto Franco's pyjamas, dazed.

He let the last note hang in the air, his bow still poised. The sound pulsed in the sudden silence. Breathing sharply again, he struck the strings with his bow, plunging like a stallion into the cadenza. With a full-throated sound, he sang; listening, he galloped and jumped. Nothing would be held in check. The song would have its way.

His black hair, glistening with sweat, whipped about his head as the song sang him hard. He swayed with the cello in his arms, his eyes half closed and his face charged with emotion. He rode full-out the frenzy of the cadenza until it slowed to a passage of lyrical sweetness, his voice simple and clear.

Babbo tilted back in his chair, stuck his fists into his armpits and wept. Mamma, at the door, shook her head back and forth, flushed.

Franco relaxed into the flow of the last movement, allowing the melody to sing itself out hauntingly, longingly. It dipped into the deep register and gently sobbed, softer and yet softer. The voice was held, and the music ended on a tone at the edge of hearing, like an imperceptible spasm of breath.

"*Bravo!*" cried Mamma, thwacking the wooden spoon against the doorpost. Babbo sat staring wonderingly at his son, tears streaming down his cheeks. Then they both looked at me for my reaction.

I couldn't even look up. Every nerve in my body was in a state of sweet agitation. I tried to scoot into a more decorous position, but I couldn't seem to extricate my hand from Franco's pyjamas. Half-lying on his bed, my face hot and my arm lost beneath his pillow, I gazed up helplessly, unable to speak. Franco chuckled, his eyes luminous and tender.

"Did it please you?" he asked finally.

"*Si,*" I stammered, tremulous. "*Mi piace molto, molto!*" Our eyes met, the only two people in the world.

"Now it's your turn," he said quietly, laying his cello on its side and reaching behind him for my flute.

All evening we played for each other, going through our repertoire. After one sonata, I was reduced to improvisations, but he insisted we continue to take turns. At midnight we started on duets, but Babbo poked his head in the door and apologetically asked us to stop.

"The neighbors..." he said.

Giddy and flushed, we left the house and wandered the dark streets like innocents in paradise. The neighborhood was quiet; we hugged passionately in the shadows of every alleyway, kissed madly behind shuttered vegetable stands. At three in the morning, we were still wide awake and brilliantly witty. Everything was funny and the night was forever. The world existed for us, and we existed for the world. Nothing would ever make us part.

Except that in two days Franco had to leave for a one-week tour in Switzerland.

"I'll come," I declared. He regarded me with a pained expression.

"No. It's impossible."

"Why?" I asked, taken aback and hurt to the quick.

"The life is too grueling."

"But we'd be together!" What could be too grueling - sleeping on hotel floors and standing in the backs of concert halls?

"But we wouldn't be together," he tried to explain. "There's no time - we rehearse all day, perform every night and then sleep on the bus."

"I can do that," I persisted. Anything would be preferable to being without him for a whole week. He leaned forward and kissed the bridge of my nose.

"Listen - please?" He took my face in his hands and spoke pleadingly. "Mamma is going to Cusercoli while I'm gone. She wants you to come with her to meet the family. It's beautiful in the hills - it really is - and then you will know where I come from. That means a lot to me, Marta." Lifting my hand to his lips, he kissed each knuckle one by one. "Then," he continued huskily, "will you come and meet me in Bologna?"

"Bologna?"

"For a week. We'll have a whole week together in Bologna, and," he whispered, lacing my fingers through his, "in Bologna we can practice for the concert at Sant' Apollinare in Classe." His face, by streetlight, was full of mischief.

"What concert?"

"Kiss me and I'll tell you," he replied merrily. We kissed until I pulled away from him.

"Tell me," I demanded.

"Once more," he teased.

"That's bribery!"

"You're right!" When we emerged, quite breathless, I stepped away from him and crossed my arms over my chest. His face was the most beautiful face I had ever seen.

"Now, tell!"

"Yes, I'll tell you all, *mia cara*. There is a ceremony at the basilica every August at which I always play. This year - due to the, ahem, intervention of a certain *violoncelliste* - the Americana has been invited to play as well." He twinkled with fun. "I presume that you will accept this, ahem, engagement?"

"But Franco...!"

"Wait, there is more. You will not be paid for this performance, but then, neither shall I. The *padre* has offered to recompense us with as much *vino* as we can drink..."

"But Franco, I'm not good enough!"

"Yes you are," he corrected me, "and furthermore, you will have time to practice your parts in Cusercoli!"

"You've thought everything out, haven't you?" I accused.

"Your scores are back at the house," he whispered provocatively in my ear. "In Cusercoli, you can learn them, and in

Bologna, my love, we can practice..."

So I went to Cusercoli with Mamma. The girls remained home to take care of Babbo, Franco took the early morning train for Bologna, and Mamma and I boarded a bus for the hills, our arms loaded with gifts for the relatives.

The bus rumbled out of Ravenna, shifting gears noisily as we climbed past the outskirts of the city toward the hill country of Emilia. Settling back for the four-hour ride, we stared out the bus windows at the changing countryside and its landmarks. Mamma pointed out the road which led to Babbo's village; a tiny church famous for its frescoes; a grove of trees famous for its mushrooms.

In every field and vineyard, men and women at work straightened as the bus lumbered by, and waved. By roadside doorways, kerchiefed women with sun-browned faces shielded their eyes and watched us go by. Skinny chickens, unaccustomed to motors on their roads, scattered out of our way as the bus rattled higher into the hills. These were Mamma's hills of home, and she grew increasingly more animated as the river disappeared into a deepening gorge and the small towns gave way to open, green slopes with an occasional roadside village.

"That's our well! That's the path to the river! That steeple up there - that's our church!"

When the bus wheezed to a halt before a ramshackle cluster of cottages hugging the roadside, Mamma pulled me to my feet, calling excited greetings to a knot of women gathered there to meet us. Elbowing our way down the crowded aisle past bundles and live chickens, we all but fell off the bus into the arms of the waiting women. While they hugged and kissed us, exclaimed and kissed some more, the bus took off in a noxious cloud of exhaust leaving us, rumpled and excited, in the little village of Cusercoli.

All of Mamma's people came to greet us that night for the welcoming feast. Pasta, veal, cabbage, eggplant, bread and wine was brought on in profusion, and the wine and conversation flowed all night - in a dialect I could barely understand.

"Eat, eat!" I was urged by Franco's aunts and uncles and cousins. Mamma duly translated for me, as Franco had done at home. In every face I caught a hint of Franco: a hairline, the curl of a grin, the shape of the nose. I was fascinated each time it appeared. They also were fascinated, never having seen a foreigner before. Mamma translated back and forth - especially when it was something about Franco - and then everyone laughed. She told them I would play my flute for them, and they all applauded. The children stared in wonder and touched the cotton of my dress. All of Franco's relatives watched me eat, smiled broadly at my compliments, and commented about my looks.

His presence was close - in his kitchen, his people, his countryside - but he, himself, was conspicuously not there.

The children, the next morning, were given charge of me. While the men went to the fields and the women caught up on family gossip, I was marched by the children to the schoolhouse, the church, the river, the shop. This was where Franco had gone to school; here was where he was christened; here was his old swimming hole. I met the priest who taught him catechism and picked tomatoes for lunch from his family's field.

The children laughed at my attempts at their dialect, and corrected me gravely. I tried speaking in patois, using Italian and the few words of their dialect I had learned, but they stared at me, uncomprehending.

"That's the way Americans talk," they explained to each other, as if America were a province as far away as Milano.

By the end of the third day, I was exhausted. I had seen everything there was to see, and could converse with nobody but Mamma. At night we slept, along with five other women and girls, in two enormous beds pushed together. Mamma and I shared the bed in which Franco had been born, and the others crowded onto the remaining bed. They all talked, until very late, in low voices about people I didn't know in a language I couldn't follow. At first I strained to catch a mention of Franco, but then I drifted. In the bosom of this simple family exchanging news of one another, I realized that I had not given my own family a thought for weeks. I could hardly imagine Franco existing in the same world as my father. If Mamma had any idea of the family I came from, she would not lie trustingly beside me in the safety of her girlhood bed. I couldn't betray such a trust - tomorrow, I would write my parents a postcard.

But oh, how I missed Franco. I would conjure him up by practicing my part for the concert at Sant' Apollinare. Sitting by the river, or in the shade of the church, I would take out my flute and play. The children surrounded me, wide-eyed. They listened intently to my scales, applauded when I played fast chromatics, loved the high tones and asked for repeats of the melodies. When they recognized a phrase, they congratulated themselves.

I played my parts over and over, and had them sing each phrase back to me. They loved the game, and by the end of the week the children in the village came from wherever they were at the sound of the flute. I was like a Pied Piper, and in no time at all I knew every note of my music by heart.

So did the children.

There were tearful goodbyes, hugs and kisses all around, and armloads of farm produce to take back on the bus with us to Ravenna. We hung out the windows until the bus cleared the bridge, calling out names and throwing kisses. The children ran after us in bare feet, waving and shouting until the bus chugged around the bend and gained speed on the downslope.

"*Ciao!*" they yelled in high-pitched voices. "*Ciao!*" We hung out the windows until the last of them was out of sight, waving our arms. Then Mamma settled back in her seat and sighed, her eyes already misty with nostalgia.

As we sat back for the long ride home, I asked Mamma to tell me about her people, and about how she had met Babbo, and about what Franco was like as a baby. For an hour she talked wistfully, remembering a poor but happy childhood in those hills she loved so much. Babbo she had met when he came to help with the haying - how handsome he had been, how strong.

"Like Franco," she said, smiling at me. "But not like Franco. Franco is better than we are - we are simple people, you see. And our first son is much cleverer than we..."

"You are the kindest people I have ever met!" I told her fervently, squeezing her hand in both of mine. "He gets his goodness from you!"

"Babbo, *si*," she laughed. "He is gentle and kind - an artiste, but he never had the chance. He is different from most men," she glanced at me meaningfully. "And Franco is like him, *si*."

"Franco is wonderful!" I exclaimed with a bit too much passion, feeling embarrassed. We sat side by side in silence as the bus lurched its way down the mountain, each picturing a man - she the father, and I the son.

"You like our Franco, no?" she asked at last.

"I - I love him!" I blurted out, amending it immediately with, "I do like him a lot, *si*."

"He likes you too," she said mildly, keeping my hand tucked warmly in hers. "That's very good."

I spent the night sleeping in Franco's room - in his bed, upon his sheets, under his blankets. His smell penetrated the bedclothes and I nuzzled in his pillow until I felt dizzy. Sleep, however, wouldn't come. I itched; I flopped onto my side, my stomach, my back. My arms kept getting caught under me. I sighed until my throat was dry, then had to drink some water, then had to pee. I went out onto his balcony and brushed my hair, fantasizing him standing where I was and myself on the balcony opposite. The clock said one-thirty.

    I scribbled love notes and hid them in his shoes, his pajama pocket, his music. Then I lay down and shut my eyes tight. But sleep wouldn't come - I worried that Mamma or one of his sisters might find the notes and I jumped out of bed to collect them all again. I looked at the clock; it was one-thirty five.

    At last I dropped into a fitful sleep, only to awaken at four thinking I had overslept. What if I missed the train? By dawn, I was spent and in the mirror, looked gray. I felt as if I had spent the night treading water.

    Babbo knocked on the door at seven to awaken me, but I was already dressed. I smiled wanly, and accepted some coffee. A pile of gifts for Franco- cherries and mushrooms from Cusercoli - got stuffed into my backpack and at seven-thirty I took off for the station at a run.

    The train, Lord help me, was late. Then it broke down a few kilometers outside of Ravenna and sat stranded on the tracks. When it limped, finally, into the next station, the workmen were out for coffee. I got out with some others to see what was wrong, but the stationmaster told us they would return soon. While the others buried themselves in the morning paper, I sat hunched over, my stomach knotted into a ball.

    The train eventually started up again, but wheezed again to a halt. Again it got going, but slowly, straining to gain some speed. We all cheered it on, only to moan in chorus when it lost its momentum, but at least it didn't stop. It kept a maddeningly slow pace - click-and-a-clack - all the way to the next stop.

    Each time it appeared to flag, I held my breath and urged it on. We were already almost an hour late. What if he thought I wasn't coming? What if he thought I had seen his village and now thought I was too sophisticated for him? The train picked up a smidgin of speed and I prayed. Then it bucked and jolted to a stop.

    Surely he wouldn't wait.

For a full twenty minutes we were stalled out in the middle of the line. The other passengers made the best of it, pulling out flasks of coffee and making jokes about the railway system. They, of course, would only be late for work. For me it was the end of the world. Clinging to my seat, I prayed for Franco not to give up on me.

As if hearing my plea, the train lurched again into motion and the wheels turned steadily until it was fairly humming along the tracks. The engine puffed and sent out smoke and the train neither slackened nor stopped, but kept chugging along the tracks until it pulled into the sooty cavern of Bologna Station - two hours late.

My knees were weak and I trembled lest he not be there, but I saw him running, threading his way through the crowd, leaping over valises to reach me. We met with a quick, hard embrace, hanging onto each other tightly and swaying as the crowd ebbed all around us. By the time we let go, there was nobody else left on the platform.

We rode our time in Bologna like a river, dipping and swelling from night to day to night without a break. Everything was enchanting and we were oblivious to everything but each other.

I felt as if I were the consort of a prince. Everywhere we went Franco was adored.

"*Buon giorno*, Franco!" I would hear from shopkeepers, tram conductors, children in the street. Through him I met sausage-makers and opera singers. As Franco's friend I was welcomed, and as Franco's American girlfriend I was an object of avid, eager curiosity on the part of them all. Even the gatekeeper at the Conservatory of Music knew about me.

We spent a whole day there, alone in its empty rooms. The students were gone for the summer and we had the whole place to ourselves, from the theater to the organ loft.

On the stage, we waltzed wildly until we were out of breath, falling into a dizzy heap on the raked floor and staying there to talk.

"Dancing has always been my dream," I confessed, telling him of the dances I always made up in my head. "I think I'm meant to be a choreographer, because I can't stop making up dances."

"Dance for me," he said seriously.

"Right now?"

"Right here," he declared, scooting to the side of the stage where he could watch without being in my way.

"I'm self-conscious," I mumbled after several moments of standing in the center of the stage not knowing what to do.

"Take a deep breath," he said, "and just let it come." I closed my eyes, felt my body shift to the right and hearing the beat in my head, danced to its music as I had done as a child. My limbs shook loose and my arms spread to the sides, bending and turning. My dance took me to every corner of the stage, at times shy and at times exhilaratingly free. Then I worried Franco must be bored, and I brought the dance to an end with a mock curtsey.

"Don't stop!" he urged, tapping out a beat on the boards. "I'll be the music." To his beat now, I moved into my dance again, surging towards him and away as his drumming grew more heady and our collaboration became more of a duet. I stamped, teasing his syncopated rhythm, and he thrummed his beat back at me until we were both out of breath and I flopped next to him in the wings, laughing.

Later, we climbed up to the organ loft and practiced chorales - he taught me the pedals and he played the keys - until the whole conservatory rang with crashing chords. Tiring of that, we went and sprawled on the floor in the listening room, playing every student recording he had ever made. I tried to imagine a young Franco who had never heard of me, but the notion was unthinkable.

He listened critically to his own playing with rapt concentration, his body pulsing to the tempos of each piece. The raw sounds of the younger student gave way, with each recording, to the rich sonorities of the more mature player and I could hear the development of the depths and subtleties of his art.

"That's beautiful!" I exclaimed at the end of one of his senior quartets.

"Late Beethoven's impossible," he murmured shaking his head, his eyes faraway as if his ears were still hearing the music. "We made a mess of that one."

"Sounded good to me," I countered, rubbing my nose against his arm and humming, into his sleeve, a melody from the last movement. "Every sound you make is gorgeous," I teased. A low rumbling started in his throat and rose into growls and squeaks and threatening roars. I pretended horror and ran away from him while he chased and grunted, tickling me until I got away again.

"Not every sound!" I protested, laughing weakly against the wall. Arm in arm we staggered through the halls making funny noises and for the rest of the day we sat cross-legged on the common-room sofa making faces at each other and weird-noise duets, collapsing into laughter as we outdid each other with our improvisations.

On the fifth evening Franco took me to meet his friends. We walked through the city in a light drizzle, fingers entwined and milky in love. Droplets of rain tipped his dark hair like a halo.

"They're going to love you," he assured me.

"What have you told them?" I asked. We stopped to look at ourselves in the reflections of a shop window. In the evening light, we both looked Italian.

"I refused to tell them anything. I said you were indescribable." We waved to our reflections and continued on down the street. "I told them to be prepared to be overwhelmed," he teased.

"I can't live up to that," I protested, bumping him with my hip. He bumped back and we broke into a run, stopping at the streetcorner for a kiss.

"Oh yes you can..." he sang, leaping over a sidewalk puddle and dragging me with him. "Because there's something I've never told you, that I have told them." I stopped short.

"What?" I demanded. He faced me, regarding me as a painter might study his model.

"That you are the spitting image of one of the *Madonnas* in the Uffizi Gallery - a sixteenth century. They're all so bursting with curiosity, they can hardly stand the suspense."

"Oh Franco, quit it."

"I'm not making it up, I swear. When you're in Firenze, you can go see it for yourself. Why else did you think I picked you up on the train?" He winked archly and pulled me across the street.

"And here I thought you were just being a gentleman, and helping me find my way."

"And wasn't I the perfect gentleman?" he asked archly, blowing a droplet of rain off the tip of his nose.

"Franco, *Dio mio*! You're going to freeze her to death!"

We were greeted at the door by Luisa.

"Look at you - you're both drenched!" She closed the door behind us and ran for towels. "Get them some wine! Here, come in where it's warm. Franco, you're a fox! Look at her - keeping her from us all this time. We wanted to come and break down your door!"

The others crowded around to greet us, offering two-cheek kisses and all talking at once. I was handed a glass of wine, wrapped in a woolen shawl and herded into the room of strangers who were Franco's Conservatory friends.

"Here's Bruno, and this is Elena. Meet Ugo, Stefano, Maria... and come, I want you to meet my favorite person in the world, Luisa's grandmother." Franco guided me into the kitchen where the parents waited, his face lit with excited smiles. He had told me about this old woman - his godmother, he said. She, more than anyone, was his teacher.

"Not of music," he had told me gravely, "of life."

"Signora," he said now, bowing to the calm, white-haired lady in black who sat with her hands folded in her lap and an expectant smile on her face. " May I present Marta." Warmly, she enfolded both of my hands in hers and gazed at my face. Then rising smoothly from her seat, she took my face in her hands and kissed me softly on both cheeks. Then she gazed again, thoughtfully, and nodding, turned to Franco with a gentle smile.

"*Si*, Franco," she said softly. "You are right. It's the inside look as much as the face."

"She does, doesn't she?" exclaimed Luisa's mother, taking my chin in her hand and turning my profile to the people crowded in the kitchen. "It's in the eyes - and the mouth..."

"It's more than that," declared Grandmother. "It's the expression..." While the others continued to appraise me unabashedly, she went out into the garden, and returned with a long-stemmed red rose. Standing before me, she offered me the flower.

"*Per la Madonna*," she said, with a little bow. For a moment the room was hushed. I had never been the object of a tribute before, and was not sure I knew how to be gracious. Accepting the rose with a return of her bow I breathed in its fragrance and held it to my heart.

"*Grazie*," I murmured, turning then to smile at Franco. Tremulously, I took his hand. His friends all sighed, everyone beamed approval, and Grandmother kissed us both, sending us back into the parlour to have our party.

For the rest of the evening we drank and laughed and sang. Franco had to tell them the whole story of how we met on the train and how he had to scour the streets for hours the next day to find me again.

"I thought I had perhaps dreamed up the whole thing," he explained. "This Madonna of the Train might have been just a hallucination."

"But why didn't you ever tell me this?" I asked.

"Maybe he was afraid of breaking the spell," offered Bruno.

"It was never the right moment," Franco confessed. "How do you tell a lovely woman that she looks like a painting?"

"Especially one that's just given birth!" Elena added, as everyone broke into general hilarity.

Later, we made music. Luisa sang a new piece of Bruno's, and he accompanied her on the piano. There was a heated discussion of Bruno's composition, and then Luisa sang it again. Bruno played another of his pieces - one of everyone's favorites - and suggested madrigals, which we sang for awhile, two to a part.

"Now it's your turn," Stephano said, pointing at me.

"Me? I can't - no flute!" I declared. Everyone went silent and glanced at Franco, who pretended to whistle innocently and examine the ceiling. There was mischief in the room; I was missing something. Casually, Franco pulled his backpack out from under his chair and slowly took out my flute.

"Franco!" I exclaimed, shocked.

"They made me..." he said sheepishly, holding back his merriment. My head swam. I couldn't play my little improvisations for this group of real musicians.

"I won't," I declared, shaking my head.

"We're longing to hear you," cajoled Bruno. "Franco says you're a natural."

"But I'm a beginner," I protested. "I don't even know any pieces..." Franco tentatively handed me my flute.

"Do what you know how to do," he said softly. "It's beautiful."

"But - I've never done it in front of people before - and all of you are professional musicians!"

"And every one of us is jealous of someone who can make music without reading it off a page," remarked Bruno encouragingly. "Please play."

With trembling hands I assembled my flute and stood to the side of the piano. The flute felt cool in my hands, then familiar. Lifting it to my lips I waited, listening for the first phrase to sing itself in my mind's ear. A song was there, tentative at first, but then flowing. I let it flow. Like sap, it rose within me and came through sweet as honey. I breathed deeply and let it sing, playing my song for Franco.

Again we found ourselves on the train from Bologna to Ravenna, but this time we were traveling together. With the cello propped up between us we stared out at the passing countryside, tired and not prone to conversation. After a week of being together every moment, we were both ready for solitude.

Franco hummed to himself, one knee braced on the seat ahead of him, and gazed past me out the window. Across the aisle, a man blew acrid cigarette smoke in our direction. My eyes began to water and I climbed over Franco and the cello to retreat to the other end of the car.

A child whined and a mother scolded and the trainwheels clacked steadily through green fields and hamlets which whizzed by in a blur, their people appearing and disappearing like colored dots against the green.

For most of the trip, Franco and I stayed apart. Either I roamed the train, or he did. When we crossed paths, we treated each other like strangers passing in the aisle, just like few weeks earlier before we had met.

By the time we reached Ravenna, however, we were both ready to know each other again. He tugged at my braid as I jumped down to the platform, handing me his cello before he followed me. Just outside the station, on the queue for tram *numero quattro*, we turned to each other for the first time that day, and smiled shyly. Again, he was carrying a cello, and I a backpack with a flute inside.

"Tell me," he asked cautiously, enunciating each word ,

DUO D'AMORE

"Do you speak Italian?" His dark eyes shone with fun.

"*Tre poco*," I admitted with a smile. "*Je suis una Americana.*"

"Oh," he said gaily, "We speak the same language. Let's talk."

In the lowering light, the road to Classe seemed oddly unfamiliar. Birds winged their way overhead through a pink and orange streaked sky to their roosts in trees that darkly dotted the countryside, and the fields, in the setting sun, looked mauve.

I sat astride the back of a borrowed Vespa, pressed against Franco's back. The friend who lent it would bring our instruments to the Basilica by car. My hair whipped in the wind, which lifted my skirts, and the motor drowned out all other sounds on the road.

"Pleased?" shouted Franco above the roar of the engine. I rubbed my cheek against his shoulder in reply and tightened my knees against the sides of the scooter. Dipping into a hollow, we went through a stretch of cool air, rising again into a warmer current which kissed our cheeks. The fields were fragrant with mown hay, and cows plodded in groups toward the barns. I held onto Franco's waist more tightly just for the pleasure of it all, and he turned towards me for an instant, his eyes bright and his face lit with wind.

In the dusky twilight, the church was dim and cool. Just inside the portals we stopped to let our eyes adjust to the light; then we walked in, feeling the columns and arches pull us towards the curved apse where the good Saint Apollinare waited with open arms. Following the forward thrust, we let the motion take us all the way to the altar.

The smiling saint, surrounded by his entourage of sheep and flowers and angels, suddenly became flooded with light as the whole altar was illuminated from the vestry. The four Evangelists glittered like jewels and on both sides of the altar votive candles flickered, sending spirals of tallow smoke up towards the mosaic.

"*Ecco!*" cried the *Padre*, emerging from the vestry in his robes. "Franco is here - welcome, my friend!" He bustled toward us, his brown habit rustling against the stone floor and his face lined with smiles. "Welcome! Welcome!" he repeated, taking both of my hands in his and shaking them up and down. "And this is the Americana - ah, welcome, my dear."

"Marta," said Franco, introducing us, "*Padre Pietro*, my good friend and teacher."

"Such an honor, my dear, to have you play at our church." he said, gazing up at the splendor of the ancient mosaics with pride.

"The honor is mine," I assured him warmly. "This is the most beautiful church I have ever seen, and it is a privilege to play in it."

"*Si, si,*" he agreed with pleasure. "Our basilica is perhaps one of the most beautiful in all of Italy. We are so fortunate to have the opportunity to preach Our Lord's Gospel here."

"And to live in the presence of so much beauty every day,"

"Ah, yes. You understand - you have the soul of an artist. Doesn't she, Franco? Ah, but Franco, he appreciates too - I have seen him cry over the beauty of his own music, haven't I, Franco? When you thought nobody saw." Franco shrugged, embarrassed, and took my hand. Noticing the gesture, the *Padre* murmured,

"Ah, yes. Two *artistes* in my church! How fortunate we are! How we shall celebrate the Eucharist tonight!"

When our instruments arrived we went our separate ways to warm up, Franco to the altar and me to the back of the church where I could view the brightly lit mosaics. Gazing at Saint Apollinare, I blew warming long tones into my flute, listening to them ring off the resonant stone walls, and off Franco's absentminded plucks as he stood talking to the *Padre* on the altar steps.

A glint of color on the floor distracted me, and bending

over I found two bits of blue glass that had fallen from the angels above my head. I rubbed them thoughtfully between my fingers and then tucked them into my pocket. The *Padre* gesticulated with gusto, pointing out to Franco where we would sit, where he would enter. Stocky in his brown robes, he presented a contrast to Franco's lean, quiet intensity. Dressed in gray slacks and a black turtleneck shirt, shifting his weight gracefully as he spoke, Franco looked the image of the artist. To me, it was as if he were outlined in light, unique and special from everything else in creation. He pointed, with a characteristic gesture of his arm, to one corner of the apse, and glanced back at the *Padre*. The *Padre* nodded, they shared a joke, smiled and shook hands.

It was just a simple exchange between two men but suddenly I was filled to bursting. Life, at that moment, was perfect. Ecstatic, I put the flute to my lips and sang out a tone that filled up the whole church and held it to the end of my breath.

Behind the altar, Franco tuned his cello, hearing my note and matching it exactly. Our notes seemed to meet in the air and resonate there. He played long tones and scales, warming up his fingers and strings as I tried out my flute in different locations: the side aisles, the back of the nave, beneath the clerestory windows. The acoustics, at each place, gave a different sound.

"The church responds!" I called out to him from the middle of the nave. He thwacked me a chord in reply which bounced off the walls and beat in the air for several seconds. I answered with a trill; he replied with a deep double stop. We both laughed, and the basilica echoed that as well.

"The doors will open in fifteen minutes," the Padre informed us, placing a vase of lilies on the altar. Joining Franco in the corner of the apse, I took my place and adjusted my music stand. We warmed up together, loosening our fingers with chromatic scales which the curved walls received and returned in a jumble of sound. When people began to arrive, I realized I had to pee.

"Nerves," whispered Franco with a grin when I looked at him questioningly. "You'll do fine," he assured me. "Just enjoy the music. Do you realize this is our first public performance together?" My mouth was dry with stagefright.

"I forgot to get water," I whispered. He licked his lips and swallowed; I did the same. When I noticed that Mamma, Babbo, the girls and most of the neighbors had arrived and were sitting up front, I realized that I couldn't remember if we played the final Rondo once through or twice. As if he had read my thoughts, Franco leaned over and whispered,

"We do the Rondo twice, then *Da Capo* from the beginning." I nodded, my hands shaking visibly. "Here we go..." he breathed as the acolytes, followed by the *Padre*, entered down the aisle, incense-burners swinging. A rustle and scraping of chairs came next as the congregation knelt onto the stone floor, intoning the first prayers.

We played the *Kyrie* in unison, repeating the notes of the sung plainsong chant. The simple melody was slow enough to give us the chance to tune to each other's intonation precisely. When we were exactly on each others' pitch, the half-dome vibrated with a resonant buzz. With each tone we listened closely for our common sound; when it rang clear, we shimmered.

The *Sanctus* was also restrained; *Et Incarnatus* was a bit more complex, and the *Gloria* began to have a lilt. We followed each chant, repeating exactly the notes sung by the Padre, at exactly his pace. During the sermon we sat with our heads bowed, our instruments at rest. He spoke of harvests being like the gathering of souls into community. His voice echoed through the church, ringing off the walls like music.

The *Agnus Dei* was a plaintive call, and by the time we played the beseeching tones of the *Dona Nobis Pacem*, my fingers itched to take off in a separate creation. But the ritual of the Mass took its own time, solemn and measured, and I held back my impulse to soar. During the *Amen*, Franco caught my eye and grinned, keeping the beat steady but clearly as impatient as I.

The last notes of the *Amen* hung suspended in the air as the *Padre* intoned them into the hushed basilica. Pause. The echoes settled, and then it was time for Communion. It was our time to play. The faithful rose from their seats, filing with folded hands and bowed heads toward the altar. Franco and I confirmed a common beat, breathed in together and played out the first phrase of our music, cello and flute.

The *Padre* held his arms high, bread in one hand and wine in the other.

"THIS IS MY BODY - TAKE IT AND EAT.
THIS IS MY BLOOD - TAKE IT AND DRINK."

The cello outlined the bass line and the flute picked it up, exploring the dimensions of the theme. We filled the space with sound, relishing every moment as it poured out from us and spread into the church.

The *Adagio* was plaintive, sweet. Playing it with delicious restraint we held back, always promising more. The people received our music, and we felt it radiate back to us as love.

In the moment of silence between movements, our eyes met and we burned, transformed by our communion. On the upbeat we breathed together and opened into the first variation on the theme. The cello made the initial statement, holding a deep, grounded pattern while the flute rose note by note into triplets, racing playfully ahead while the cello held a sure, steady beat and returning seductively to the theme before taking off capriciously again.

Then the cello took the theme, charging through its range while the flute supported with sustained high notes from above. The cello slipped up to almost meet the flute, staying just a halftone below before dropping out of reach into its rich, resonant lower octave. The apse pulsed with the sounds; I kept the flute notes high and pure, letting the cello have his day.

Sacral Chakra

The congregation surged forward to receive the Host. They took Him into their mouths, returning to their places solemnly. Such seriousness was not for us, however, and we swung into the next movement with passion, infected by each other's rhythms and dancing out variation after variation without tiring.

Then, breath spent, we started again slowly, stepping delicately around each other until the pace accelerated and we again leapt forward, excited. We swelled together and we pulled apart. We met with gladness and we held back discreetly. We breathed in sync and we shouted with the joy of it all!

Our parts were equal and our piece was new. The cello came towards the flute, confident and strong. The flute waited - I waited - to receive him; when he came, I opened and sang in full voice.

His music begged for my response; I responded with abandon. He needed my response in order to have his completion; receiving it, he resolved his rich phrase.

His completion was essential for my satisfaction, and I embraced his phrase, rounding off the movement. The circle came full round to home. We reached the *da Capo* together, replete.

Starting again from the beginning, we played the whole piece through at a faster tempo. The beat played us as we whirled through each movement at speed. Our song sang, with us upon it, and we reached the end together, our notes filled with glory until my breath, and his bow faded out into stillness.

The Mass was achieved.

We had played ourselves out. Neither I nor Franco was ready to receive the throng of well-wishers who came forward at the end of the Mass, but the whole community laid claim to us, toasting us with compliments. We were herded into the Chapter House, given wine, pinched, patted and cheered. Franco, the native son, was adored; I the Americana, was adulated. We were separated as crowds swirled around us, exclaiming and kissing and applauding.

I felt overwhelmed, and hot. Franco was on the other side of the room, besieged by his public. Over the heads of the crowd he signalled to me, gesturing towards the door. When I could do so discreetly, I snuck out.

Outside, we made a run for the Vespa, gunning the scooter through the star-studded night to the sea. The wind was cool in our faces and I lay a flushed cheek against his back, snuggling up close. He accelerated and we jolted after the headlight illuminating the road ahead of us, leaving the darkness, the church, the congregation and our instruments behind.

We could smell the sea even before we reached the coast. Spurting onto the beach, Franco cut the motor and we idled to a stop on the sand. After the roar of the engine, the silence of the night and the rhythmic splash of surf throbbed gently.

Scrambling off the scooter, we ran hand in hand down to the water, where only a wavy line of foam indicated where the land ended and the sea began. We kicked off our shoes, skirt, pants and waded in, squealing with the shock of the cold water. Calf-deep in foam we flung our arms around each other, making sweet noise and swaying together tightly.

Dizzy. We were dizzy with each other and with the night. Murmuring with impatience, we ran out of the surf out of the reach of the waves, our legs stinging with salt. The kind dark cloaked us and we sank to the sand, coming together urgently. Opening, we listened intently for each other's rhythms and finding them, we moved together, moaning.

The stars moved with us, and the sea. The wind was our friend, and all the while the world whirled and whirled and whirled.

3

KINDERLIED

Solar Plexus Chakra - Pancreas

*Taking of personal power;
moving from inertia to activity;
the propensity to shift and change;
transformation.*

On our street in Brooklyn, with its weedy lots, elevated train tracks and two-story brownstones, Aunt Sadie was famous for her curses.

With her, cursing was an art form. She honed her craft daily, using it to test her originality, blow off steam and bond the family more closely to her. When Aunt Sadie let loose, everyone on the block stopped to listen - and thanked the Lord, I daresay, that she was a member of our family and not theirs.

"*Tatteleh*," she would croon sweetly to a son who had left his ball lying on the front stoop, "the Messiah should come tonight to give you a blessing..." with a soft, deceptive smile she would continue, her voice rising,"...and He should trip over your garbage, and it should be YOUR FAULT!"

Or to one who had not made his bed, we would hear her intone,

"I pray to God you should have one hundred rooms, and one hundred beds in every room..." Here, a blanket would be stripped off a mattress and flung into the offender's face. "And every bed should have one hundred bedbugs..." A pillow would hit the ceiling with a thump.

"And every bedbug should have one hundred babies, and they should all be starving when you got into bed!"

Like a Russian-Jewish Medusa, Aunt Sadie schlepped around in bedroom slippers and a ripped housedress, her frizzy hair jammed with bobby pins and stuck out from her head like a corona of crazy snakes. A brastrap always hung down one arm, and the aroma of chicken fat and onions clung to her skin even through the stench of her cigarette smoke.

I never knew her not to be talking, and I never knew it not to be loud. Her mouth moved continually - muttering, yelling, eating, smoking - and a spate of Yiddish meant that we kids had better run, either towards her or away, depending upon the circumstance.

"Lucky! Teddiecoo! Sollie!" the whole neighborhood would hear her yell as she trudged up the street from the store. (It would be twenty years before it dawned on me that my cousin Teddiecoo's real name was Theodore.) Staggering under a load of groceries and a gallon jug of Javel Water , her coat held together by safety pins and her slippers coming off her feet, she would holler,

"Get out here help me carry or I'll smack you so hard you won't be able to sit down for a month!"

Then on Friday for *Shabbos*, like a religious ritual she would slosh the Javel Water all over the kitchen floor - *Shabbos* was never honored in any other way in our house - and scrub the floor until it shone. After that she covered it with newspapers 'so it shouldn't get dirty', and threaten everyone who entered the house,

"Walk on the newspapers! You dirty my floor, I'll dirty your head!"

By the middle of the week, the newspapers were wadded with mud and scattered through every room in the house. Then she would trudge home from the store with a new bottle of Javel Water and dump it, like a yellow deluge, all over the kitchen floor again.

Despite everything, everyone in the house was totally dependent upon her : the downstairs family - Uncle Max and my three cousins, Lucky, Teddiecoo and Sollie , and the upstairs family - my parents, my grandfather and me, Marta, (called by Aunt Sadie, Martingcoo.) Like the Fairy- Witch of the folktales she provided refuge, advice, money and pickled herring to anyone in need. A pot of chicken soup bubbled incessantly on her stove and her door was opened to every poor soul who stumbled by, no matter who.

But when the lost one found his own feet and no longer needed her, it was worth his life to try and leave. Independence, in her eyes, constituted betrayal. Those who stayed could count on her solace forever; the others, to her dying breath, she never forgave.

"Go downstairs to Aunt Sadie until Daddy comes home," my mother said, steering me out the door of our apartment. She let me find my way down the dark staircase alone, closing our door, and the light, when I reached Aunt Sadie's door.

My mother's face was puffy with crying, which made my eyes feel hot and scratchy and my throat too tight to talk. I went quickly, scared, and I didn't look back.

"Come in, Martingcoo, shut the door, it's cold."

A couple of neighbors had gathered to taste Aunt Sadie's chopped liver and listen to her latest stories. I snuck in around them and parked myself near the mop and bucket by the stove, where it was warm.

"I should drop down dead if what I'm telling you isn't God's honest truth." Smoke poured from Aunt Sadie's nostrils like a dragon and her hands, chopping liver in the wooden bowl, shook. The boys wrestled each other for the place closest to the food and the neighbors had perched themselves unsteadily atop the piles of ironing that graced every kitchen chair.

"You won't believe - they were fighting, these two floozies, right over the grave!" Aunt Sadie chopped vigorously to emphasize the point, hitching her brastrap back onto her shoulder with a greasy finger. Teddiecoo leaned towards the bowl and she slapped him away.

"Who? Who were they?" everyone wanted to know.

"Who?" she repeated, shoving an errant breast back through a ripped armhole. "How should I know? Did I say I knew these people?"

Aunt Sadie went to funerals the way other people went to

bars. Her best buddies were an Italian couple from across the street - *the prostitute and the undertaker*, she called them - and her favorite way to spend an afternoon was at some stranger's funeral. From these she would arrive home refreshed, her eyes bright and reddened, her dress askew on her broad hips and her lipstick smeared in streaks around her mouth. After such a good cry she would laugh a lot, and everyone would gather to catch her at her best and listen to her unbelievable stories.

Uncle Max flushed in the bathroom and came out into the kitchen, blinking. I squeezed against the stove so he could get through, and he laid a hand on my head, muttering,

"What's she talking about?"

"Two floozies...fighting...," I ventured, actually having no idea what she was talking about. I didn't want to know, either. I wanted to be upstairs with my mommy who told me she didn't feel well, I should go down to Aunt Sadie. Whose cigarette was now about to drop a curl of ash into the chopping bowl. I lunged out to catch the ash before it fell, and banged my shin against the bucket. The ash dangled and then plopped onto the table instead of into the chopped liver. I felt ashamed. Tears spurted to my eyes and I turned to the stove to hide them. Nobody noticed; their eyes were all on Aunt Sadie.

"So what happened then?"

"Wait. Wait," she assured them, playing to her audience. "Max, I forgot bread - go get me..?" From her cleavage she pulled a bill and stuffed it into his hand. He shrugged into his overcoat and I leaned against his legs.

"Can I come?" I asked.

"Where's your coat?"

"No Max, leave her. I need the bread fast." She scraped at the chopped liver as Uncle Max left, resuming her story. "The wife, she was one. The other, she must have been his tootsie."

"No!" they all breathed. "A wife and a tootsie, *both* at the funeral together...?"

"*Goyim*," Aunt Sadie remarked offhandedly, slopping more chicken fat into the bowl. "Not Jews. You should see what they wear - minks like it was going out of style, hats with feathers they could poke your eye out...*vey iss mir*..."

Uncle Max returned shortly with the bread, plopped it down on the table and unbuttoned his overcoat.

"So what about the wife and the tootsie?" everyone wanted to know.

"It was a young tootsie, like a daughter more than a girlfriend..."

"So maybe it was a daughter, no?"

"No," replied Aunt Sadie with authority, "that was no daughter - Max, I forgot to tell you cream cheese." Without missing a beat she pulled another bill from her bosom and handed it over, leaving a shiny splotch of grease at her cleavage. Uncle Max sighed, got back into his overcoat and hat and shuffled to the door. I followed him.

"You can't," he said, even before I asked. Teddiecoo snuck a finger into the chopped liver and got his hand smacked.

"Ma, get to the point - I'm starving!" Lucky complained. Sollie jabbed him in the ribs, giggling. They fell to the floor in a clinch, and Aunt Sadie stopped the wrestle with a kick.

"So these two - ladies - are pulling each other into the open grave...," she went on, chopping, talking and kicking at the same time.

"Noooo!" they all sang in a chorus.

"I should tell you something it isn't true?" she asked offended. "This is God's holy truth, I should hope to die if it isn't..." She placed the liver-crusted chopper across her heart and closed her eyes reverently. Teddiecoo made another grab for the liver and was threatened with dismemberment.

"The tootsie," she continued whispering suspensefully, "her coat comes open and you'd never guess - she's expecting!"

"Noooo!" they sang again, their hands over their mouths.

Expecting. Like my mommy. Was that bad?

"Then this priest, what does he do, he almost faints and falls right into the grave, you wouldn't believe..."

Right then, Uncle Max came back. I wanted to ask him if it was bad to be expecting; I wanted to ask him to take me upstairs again. I pressed my back against the stove and bounced against where it was warm. Aunt Sadie took the cream cheese and went on talking.

"So the wife and the tootsie are pulling and kicking, I'm thinking one of them is going to land right in the coffin, and the priest looks like he's about to vomit, Max, I need carrots..."

Uncle Max's overcoat was still cold from the outside; his nose dripped and the brim of his hat made his ears stick out. He looked hungry. My stomach felt too sad to be hungry, but I wiped my nose with the back of my sleeve, even though it was Uncle Max's nose that needed it. He shook his head and said, in his gravelly rumble of Yiddish and English,

"I went already twice - you want three things you tell me once. I'm not schlepping again."

"Max," she entreated, as if speaking to an idiot child, "it's for the *geffilte* fish." As if that explained everything.

He went, and so did I. Both of us left unnoticed. I crept up the staircase in the dark to our door and curled up in the corner, pretending I was cuddled in my mother's arms. It wasn't time for me to be back inside so I closed my eyes and fell asleep, waiting for my father to come home.

"I found her out in the hall!" he exclaimed, half-dragging, half-carrying me into our apartment. "What's going on?" My father was very angry with my mother, and this time it was my fault.

"She was with Sadie," she replied in a little voice, not looking at him. She took me into her arms, but didn't look at me either. "I didn't know she came upstairs."

Our kitchen, unlike the noisy kitchen downstairs, was dark and silent. The only sounds were my parents' breathing and the crackling voice of the evening newscaster on the radio. My grandfather sat scrunched up close to the console in the next room, his forehead pressed to the speaker. He was crying- again - and wiped off his tears with the back of his hand.

"Why does grandpa still listen?" I asked in a tense whisper. All he did was cry when he listened to the news, but he kept listening to the news anyway. My mother sighed and nudged me towards my father, who held me too tight.

"Why does he still listen?" I insisted, pulling out of my father's grasp and grabbing hold of my mother's skirt. But she stared above both of us, her eyes swollen and staring at something I couldn't see.

They listened to the news every night when the war was on - the upstairs family and the downstairs family. But now the war was over. My Uncle Saul, my mother's brother, never came home 'with the boys'. It was over. So why did my grandpa still listen?

"Turn it down, Pa," said my mother in a low, sad voice.

"Hey, c'mon, let's have a little smile," my father entreated, awkwardly reaching for her above my head. But she pushed him aside and nudged me ahead of her towards the bathroom, her hands icy on my arms. In the dark, I was almost afraid of her.

My father followed, trying to hug her again in the bathroom.

"Leave me be!" she hissed, shouldering away from him as she held me against the sink.

"What the Hell's the matter?" he spit out, keeping his voice low so grandpa wouldn't hear. "You're becoming impossible..."

"Just leave me," she said again, almost crying. With an angry twist she turned on the faucet and put my hands under the running water. Then she rubbed them hard.

My father stayed by the door, watching her closely and pretending to smile. I could always tell when his smile wasn't real because then his black moustache stood out like a gash above his lips. His eyes, even his cheeks and his dark, wavy hair, looked hungry to me. Sometimes, when he looked that way, he would bite my arm in play, hurting me.

"Come here, you," he persisted, making believe she was being coy. Too roughly, he pulled her towards him and I felt her stiffen and press my arms too hard against the sink. Their legs knocked against me as she struggled out of his embrace, tossing her head back and forth to avoid his wet kisses. But he was the stronger and she finally submitted, with disgust, to a sloppy kiss before pushing him away from her.

But his eyes were still dark with needing and he reached for me instead, nuzzling at the back of my neck with a hungry tongue. A tingling shock made my body shiver, and I shrank away from him too.

"Oh, for God's sake," my mother complained, covering my body with hers against the sink and offering my hands again to the now scalding hot water. Shrieking, I pulled my arms back and burrowed with relief into her swollen belly, letting go of the sobs that had choked my throat for many weeks. For awhile she held me against her, and then turned me back to the sink.

"Use soap," she said, her voice again cold and dull, "and dry your hands when you're through." I put my hands gingerly under the flow from the Cold tap, swallowing my tears and hiccoughs. She walked out of the bathroom, right past my father.

"And don't cry," she said.

The water ran into the sink, leaving a smear of rust, like blood. I swallowed hard, coughing a little as if my throat were clogged with dirt, and my eyes followed the path of water over the rust until the hard place in my chest began to dissolve.

Around my finger the water puckered, rippled and ran smooth. The pain melted and I felt it lower down. Squashing my hand against the faucet, I crushed the water into a wild spray that wet the room. The shock of cold down the front of my shirt helped me to breathe. I did it more, gasping with the quick cold until my whole chest was numb.

The sadness inside me softened and turned to hot grease, like Aunt Sadie's rendered chicken fat on the stove. Swallowing it down hard, I held it low in my belly until I could clamp it down tight. Then I shut an imaginary hatch over the pain until the feeling went away. After that, I couldn't even remember why I was sad.

By the time I left the bathroom and went into the kitchen, my hands were wrinkled and dry, my shirt was sopping wet and I no longer felt like crying. In fact, I no longer felt anything at all.

Grandpa lived with us, but Grandma didn't. She lived in a wheelchair in THE HOME FOR JEWISH INCURABLES in the Bronx.

We called it THE HOME - not an inaccurate name, as Grandma had lived there since the age of twenty-nine when she had been stricken with multiple sclerosis and paralyzed from the neck down.

At first, Grandpa and her sister, Aunt Sadie, had tried to take care of her in the house - but by that time, there were two children to care for, too. When she became incontinent as well and had to be lifted on and off bedpans, it became more than they could handle. Already, at the age of nine, my mother was staying home from school to tend the baby, Saul. The task was bigger than they were and finally they had no choice but to send her to an institution - THE HOME.

"You can believe she didn't go willingly," my mother had said, her elbows on the kitchen table, one finger fitfully twirling a lock of hair. "She fought us every inch of the way - and hasn't forgiven any of us since." Pressing her lips together sadly, she had tucked the loose strand of hair into her bun, and shrugged,

"But what else could they have done?"

Solar Plexus Chakra

I remember the long subway rides to THE HOME with my mother, my grandpa and my young Uncle Saul. We went every single Sunday, dressed in cotton in the summer, wool in the winter. Not Daddy, though. THE HOME made him sick, he said. So Grandpa or Uncle Saul carried me, holding me against their chests and covering my ears when the train came thundering terrifyingly into the station.

Even now I could walk the three blocks from the subway station to THE HOME in my sleep - and do - past the red-brick apartment houses like windowed fortresses, each with its cluster of *babushka*-clad ladies sunning themselves on folding chairs by the entrance. Their skirts must still be hitched above pasty knees, their eyes still following every passerby wistfully.

At the corner we would wait for the light, cross in front of sputtering cars and come to the broad steps of THE HOME FOR JEWISH INCURABLES. Across the Avenue, the back fences of the Bronx Zoo offered tantalizing glimpses of long snouts and twitching tails. By the time we reached the front entryway of the hospital, I had to be prodded or picked up to get me inside.

"Could we go to the Zoo - after?" I would ask, projecting myself into the cool green shade of the Zoo's shrubbery and breathing in huge gulps of fresh air to last me the whole visit. But no matter how deeply I breathed, it was only a few steps into the lobby before I had to gulp in another breath, taking into myself the sour stench of disease and urine which permeated the very walls of THE HOME.

The lobby was like a shadowy cavern echoing with the croaks and spastic shuffling of those patients ambulatory enough to get themselves downstairs. I had known them since birth: the blind and dumb mute by the candy stand, the hoarse-voiced talker always waiting by the entrance, the lurching dribbler who followed us to the staircase. While Grandpa stopped to greet them, I ran ahead to do my dance on the steel stairs.

Banging my feet down on each step, I established a rhythm before the others came to confuse the beat. Then when their footsteps rang on the steel stairs along with mine, I listened for our combined music so I could create my dance.

Dinkity - dump - bump diddle dunk; Dinkity - dump-bump diddledunk.

Skipping to make up beats, or holding spaces to make the song perfect, the dance had to finish at the last step before Grandma's ward, or I lost a point.

Patients lined the corridor in their wheelchairs like passengers on a cruise ship, but the ocean they looked upon was each other and whoever came in through the door. Their eyes, dimmed by illness, followed us hopefully as we emerged from the stairwell.

"Over here..." they would cry out, their wasted arms reaching for us. "Beautiful child, come give me a kiss..." We held a continuous smile as we made our way down the hall, but did not stop. Every minute at THE HOME was for visiting Grandma and she, as always, was on the outdoor porch.

Like a veranda running the full length of the ward, the porch was blessedly open to the sky. Even in mid-winter, when nobody else came out, Grandma could be found on the porch in the wind by herself.

When the weather was nice, many patients huddled in their wheelchairs, talking to each other and watching the doorway for visitors. Those who expected family felt more secure and so they sat in patches of sun; those who did not took their chances by the door, making grabs for attention from every bit of life that walked through. A child, naturally, was especially prized and they clutched at me with crabbed fingers the moment I appeared. By the laws of the place, I was their hostage.

"Hahhnh," they would stroke me longingly, their breath sour in my face. While Grandpa held onto me, I got passed from one wheelchair to another so each patient could get me for a few seconds of palsied fondling. Their armrests dug into me; drooling, they kissed me wherever they could reach. Their filmy eyes were lit with the wanting that my very child's being provoked. They sang to me with putrid breath, leaving spittle on my face that I would not wipe off until I thought they couldn't see.

Some patients never noticed our arrival. They were the 'keeners' who sat alone facing the wall and railed against a God who would not let them die. Their cries, high-pitched and desperate, rang above the other sounds of the place like a plainsong chant that went on and on and on.

Grandma was something of a 'keener' too, but her complaints were for us, not God. She wanted out of there, and she wanted it *now*. She would start weeping as soon as she sighted us, her voice a high whine and her mouth clenched in a tight-lipped grimace. Captive in her wheelchair, she formed an immobile pyramid of flesh swathed in blankets, her seat a hard chrome bedpan. Only her face had motion, and as soon as we arrived she used it to cry, to complain, to talk, to sing, to laugh - and to scold.

"You're late."

"No we're not, Ma," my mother always said, leaning over for the kiss.

"You are." Then she would wink at me, her coquettish eyes hinting at the feisty beauty she once had been. Then she would gaze at each of us with pathetic longing, while Grandpa lifted me for the kiss. With a force that always surprised me, she would latch on with her lips and hold me there until I felt faint. Helpless, I would brace my knees against the rubber wheel and shut my eyes tight so I couldn't see the sadness of her wasted life on her tear-wet cheeks. When she finally let go, I would scramble down, flustered with sorrow.

"Where's your Daddy?" she would ask slyly. This was for my mother, who would make a point of ignoring the question while nudging Uncle Saul closer for the kiss.

"He's too busy working, right? He doesn't have time..." Fixing my mother with her eyes, she went on, "He'll come maybe next time, right?" Her face again flowed with tears, which grew into sobs and finally, rage.

This was a lousy prison - why couldn't she come home? The food they gave you was *dreck*, the doctors ignoramuses... Then Grandpa would bend over her and fold her useless body in his arms, stroking her once-lustrous hair and murmuring soothingly in her ear. That was the cue for my mother and Uncle Saul to take me for a walk around the ward.

Trailing behind them, I ran my hands along the high beds, staring at the wasted bodies of sleeping patients. I walked at their pace, but in my mind I ran up and down the rows of beds, pulling patients out of their covers and making them stand up and walk.

"Get up!" I wanted to scream. "Just walk! You can run, I know you can. You're just pretending!" My body ached with holding back. I wanted to fling myself around, shoving over wheelchairs and jumping on the beds. In my heart I took flying leaps out the windows, dragging sick people with me, yelling at them to fly.

Nobody would have guessed at my imaginary crimes.

My grandfather had also committed crimes - imaginary crimes and real ones as well. As a teenage revolutionary in Russia, he had been given a gun and told to shoot the local *gendarme*, which he did. In the back, while the man was pissing against a wall.

By the age of seventeen he was an outlaw. I suspect he had no illusions about getting away with his rash act, but knowing him I think he hoped to make up for his youthful crime with acts of virtue and courage in the new country of America.

In New York, he continued to work for the great revolution. He organized fellow workers, taught refugees in evening school, married a beautiful comrade and fathered a daughter and a son. But

Solar Plexus Chakra

the murder he had committed in his youth would stalk him like a vengeful shadow, as the paralysis of his gorgeous, feisty wife was only the first of the disasters to befall him.

Shortly after she fell ill, her mother, *Bubbe*, was run over by a truck. *Bubbe*, the first of that family to come over from Russia, was the matriarch of a clan that included six rambunctious daughters, of which Sadie was the eldest and my grandmother the youngest. This clan expanded with each boatload of refugees arriving from Europe and they would arrive, in tattered coats and *babushkas*, and show up at Bubbe's door. They were fed, housed and counselled until they found jobs, and then were sent out on their own to do the same for others. Everyone loved *Bubbe*. From her tenement flat in East New York, she presided over a small world.

But it would all end on a sunny Friday in the market on Delancy Street. The truck hit her straight on, tossed her down and dragged her the length of the block beneath its wheels, the chicken for *Shabbos* still dangling from her wrist in a shopping bag. When they got her out, both she and the chicken were gone.

Young Sadie, after their mother's death, took over the role of matriarch, but she was not yet formed - nor was she the same kind of woman as *Bubbe*. She ruled with an unrelenting grip what her mother had held in a firm, but tender, hand. What had been an extended family - a community - began to dissolve into warring factions.

Then came the Great Depression. Amongst those who lost their jobs, and thus their cold water flats, were my grandfather and the two children. They had no choice but to move in with Aunt Sadie and Uncle Max, becoming orphans in a family that was now less than kind to orphans.

Meanwhile, my grandfather's bride from Lithuania gathered bedsores in the Bronx. Rage massed like thunderclouds within her as her lovely body grew flaccid and slumped, a lump of wasted flesh, into a wooden wheelchair which her useless arms could not even push.

And then, as if all this were not enough, came my grandmother's curse. This was a real curse, not an excuse for inventive release, like Aunt Sadie's. It was this curse which ushered in the next string of disasters in our family which, as they occurred during my lifetime, inevitably became mine.

It happened, oddly enough, during a morning bath. The nurse who bathed my grandmother also had a son and the two women, over the years, gossiped about their children. The nurse had a special fondness for this unfortunate and beautiful woman, crippled from the neck down in her prime, and bathed her daily, and talked with her.

Both boys at that time had reached draft age and with the war now raging in Europe, the women were terrified of their sons being called to the Front. Saul, as the son of an invalid mother, was not obligated to serve, but the other boy, of course, was.

As I have heard the story, as the woman soaped my grandmother and told her, in hushed tones, that her boy had been drafted, the two women had cried and Grandma had slipped, for an instant, out of the woman's slippery hands.

Startled, her pent-up rage had let go and she erupted like a volcano in full blast.

"Bitch!" she shrieked over and over. "I pray he never comes back from the war!"

That son came back. Saul did not.

He enlisted, despite the fact that he didn't have to. By his twentieth birthday he had been sent to the Front and wounded in action.

"He was so gentle - not a fighter...," my mother, for years, would moan.

In the army hospital his wounds became septic. In a few weeks the infection had spread; in a month, he was dead.

"He didn't have to go...," my mother, still in shock after years, would whisper.

A Purple Heart for bravery came in the mail. With it, a tufted mat in purple and yellow for Easter - made by Uncle Saul in the hospital, they said.

"He never made this...," my mother mumbled, her mouth quivering and her eyes unblinking. She put the mat in a drawer.

"He didn't like purple..." I took it out and fingered it wonderingly. Finding me with it, she snatched it away and hid it deep in the bottom of another drawer, underneath the tablecloths. For years, when she wasn't looking, I would remove it from its hiding place and feel the tufts, wondering sadly about my uncle.

As my grandmother's curse was considered the cause of Saul's death, she was never told that he was dead. She knew immediately anyhow, of course, keening through clenched teeth even before the telegram and the Purple Heart had arrived at our house.

But his name would never be mentioned to her again, no matter how much she wept and cajoled. All information about the family outside, good or bad, was not to be spoken to her. The few times I slipped, responding to her questions about a cousin, or my schoolwork, I was punished.

I wonder, now, about my grandfather's complicity, and how he was able to resist her tireless proddings. Perhaps he also blamed her for Saul's enlisting, and could not forgive. Maybe he was horrified by the power of her curse. Or perhaps, after Saul's death at twenty, he felt beaten by fate and gave up the struggle. In my memory, his strong-boned, craggy Russian face has sad, green eyes and a bland, American smile. The fiery, young revolutionary was a man I never knew.

I was close to six when Uncle Saul died. Afterwards, my mother seemed to lose the glue that held her together. For weeks, she sobbed inconsolably. Then she sat and stared at the wall. Although she almost never left the house, it was as if she was no longer there amongst us.

My father was scared. She was out of control with grief, and he didn't know what to do. It was as if she had left us - her husband, her six- year- old daughter, and her new baby girl. The only thing she could do was mourn her brother.

"That's enough!" he lashed out at her one evening when he came home to a hysterical wife, hungry children and no supper on the stove. His black eyes were frenzied. She backed away from him and pressed against the wall, cowering. I also backed away, hoping the wallpaper would suck me in. Roses in a garden, innocent and pink.

"You've been crying for four weeks straight! I've had enough! You've got to stop it right now!" He stamped his foot again and again and she stared, unseeing, right through him. She didn't breathe. Neither did I, until he stomped out of the room. She kept staring at the space where he had been, unblinking. And she stopped crying - cold.

Her tears went away, but so did my mother. She was there in the house, but instead of a mother there was a cold, distracted stranger. When she looked at me she stared, but did not see me. Her hands felt dry, and she never spoke except to rebuke. In my memory she fades at this point, as if she went into a room and shut the door behind her, which I suspect is in essence just what she did.

My baby sister, Simone, and I were put into Aunt Sadie's care. Aunt Sadie now had three boys and two girls to look after. The boys were a handful, and Simone an infant. I, at six, tending to be quiet and to keep to myself without getting into trouble, was left to fend for myself.

Every day I crept up the dark staircase and gazed at the locked door of our apartment. Lying on my stomach on the landing, I would peer through the crack under our door and look for my mother. If I saw her moving about I would call, under my breath, "Mommy....Mommy..."

If I didn't see her I would gaze for a long time at our empty kitchen. Once she was there scrubbing up and down at the walls, her arms wet with dirty water and her face white and hard. I started to call, and choked on my voice. She turned towards the door, her eyes blazing as if they had blood behind them. I flung my arm over my mouth and scrambled down the stairs as fast as I could go, rushing into Aunt Sadie's arms and clinging to her housedress for the rest of the day, never making a sound.

Of that time, between the ages of about six and eight years old, I remember almost nothing. I know, as history, that the Second World War ended; that my sister Simone was born. I know that my long braids were cut off and that I broke my front teeth falling on the sidewalk. I know this because of the continuing evidence, not because I have any recollection of them occurring.

Like everyone else in the house upstairs and downstairs, I was preoccupied with sorrow. I withdrew, like my mother and my grandfather, until I was barely there at all. Where I was, I have no idea. All I remember is numbness and humiliation, as if my very despair was something to be ashamed of.

I tried to be invulnerable, to want nothing. Mortified by my own needs for food, care, comfort, I disowned them. I learned not to cry, choking down tears every time I swallowed. With the force of six- year- old muscle, I crammed down sadness until it was far out of reach.

Since I needed my parents desperately, I hid from both of

them. They were not safe to love, so I unlearned how to love. Like an abandoned puppy I crouched in dark places and ran away from possible refuge. Wary and fearful, I gradually slowed down, body and mind, to the stolid halt of the deeply depressed. My body grew numb, my brain unwieldy. The flow had been obstructed and the drain clogged. I held onto my sadness hard, and like the sleeping princess went to sleep behind a barrier of impenetrable thorns.

My father was also depressed. Desperate for love, he came to me. He would pretend to chase me in play, grabbing for me the same way he grabbed my mother, biting me and sucking on my neck, holding me much too tightly against him. Helpless to resist, I submitted to his wet kisses and sloppy fondling, my stomach and groin aroused to feel things I was much too young to feel. Loathing myself in his caresses, loathing him and loathing my mother, who turned away from us in disgust, I would go numb in his painful grasp. Retreating, I was no longer there. My body - limp, nauseated and violated - was left to fend for itself without me.

Snapshots from this time show an unkempt, heavy child with uncombed hair and unsmiling lips held tense over broken teeth. When my father is in the picture, I am pulling away from him, belly out-thrust and eyes guarded. There are no pictures that show me with my mother. By the age of eight I was on my own; childhood was virtually out of the question.

The end of the War and the birth of my new sister Simone occurred at the same time. While the rest of Brooklyn welcomed the boys home and mourned those, like Saul, who would never come back, we all gathered in the upstairs bedroom around the new baby.

As the center of both families' attention, she gave us an opportunity to regroup and to heal. She was the only one who could make everyone - even my mother - laugh. As if she understood the importance of her mission, she radiated love and laughter, her little face dimpling sweetly for everyone who glanced in her direction.

As my mother was still unstable after her brother's death, it was Aunt Sadie who took on the raising of Simone. Simone was the daughter she had been waiting for, the child of her heart; she staked her claim and brooked no opposition. But Simone, from the very beginning, made it clear that she was her own person; she would belong to nobody but herself. By the age of two she had everyone - even Aunt Sadie - baffled, and could slip away unnoticed and raise havoc in seconds, where nobody thought to be looking.

My mother, still deep in mourning, had no energy to cope either with such an inventive, irrepressible child, nor with Aunt Sadie's passionate claim on her. Trapped with both of them and still filled with unexpressed rage, her response was to anger easily, striking out at every provocation either of them offered - which were many - and to take it out on the most vulnerable one, Simone.

My sister, though, despite the fact that she was barely walking, knew how to fight back. Hated, she made herself hateful. She refused to eat; spit on the floor; wiped her little nose on the walls.

It was not long before the two of them were bonded by mindless violence- the kind of household violence that seeps into every cranny of daily life and covers every surface like a layer of dust. Mother and child, their clamor was inescapable, incessant. Their battle took over my life, and ruled it. My sister, it was clear, was in danger; I, as the elder, had to protect her.

If I had had the maturity and wisdom of the Buddha, I could not have effected peace between the two of them. They both seemed wedded to the combat and dependent upon its excitement. Their attention, from the beginning, was focused upon each other; I was incidental. More and more ashamed of my ineffectual anxiety, I retreated from their fights impotently, absorbing the poisons that they, scrapping and yelling and crying, were able to get out of their systems.

As she grew, Simone's ability to get into trouble became more ingenious. I followed her, my throat in my mouth, and tried to neutralize her misdeeds. Like a guard on the football field, my job was to cover the player with the ball. But if the player poured water from the window onto the landlord's head while I was at school, what could I do? If the player, in the summer, painted the radiators with cod-liver oil, who would believe me if I said it was me when the heat came up, stinking of fish, in the winter?

Only in Aunt Sadie did Simone meet her match. Between the two of them ran a single thread of spirit. By the time Simone was three, it was clear that they were cohorts, and my mother knew Sadie too well to chance the havoc that the two of them, together, could wreak. So with a supreme effort of will she began to pull herself together, reclaim her children and put on her lipstick when she went out to the store. Our time spent downstairs with Aunt Sadie became rationed.

Eventually, the two families in the house settled into an uneasy semblance of normalcy. My mother cooked and cleaned the apartment, took care of my sister and me and sometimes went out for walks. My father went to his office, came home for supper and kept trying to put his arms around my mother. When she pushed him away, he sometimes came to me.

Every morning my grandfather and Uncle Max left for the factory; Aunt Sadie cooked brisket and huge pots of cabbage and sent my cousins, in a flurry of kicks and curses, off to school before she left for her funerals.

I, during this period, took for granted I was not like other children and in kindergarten only pretended to be a child. I knew better than to be interested in jump-rope and dodge-ball. Preoccupied with the gravity of things, I stood alone in the schoolyard during recess and only mouthed the words to the songs the school sang at assemblies.

I lived in my head, and in my head, I danced. I craved these imagined dances the way a bee craves pollen. While plodding heavily around the corner to school, I saw myself leaping splendidly through space. While the others jumped rope in the playground, I sat stolidly on a bench and envisioned myself flying weightless through the air, my feet barely needing to touch the ground. Lying on my back in my bed, I dreamed of spinning and twirling, my skirts sweeping gracefully behind me, my face tilted to the sky.

Once, in a timid mumble, I asked my mother if I could take dancing lessons. She stared for a moment, then laughed unkindly. I dared never ask again, knowing that my size and my demeanor were not those of a little girl who danced, although a hundred times it was all but out of my mouth before I remembered.

Instead, I sat on the sidelines and watched the other kids play. As they ran, I felt in my own body the bending and straightening of their legs, the quick pumping of their arms, the twisting of their torsos. Rapt, I watched games of Stickball, Giant Step, Territory, my rooted body memorizing the moves of a slow-pitched ball, the reach for second base, the twirl of the Umbrella Step.

In bed at night I would try out everything I had seen, sliding my arms along the sheets to catch an imaginary ball, bending my legs up and lowering my head as if to start running...

...running in a forest with 'my people'. We climb a tall mountain and reach the top just as the sun is setting. We are tired, but happy. The whole forest is brightly lit.

"Are we stopping here?" I ask. An adult smiles at me and explains that we must go down into the valley before we stop. When we get there, we will be home.

In the valley it is beautiful and we all gather together around a fire. The air is leafy and green and fresh. I am loved. This is where I belong.

But then they put out the fire, and we have to keep walking. I want to stay...I'm tired...It's night...I don't want to leave...I don't want to be alone...

I awoke with a pounding heart, bereaved. That was my real home and those were my real people. I reached backwards into my dream for them, but they dissolved, leaving me in a treeless darkness that did not know my name. Tensing, I tried to bring it all back, but all that remained was a haunting smell of fresh earth and woods. I sucked it in until even the smell faded away in the Brooklyn night.

Every morning, Teddiecoo peed into a milkbottle. He was a diabetic and the milkbottle ritual was designed to test his urine for sugar and give Aunt Sadie an excuse - if indeed, she need one - to spread more newspapers on the kitchen floor.

I wasn't allowed to watch him pee, but as soon as he handed over his yellow froth, still steaming in the milkbottle, I could join her at the sink and watch her try to pour it from the wide-mouthed milkbottle into a narrow test tube. Her hands always shook and so more urine reached the sink than the test tube, but there was always enough that hit true to continue the ritual.

"Hurry, Ma!" he would complain from the bedroom, hopping up and down in his underpants. "You want me to freeze to death?"

"Yeah," she would mutter, heating the test tube unsteadily over the front burner. I always expected her to spill it into the stove. When the urine turned brown or red, she would pull it away from the fire and flush it, in a stinking sizzle, down the kitchen sink drain, and get the syringe ready for his injection.

It always took several jabs at his thigh before the needle went in straight, and the whole time she aimed unsteadily she scolded him in advance for the sins he was sure to commit during the day.

"You put anything into your mouth I don't give you, I'll break every bone in your body." Swabbing, she poked the needle a good two inches away. I handed her the alcohol bottle again.

"I won't!" he yelped, rubbing his thigh. "Do it already!"

"I'll do you," she threatened, pinching his flesh to improve her aim. "You dare touch that *dreck* at Eugene's house - don't think I don't know what you go eat there..."

"You finished, Ma?"

"I'll finish you like you'll never remember you got started," she declared, pulling out the needle with a flourish and brandishing it in his face. He laughed, teeth chattering with cold and his brown ringlets every which way on his head.

Twenty minutes later he was tumbling down the stoop to get to school on time.

"Go already!" Aunt Sadie yelled from the doorway, having pushed him out after a spit-and-finger face cleaning. "Go put something into that head so you don't grow up a *schlemeil* like your father!"

Uncle Max, a *schlemeil*? Teddiecoo skipped off, giggling like a maniac. At that moment I wanted more than anything to be sitting quietly on Uncle Max's lap.

"Aunt Sadie?" I asked in a tiny voice, scraping at the peeling paint of the door with my thumbnail. "Do you love Teddiecoo?"

Schlemeil meant dumb, stupid, mean. You called other people *schlemeils*, not your own family.

She regarded me curiously, breaking slowly into one of her rare smiles, and caressed my head with a trembling hand.

"Of course I do, *mammeleh*," she said in an unusually gentle voice. "That's just the way we talk."

In that moment, though, I believe that both she and I knew, for the first time, that by saying *we* she was not including me.

Everyone knew that Teddiecoo ate whatever he pleased, despite the warnings from his mother and the doctor. He snatched food from the icebox, bartered treats in the schoolyard, filched chocolate from the candystore.

Occasionally his timing was off, and he got caught. Aunt Sadie would hear the furtive squeak of the icebox door, or sneak up on him in the street as he munched a Hershey Bar. Then he would run away as fast as a rabbit and she would chase him up and down the block, her mouth pouring threats and one shoe held high in her hand to hit him when she caught him. Dodging under hedges and behind garages, he would finally outrun her and disappear.

"I'll kill you when you get home!" she would shriek in defeat, the shoe still upraised. "Don't bother to come home! Ever again!"

Each time I worried that this time she meant it; that this time he would stay away and never come back. Sometimes he was still not home well after dark and we would all really begin to worry that something had happened. Frantic, the adults would prowl the streets calling his name, call the police, the hospital, the morgue. But while they were all gone he would come sneaking in, his eyes bright with mischief, and seat himself at the kitchen table until they returned, his face a mask of innocence.

"Aunt Sadie, he's here!" I would yell out the window. "He's home!" Moments later she would burst through the door, her cheeks wet with tears, and smother him with kisses. Then she fed him a meal to make up for any he may have missed, following that with a walloping loud enough to hear two houses away.

"You finished?" she would threaten as soon as his plate was clean. "Now get over here so I can kill you!"

After supper, the boys and I would lie on the floor in the upstairs livingroom and listen to the radio shows - "The Lone Ranger", "Fibber McGee and Molly", "The Shadow".

"Who knows what evil lurks in the minds of men? The...Shadow...Knows...heh heh heh..."

As the voice echoed into the dark tunnels of a terrifying abyss, my body went stiff and my mind faded away. I was literally too scared to move. I lay on the floor, rigid and unresponding while my cousins tickled me and thought it was a joke.

"She wants to be carried like an eensy-weensy baby," teased Lucky, winking at Sollie to grab my feet while he grabbed my arms, and swing me to wake me up. But I didn't laugh or fight. Only when Lucky carried me roughly and dumped me in my bed, did I relax into a stupor and fall asleep.

At first the family assumed I was being "good" when I went still and silent like that.

"See how nice your sister sits in a chair?" they would admonish the naughty Simone. "She's a good girl, doesn't bother anybody," beaming approval at my paralysis.

Eventually though, it occurred to them I was a bit too good - stupid, in fact.

"Keep your wits about you!" my mother would sigh in exasperation, as I stopped stock still between the kitchen and the hall. "Wake up!" my father would hiss as he entered my room to find me drooped into senselessness.

"She's sick," they decided at last, and made an appointment with an important specialist in the city, leaving Aunt Sadie to take care of Simone, who screamed like a banshee, wanting to go to the specialist, too.

The office was in a tall building that had halls and doorways on every floor. Entering one doorway, a nurse ushered us in to a darkened side room that held a high table and revolving drum covered with graph paper. I didn't like the smell and was astonished that she knew my name.

"What's that?" I asked about the humming, fat cylinder alongside the table as the nurse took off my shoes and laid me down.

"Nothing to worry about," she said, pushing on my chest and lowering a suffocating mask towards my face. Panicked, I tried to scramble off the table.

"Whoops!" she exclaimed, grabbing my arm and clapping the mask over my nose and mouth. "Breathe deeply...."

The numbness crawled like stinging pins up my legs and into my belly. Suffocating, I dropped into dense sleep.

Doors...up a long hallway...which one should I enter? Which one is safe?

At the far end, a scratched, black door. Not like the others, and open a crack. I slip inside.

It's not an office, not an apartment, but a huge cathedral with vaulted ceiling and tall columns of stone. Stained-glass windows light the nave; organ music leads me towards the altar.

A choir sings and the music beckons me forward. I go, feeling awed and welcome here. Down the aisle, step by step, the music leads and I follow.

The music beats to the pulse of my heartbeats.

Music...heartbeats...music...footsteps...music...my heart pounding...music...the revolving drum...the drum...the drum...

The music stopped as the revolving drum was switched off. The cathedral faded. Terror returned as I struggled against the choking mask, against the nurse, against the doctor. Gasping, I tried to escape.

"Didn't she do well, now?" chirped the nurse, still restraining me so the doctor could examine me.

He poked and prodded; called my parents in and spoke to them in a low voice. They looked worried.

"What's wrong with me?" I asked, and when they did not respond, asked again. "What's wrong with me?" The nurse absentmindedly patted my thigh, and smiled.

"You're fine, honey" she said brightly, turning away and writing on the chart. "You did just fine."

"Did you find out what's wrong with me?" I asked again

on the way home. My mother looked at my father and my father looked at me. I was scared by the serious look in his eyes.

"It's your metabolism," he said. I had no idea what 'metabolism' meant, "but it's going to be alright." I almost asked him for an explanation, but I didn't because something in his expression warned me that he didn't know what 'metabolism' meant, either.

I was going to ask Aunt Sadie when we got home, but the chance never came since a crisis was in progress that would occupy everyone's attention for at least the next two weeks. Simone had locked herself in the bathroom.

"Don't worry - she's alright!" was Aunt Sadie's hollered greeting as we drove up. The buttons of her housedress were undone and her hair seemed to stand straight out in all directions. She flung a hand over her mouth as my father leaped out of the car, stubbed out his cigarette on the sidewalk, and vaulted up the front stoop of the house. My mother, in high heels, followed close behind.

"The Fire Department's coming!" Aunt Sadie shrieked. She had pressed herself against the downstairs bathroom door, her arms covering it to block our way. Her eyes were wild.

"Let me in!" demanded my father, trying to push her away. But Aunt Sadie would not be moved. He pounded with his fists on the door above her head.

"Are you in there, Simone?" he shouted.

"Of course she's in there," Aunt Sadie yelled above his voice. "That's just the trouble!"

My mother pressed her knuckles to her lips and leaned weakly against the wall for support. Aunt Sadie blew her nose on the hem of her housedress. "She won't come out!"

"I'll get her out," my father declared, pulling the doorknob towards him and then pushing hard against the door with his knee. Nothing budged. From inside the bathroom came a whimper, then a high-pitched giggle. Everyone suddenly shut up and listened.

"What *bubbeleh*?" cajoled Aunt Sadie, her ear to the keyhole. "Come out, Shimoncoo..." Another giggle. We held our breaths, but all was silence again.

"Turn the little key, pumpkin," coaxed my father. "Let Daddy come in, O.K.?" Simone whimpered again, and the whimper grew into a frightened wail.

"I'm breaking down the door - watch out!" announced my father with grim resolve, stepping back and leading forward with his shoulder.

"You'll kill her! You'll kill her!" screamed Aunt Sadie. "Shimicoo, get into the shower so he won't kill you!"

My mother yelled at Aunt Sadie, Aunt Sadie shouted at Simone and my father grunted as he tried to force open the door. I called out, over all their voices,

"If we go away, will you come out yourself?" Silence. Everyone listened for her response.

"Can't."

"Why?"

"Locked."

The yelling started up again but from inside came a rustling of the key in the lock, and a snatch of song. My father rattled the doorknob.

"Do it again," he coaxed through the keyhole, picking fitfully at his cuticles and drawing blood.

"Can't."

"Try again, *bubbeleh*...," wailed Aunt Sadie just as three firemen, in full gear, came in armed with axes. Half the neighborhood followed close behind.

"Where's the baby?" they asked grimly. The neighbors held onto my mother's hand.

"EEEEEE!" screeched Aunt Sadie, pounding on the door with both fists. "Turn the key, Shimkeecoo, quick! They're going to kill you!"

"She's in there, officers," my father informed them

unnecessarily. "If she's in the bathtub, you could crush her with the door, but she might be in the shower - if you can wait till we get her to stand in the shower..."

"Could you wait in the kitchen, sir?" suggested the head fireman, herding my father, my mother, Aunt Sadie and all the neighbors into the kitchen. I was the last to go. They all lit cigarettes, until the kitchen was filled with smoke, and I reasoned that if they should set the house on fire, at least the firemen were there.

We all peered down the hall to where the firemen stood plotting how to rescue Simone.

"As long as they get her out alive," Aunt Sadie swore, "I don't care how much it costs me a busted door. Shimonaleh..."

"Oh, shut up!" my father swore under his breath, puffing frenetically on his cigarette.

The firemen conferred, lay down their axes, unhinged the bathroom door and lifted it out neatly. Moments later, with all of us crowding into the hallway, they emerged with their prize - a naked, shaving-cream-and-toothpaste covered Simone wriggling happily in their arms. Still absorbed in smearing it all over herself, she rubbed lather into her hair, her chest, her vagina. Playing to her captive audience, she blinked it coyly out of her eyelashes and blew it, with great elan, right out of her nose.

For a moment everyone was too shocked to make a sound. But then Aunt Sadie had hysterics, slumping helplessly against the wall, her hands holding onto her breasts to keep them from jiggling. For years she would tell the story, collapsing with laughter each time:

"She was so slippery you couldn't get your hands on her!" Snorting and cackling. "Her little panties were crumpled in the bottom of the hamper, we couldn't find them for weeks..."

Simone, by the time she was five, had properly examined the secret contents of the hamper, the refrigerator and all of Aunt Sadie's other hiding places in the house. She knew, since the day she locked herself in the bathroom, not only about the knotted nylon stocking crammed with money in the bottom of the hamper, but about the wad of bills stashed under the rug in the livingroom, the loose change in the herring jar on top of the dresser, and the bottle of Slivovitz behind the claw foot of the bathtub.

I was much less astute. It took me years to understand why I would sometimes find Aunt Sadie in the bathroom, one hand behind her back and her breath reeking of whiskey. Wiping off her mouth with the back of her free hand, she would twinkle at me strangely and demand,

"Whattcha doing here? Cancha see I'm busy?"

Thirty years later, when Teddiecoo phoned across the country to tell us of her death, Simone would mime her perfectly - legs wide apart, head thrown back and an imaginary bottle held to her lips. When Simone wiped off her lips with Aunt Sadie's gesture and shook her head admiringly at the imaginary bottle, we didn't know whether to laugh or to cry.

"Believe it or not, she's gone," Teddie announced. By then, his mother had outlived all the men in her life, antagonized most of the women, and had not spoken to my mother, Simone or me for almost twenty years.

"Go look in the hamper," Simone told him wryly.

"What for?"

"Just go look. You'll see. In the bottom right hand corner." In the background, we heard him rummaging.

"Holy Mackerel!" he finally exclaimed, returning to the phone with the knotted stocking in hand. "How the Hell did you know?" He counted out more than eight- hundred dollars in small bills.

"How the Hell did you not know?" retorted Simone, her eyes growing misty, and a small smile lingering on her face.

It was a dreary Sunday in early winter, and after breakfast we were all going to the THE HOME to see Grandma - even my father. Simone, at five, balked before every visit and my mother, in the last weeks of her pregnancy with a new baby, was heavy and impatient.

I, at ten, felt myself the anchor of the household. My mother and sister bickered incessantly; my father postured like a movie actor who had lost his lines, and my grandfather stayed away as much as he could. With Aunt Sadie and Uncle Max as the only other adults, it was clear that the whole place depended on me.

"Don't wanna go!" pouted Simone, twisting away from the shoes my mother placed at her feet. Stamping defiantly, she flung her elbows this way and that, striking my mother accidentally in the side of her swollen belly. My mother's lips went white.

"Don't wanna go!" Simone repeated, blinking in anticipation of what was to come.

My father strode furiously into the bedroom, his eyes flashing and his moustache a dangerous gash above tight lips. Simone did not flinch. Everything in me wanted to slither into a sea of sand, but if my sister were being attacked by a ferocious tiger, would I run away? My stomach sinking and growing hard, I stayed.

"Won't go!" she insisted. He roughly grabbed her arm, and she shook him off with contempt.

"Oh yes you will, young lady." His teeth were clenched in what almost looked like a smile. My knees locked; I prayed for it to not be happening. My rage flicked from my father to my sister, and back again. Then to myself, for my impotence to stop it.

"Won't!"

"YOU ARE GOING." By the bed, my mother's fists were clenched.

This was my family.

"Why should I go, if you don't?" Even at five, my sister shot straight from the hip.

"Watch it, young lady!" he shot back warningly, forgetting

she was a little girl of five. My head said things in a scramble - words I had never allowed my lips.

She's a baby! it shouted at him. *Run away!* it shouted at her. *I hate you, hate you, hate you!* it shouted guiltily at all three of them.

My mother, ashen, teetered at the edge of the bed and sank down heavily.

"Daddy is coming," she mumbled, beaten. One of Simone's shoes dangled from her hand.

"I always come when I can," he lied.

Are you lying on purpose, or do you not know you're lying? I asked without words. Simone gave a kick at the air and stuck out her lower lip.

"Won't go."

"Yes you will."

"Why?"

"Because I said so."

"No."

"Get dressed!" His voice cracked alarmingly, and I stepped closer to Simone. Suddenly roused, my mother snarled, rose off the bed in one motion and smacked my sister with all her strength.

Simone was knocked to the ground and my mother, with her fist to her mouth, rushed out of the room sobbing. My father ran out after her, slamming the door behind him.

Simone lay still, almost peaceful. There was no sound from her, not even a breath. She pinkened, then grew red, then blue. Her eyes gaped, staring as she struggled, without a motion, for breath. Crouching, I shook her shoulders and breathed for her.

"Breathe!" I begged her. "Please breathe!" Her eyes popped, and at last she sucked in an enormous lungful of air. And let it out with a curdling howl that rattled the windows. Shuddering, disconsolate, she sobbed. Such a small person; such misery. She was drowning; I would drown with her. She was gasping for air; I would breathe for her. If she died, I would die too.

When her sobs had faded into sighs and then into hiccoughs,

I whispered,

"It's by car, not train."

"I don't care! I won't go. I *hate* it there!"

"Me too," I said, admitting it for the first time in my life. "But we have to."

"But why?" she pleaded, her whole body heaving and her breath catching on the words.

Why, indeed? I had no answer. In ten years, it had never occurred to me to ask that question.

"I don't know," I replied at last. "I only know we have to."

"Won't go," she repeated, but this time with a little less force. I straightened out her socks, helped her put on her shoes, and looked all over the room for the blue barrette for her hair.

In the end she went, of course. We all did - the four of us, with Teddiecoo, in the car, and Aunt Sadie and my grandfather, by subway. Except for Teddiecoo, we were silent. We stared out the windows, pale and red-eyed, first at the bleakness of Brooklyn and then at the bleakness of the Bronx.

My father sat stonily at the wheel, puffing on one cigarette after another and swerving full speed around people crossing the streets. In her full lap, my mother's hands were clenched. Her wedding ring, I noticed, was much too tight for her swollen finger.

This time, I didn't ask if we could go to the Zoo afterwards. In fact, I was never to ask to go to the Zoo again, but would make it the first stop, twelve years later, on my honeymoon.

At the entrance of THE HOME Simone again set up a scream of protest. My father angrily hauled her, kicking and yelling, into the dark lobby but she twisted out of his grasp and ran right out again. I hurried ahead, leaving them to their own devices. They would never dare strike her in public. The stench of disease hit me right away, but I no longer tried to fill my lungs with fresh air before going in. The smell, I had learned, could be ignored if I breathed quickly as soon as I got there.

I was growing up.

Alone on the steel stairway, I jumped right into my steel-steps dance, establishing a rhythm with my feet and adding arms and head and shoulders.

Dump   Dumpa dump   Dump   Dumpa dump   Dump Dumpa dump.... Swinging my back leg forward, I clapped the beat with my hands, flicked my head up and balanced.

Dump   Dumpa dump   Dump   Dumpa dump   Dump Dumpa dump... I shifted my weight, leapt onto the other foot and landed with the beat on the next step. Perfect.

Dump   Dumpa dump   Dump   Dumpa dump.... Rippling my spine like a snake, I hung onto the stair rail and held my back leg straight out behind me. In my mind, I saw a ballet dancer doing the arabesque, her leg high in the air, her toe pointed. Then she would leap and run in a great circle around the stage. Her arms would float above a tiny waist, her tutu would bob in chiffon layers, her feet would skim the stage lightly...

"Where's Mama?" Dolly asked with a toothless grimace. The half-wit from my grandmother's ward stood at the landing, her hands on her hips and her cotton stockings sagging. In her stained housedress she smelled like sour carrots. "Where's Mama?" she cackled again.

"Downstairs," I replied, embarrassed that she had seen me dancing. It was supposed to be my secret. Dolly, a middle-aged retard, shuffled about the hospital fluffing up pillows and searching for playmates, leading every soul who would follow her to the doll collection spread out on her bed. She grinned, squinting into my face and grabbed my skirt.

"Wanna see my dolls?" she asked hopefully. I had to look at her dolls every time I came, and she never remembered I had seen them just last week. I was never allowed to touch. I nodded, as I always did, and she pulled me through the ward to her bed.

"Pretty, huh?" she asked, peering into my face. I did not find them pretty, except for one peasant doll in a paisley apron.

"Yeah, pretty," I agreed, mindlessly reaching over to straighten a Kewpie doll that had fallen over.

"Don't touch!" she screeched. The force of the hand that flung me away from the bed was that of a madwoman, not of a harmless retard. "Go away! Go away!" she raged over and over. Her toothless face crumpled into tears and terrified, I ran through the ward and out onto the porch to where my grandmother waited in her wheelchair. Taking a deep breath, I opened the door and stepped onto the veranda with a bright mask of a smile on my face, swallowing down tears that would not be shed for thirty years.

Aunt Sadie was already there, and Grandpa. My grandmother sat between them, waiting for us, her face bathed in tears. She was the only patient on the porch.

"Marta, where's Mama?" asked Aunt Sadie, sounding just like Dolly. Her lips, around her cigarette, were blue with cold, and she pulled her coat more tightly around her, shivering.

"Downstairs," I said, going over to Grandma for the kiss. Grandpa sat up close to her wheelchair, his back to the wind and his hat pulled down over his ears. My grandmother, wrapped in shawls and blankets, was the only toasty one among us. "Simone had to pee," I lied. With a useless finger, she latched onto the belt of my skirt and pulled me towards her. Her bedpan badly needed cleaning. I bent over for the kiss.

When the others finally arrived, she was whispering in my ear to tell her the real truth about why Uncle Saul never came anymore.

"He's dead, isn't he?" she demanded, her finger still hooked in my belt. We went through this every time. "They don't want you to tell, right?"

I looked down and memorized the terra cotta tiles of the porch.

"Hi Ma," said my mother wearily, coming over for the kiss. I prayed she had not been listening. My father prodded Simone ahead of him, pushing her with his knee at every step and Teddiecoo followed behind, furtively wiping sugar from his face. Simone's whole attention was on a red lollipop held tightly in her hand.

"Isn't it too cold out here?" My mother pulled her coat around her protruding belly, and hugged her arms to her chest.

"What's the matter - you don't like fresh air?" retorted Grandma. This was her day and she would have it her way. Simone was lifted for the kiss; she squeezed her eyes shut and stuffed the lollipop in her mouth, gagging at the bedpan smell. When my father bent over, he gagged too.

Good, I thought without words, *then I'm glad you came.*

Teddiecoo was bored, and squatting behind the wheelchair in his coat and knickers, he took imaginary potshots at the resident pigeons.

"P'tchow!" he sang out, his finger extended towards the birds. Scanning the field with squint and finger, he took aim at Simone. Sitting on Aunt Sadie's lap and sucking on her lollipop, she pretended to ignore him.

"P'tchow!" he tried again.

I meandered along the railing of the veranda until I could barely hear their voices. Leaning my head against the balustrade, I gazed up at the overcast sky, watching layers of drifting cloud thin to reveal tiny patches of blue, and then cover them over again. Some birds sailed by in pairs, carried by currents of wind.

In my head, a tune began. I felt my fingers follow it, and then one foot. My arm felt like fluttering out, winglike, in time to my song. A dance was starting - if only nobody was here I'd lean to the left, bend my knee...Swing with my arm and a- one- two- three...

"P'tchow!" Teddiecoo was growing bolder; Aunt Sadie

gave him a whack. He ducked around behind her and gave my sister's curls a tug.

"Ow," she complained mildly.

"P'tchow!" he cried again, quickened by her response. I let my tune fade away and edged closer to them so I could distract my cousin before things got out of hand.

"Leave her alone or I'll break every bone in your body," Aunt Sadie threatened.

"P'tchow!" he squealed, ignoring her and pulling Simone's hair again. Snorting happily with success, he lurched away, and then back to grab at Simone from the front. She sucked on her lollipop, hardly deigning to look up. Sweetly giving it an adorable, pink-tongued lick, she turned to Aunt Sadie, dimpled and said,

"Teddiecoo ate up the free peppermints at the candy stand, and now isn't his diabetes going to get sooo sick...?"

Bedlam ensued. There was not a thing I could do.

Up in the sky, three birds flew against the wind. They flapped their wings and turned, free.

The fog, as we drove home, began to burn off. As we passed Plum Beach on the bay, we stopped so my mother could go to the bathroom. In ten years, we had never before stopped at the beach.

I jumped out of the car before the ignition was fully off, and took off towards the far end of the narrow, curving strand by myself. Nobody else was there; gentle waves lapped against the shore and the air smelled clean and briny. I put as much distance as possible between myself and the family, clambering over low rocks to get to a small tidal cove littered with shells.

Fog wisps rose from the water and trailed, like filmy clouds, into bluer and bluer sky. Seagulls dipped and cried, swooping low over the water, all creamy yellow and white. I gulped in huge breaths of fresh, saltwater air and let out the sour staleness of the hospital. The sun shone warm through the patchwork sky, and I took it in like a gift.

The wet sand of the cove was ankle-deep in pebbles and seashells, and hunkering down, I rummaged for treasure. I found a perfect winkle; then a pure white pebble. Dropping them into my skirt pocket, I searched for two others like them so they would have company when I got them home.

A conch, slightly broken, roared with the sounds of the sea when I held it to my ear. I closed my eyes and listened to the sounds of another place. Maybe there things were different. Maybe there I wouldn't have to worry about my sister and the new baby too.

I slid onto my belly facing the water, and watched the waves spurt against the shore. Little bubble kisses popped in wet sand and the water rocked back and forth, like a cradle. Resting my chin on my arms, I saw the waves come in again, and again, and again...

It's never finished, they seemed to be telling me. Waves come again. Chances come again. Again and again and again and again.

From the distance, I heard my father's whistle. Not yet! Raking the shellpiles with my fingers, I picked up an oyster shell, all pearly inside, and a spoon-shaped mussel. A long, pointed spiral came to hand, and I turned it over and over. It was the most beautiful thing I had ever seen, gracefully spiralling until the top flared, like a flower.

It was the treasure - my sign. If I found a treasure, then my time would come. The waves keep coming.

My father whistled again, closer this time. Sighing, I stood up, brushed sand off my skirt and climbed slowly back onto the low rocks. But my father stood there right above me and taken by surprise, my feet turned to lead and my mind slipped into darkness. I tried to will my body back, but I couldn't move or speak. Only my hand, clutching the spiral shell, registered feeling. All the rest, except this thin, high wail biting into my palm, was blank.

"I found her!" My father's shout burst into my head,

reverberating. I tried to open my mouth, and felt screams rise like fireworks in my chest, never reaching my mouth but getting stuck, as pain, between my heart and my throat.

I had to be carried to the car, and slept all the way home. The spiral shell remained clutched in my hand when we turned onto our street and I awoke abruptly by being hurtled off the seat when my father gunned the engine and slammed on the brakes.

My heart thudded in my mouth. My mother glared at my father, afraid, and Simone had again set up a howl. Out on the street, the kids in roller skates scattered to the sidewalks and watched our car continue up the block. Out the back window, I saw them make the 'crazy' sign with their fingers, slowly going back to their game with expressions of derision and disbelief. The guy had tried to run them down!

He didn't mean it that way! I wanted to yell out the window, making it alright. *He's just in a bad mood because Simone was bad and he had to go to the hospital. It stinks there!*

But I knew I would never say a word to them, even to Lucky and Sollie, who made the crazy sign for my father along with the rest of the kids.

Remember this, I said to myself as I stepped shakily out of the car by our house, the shell tight in my sweaty grasp. *You are ten years old and you hate your father, and you promise that no matter how bad you feel ever in your life, you will never use it to be mean to people.*

With the vow, a spot of warmth began to pierce the cold, hard pain in my chest. I stopped at our steps, undecided. I could either go inside with the family or stay on the street where the kids gossiped insultingly about my father. It was like making a choice between horseshit or vomit. I opted for the street, and leaning against the fender of a parked car, watched the kids play hockey.

Elihu skated low to the ground, taking long, smooth strides. With his sawed-off broom handle he hit the tin-can puck and sent it spinning. It hit the ground with a *ching*. Helen skated in, stole it and flipped it quickly in the other direction, while Lucky and Sollie both banged their sticks around the clattery puck, breathing hard with concentration.

They had forgotten about my father. Not so easy for me. Lucky made a lunge for the tin can, whacked it hard and skated after it as fast as he could. Suzie fell down, squealed, and picked herself up to chase Lucky. Their cheeks were all red, their eyes bright with the fun of the game. If only I could play...

I could feel in my body every one of their long-legged strides, their lunges for the puck, the exhilaration of speeding down the street on skates with wheels. Twitching inside with the longing to move, I held myself as still as I could.

A warm, wet nose nudged my hand, and I reached down to pet Helen's dog, Duke. He wagged his whole body, jumping up to lick me, and I slid off the fender so I could put my arms around him. Warm and furry, he wriggled ecstatically, washing my face with a wet, sloppy tongue. I hugged him hard, feeling the small light in my chest open a bit more, while the game picked up speed on the street.

Elihu, Helen, Lucky, Sollie and Suzie skated round and round each other, weaving and circling and turning. Their skates scraped the asphalt like music and their sticks clanged and chinged the puck as they hit it. Like dancers, they skated in pairs, moved off in different directions, making colorful patterns that kept changing but were always connected by the game.

It was so beautiful my eyes went a little blurry, and I put my cheek against Dukie's head. For a moment, the skaters formed a circle, which quickly dispersed, but for that moment they were like the hub of a huge, colored wheel that was in the center of the whole world, right in the middle of all the time of the universe. And it was happening right here on our street, on Sunday afternoon, with the kids on my block.

It was as if the circle of skaters stood in the middle of all time and all space. From them, everything rayed out like the spokes of a wheel to the ends of the world in every direction.

It was as if I could see all the ancestors of everyone back to the beginning of time. And in the other direction I could see all the children and the children after them to the end of time. The whole Universe was held in the hockey game on my street. And with me in it, even though I wasn't skating. And Dukie.

Even my family - and the new baby to be born. Even my father when he hurt kids. Even Aunt Sadie when she cursed.

Everything in the world was a part of the Whole Thing. There was nothing left out, even the horrible stuff. Somehow it all fit. Some day I would understand it.

I took in a huge breath, and let it out. Dukie wagged his tail and nudged his wet nose into my hand. I patted him, the warm spot in my chest growing larger. In my other hand I held the spiral shell.

A door inside me opened a crack, and then wider. Hope entered in. I would be alright; all things would be alright. But I had to make them alright.

I had to go home and ask for roller skates. If my father said No I'd ask Uncle Max. Then I would practice skating when nobody was looking. I'd take long strides up and down the driveway, and after I learned to skate I'd borrow Lucky's hockey stick and learn how to hit the puck.

Dukie jumped up and whimpered to be petted. I ruffled his ears and took both his paws in my hands. The game went on and Helen was down, laughing. Elihu positioned the puck, gave it a swat and sent it sailing. They all took off after it.

I watched, feeling the movement in my chest, feeling the warmth. And Dukie's. I leaned my cheek against his head, my heart pounding. I'd ask tonight. I'd keep this feeling, and ask tonight!

4
HARMONIC CLUSTERS
Heart Chakra - Thymus Gland

Learning how to love;
belonging to a group;
the urge to bond with family, tribe, community;
identification with others.

Three years after we met, Franco and I got married - to other people.

On opposite sides of the ocean, one month apart, he married Luisa and I married Kurt.

In the end, our romance had indeed been a summer romance. Our backgrounds were too different, and my need for freedom too great for me to settle into the life of an Italian housewife - albeit the wife of a cellist with the Maggio Musicale. So, after a series of wrenching partings and passionate reunions which lasted over a year, I enrolled in a course of Medieval Art History and studied for another year in France, finally returning to New York to continue working towards an American degree. It was on my first Christmas eve at home that I met Kurt.

His friend knew my friend. We had both come to hear the midnight Mass at St. Thomas Church in New York, and were introduced alongside the font of holy water by the door, two Jews out of place in a crowd of well-dressed Manhattan Episcopalians.

"What brings you to an Anglican Mass on Christmas Eve?" I had asked. A head of kinky reddish hair outlined a pair of deep-set brown eyes that regarded me with soulful attention. He was so tall he had to bend over to hear me and his beard, when he came close, smelled clean and male.

"I love New York," he replied enigmatically, stuffing big hands into the pockets of an ill-fitting jacket. "What about you?"

"I love the Middle Ages," I rejoined, laughing and

following the others into the church.

During the service we four sat together, commenting in whispers on the architecture, the music, the vestments, the congregation. While the choirboys sang, I learned that he was a mathematician, just finishing his degree at Columbia University. He said he had been born in Czechoslovakia, barely escaped during the war, and that he had an on-going love affair with the city of New York - the bridges, the buildings, the rivers. He spoke with such seriousness, such intensity; his legs, long and gangly, had no place to go in the narrow pews, and his eyes seemed to bore right into me. His parts didn't seem to match, but he added up to a person utterly different from anyone I'd ever met before. I wanted to know him.

During the singing of the final hymn he offered to drive everyone home and at three in the morning, having dropped off the other two, his car crawled at twenty miles an hour through silent, snowy streets. We were the only people on the road.

I told him about my two years in Europe, and my fascination with the Middle Ages.

"The art and the religion are so much a part of the whole life," I declared, "it seems a good period to try and understand what really makes people tick."

"You're an egghead," he declared bluntly. "Like me."

I wasn't sure whether that was an insult or a compliment, but he turned to me with a friendly grin, letting the speedometer slip down to fifteen miles an hour. By the time we reached my house our feet were blocks of ice against the floorboards of the car, and we were deep into the difference between mathematics and poetry, so I invited him in for tea.

"You weren't joking when you said you loved the Middle Ages," he remarked, speaking in a low voice so we wouldn't wake my parents. I cut another slice of cherry pie.

"No I wasn't," I admitted. "I love being in beautiful old churches, with their old stones and quietness, and to feel all that faith."

"A mixed blessing...," he sighed. I liked the way his eyes crinkled, the way he fingered his beard. He told me about his background, his family's flight from Europe, his passionate commitment to America. I listened hard, wanting to take his hand. I sliced more pie instead.

At five the dog whined to go out, and we took him out into the graying dawn; our feet - Kurt's big ones, my smaller ones and the dog's scampering paws - made the first prints in the new fall of snow.

At six in the morning we were still talking, shivering outside on the stoop under swirling snow and dabbing our runny noses with the backs of our sleeves. We hardly noticed that it was day, except that the sounds of morning had started up in the houses. He glanced at his watch, raised his eyebrows with dismay and laughed. Taking my telephone number, he patted the dog, shook my mittened hand and dashed away. I walked back into the house slowly, smiling.

I slept most of Christmas Day, and then lay in bed staring at the ceiling. The next day he called, and we took a walk across the George Washington Bridge.

"Cheap date," was my father's comment, as always missing the point.

During that winter Kurt introduced me to his city - the 'undersides of New York', he called it. We went to the beach at Coney Island late at night; watched sunsets from the rooftops of highrise hotels; birdwatched at the Hudson River garbage pier. In a blizzard, we rode the Staten Island ferry, and every Sunday we walked the span of one of the bridges leading out of Manhattan. Kurt's repertoire of the unknown marvels of New York seemed infinite. And as we explored, we talked.

He spoke of growing up poor in the city after emigrating from Europe as a refugee. He told me about his parents - how they had lived in the old country, and who they had become in the new. Fervently, he declared his intentions to be a pure scientist, teaching mathematics in the university as soon as his doctorate was completed.

In turn, I told him about my family, confessing my worst fears for my sister and brother, and my despair about my mother's passivity during all these years with her madman of a husband. I realized that never, in all the time I knew Franco, had I been able to say any of this to him. I told Kurt about Franco, about my penchant for men who were artists, about my old dream of being a dancer and choreographer. He listened, apologized for not being an artist himself, but then wrote me a poem.

We wandered and kept talking, often confounded by what the other was saying, but always probing to understand. When words broke down, we wrapped our arms around each other and felt for the other's warmth. In many ways we were a typical young couple of the fifties, talking a blue streak and mystified by what the other was saying. When he discussed the beauty of numbers to me, I felt too stupid to even ask questions; when I tried to describe the feeling of dance and music as a religious experience, he just gazed at me, perplexed.

But loving each other's selves - quirkiness and humor and imagination - we were not sure it made a difference. In fact, we thought it might even make each of us more interesting.

"I like challenges," Kurt teased when he proposed that we marry.

"Are you sure you're willing to marry into my family?" I warned, half in jest and half in earnest. He looked down at me with his deep, warm eyes, wrapped those long, gangly arms around my waist and hoisting me onto his lap just kissed me in response.

Now, two winters later and a continent away in California, we lay in bed in our rented attic room and listened to the storm outside. It thrummed with increasing intensity against the pitched roof, slashing through the cracks in the windows and jerking the empty cradle by the bed into motion. I clenched to resist the growing pain in my belly, pretending calm to avoid going out into the rain in the middle of the night.

"That was five minutes," Kurt murmured, pocket watch in hand. He rolled over onto his elbow and watched me closely. "I think we'd better go to the hospital."

"No," I muttered, nudging myself onto his shoulder to make him lie down again. Reluctantly, he lowered his head onto the pillow, only to jerk up again when a tearing crack of lightning lit the room, followed by a rolling crash of thunder. I snuggled deeper into the covers, willing myself back to sleep through the achy rumble of the next contraction. Despite myself, I gasped. Kurt timed the contraction, his hair disheveled and his face a study of concentration. When it was over he flung his long legs out of bed and reached for the phone. I was too weak to protest.

"Hello, Paul," he said urgently into the phone. "Sorry to wake you. I think this is it." The room, at that moment, lit with lightning and he laughed nervously. "Sorry about the timing..." He nodded to the voice on the other end; I scrunched under the covers, dreaming of rainswept woods, fragrant and mulchy.

"They've been coming at five- minute intervals since about midnight." I closed my eyes tighter. "Yeah," he chuckled, "she's been fighting me like mad. That's one of the signs? O.K., we'll meet you at the hospital as soon as I can get her out of bed."

"Wait!" I croaked. "Let me talk to him."

I would convince the doctor to let us wait until morning. But my body began to grow hard again, and my groan of pain was drowned out by a prolonged crash of thunder. I panted and waved the phone away, unable to do a thing until the contraction was over.

Kurt threw on khaki pants and a tee-shirt, dressing me over my nightgown in a bathrobe, parka, sneakers and a hooded poncho. I could barely move. Bundling me out into the shock of the storm, he fought wind and rain and a collapsing umbrella to stuff me into the front seat of our beat-up Ford. I sat like a red-hot lump swaddled in layers of clothes, my body burning with its insistent burden, going hard, then soft, then hard again. Kurt splashed his way into the driver's seat, pumped the engine to life and took off like a maniac. I began, uncontrollably, to giggle.

Screeching around our corner, we sped through the raindrenched streets, the rain pelting the car like bullets and the roads knee-deep in puddles. Great arcs of spray hit the windshield - more than the wipers could handle - and Kurt accelerated to make them go faster.

"Too fast!" I gasped, ducking away from each onslaught of water and holding onto my burning belly. He slowed down a bit, and I braced for the next contraction.

"How're you doing?" he asked as we barged through another wall of water.

"O.K., but you don't have to go so fast. Nobody's chasing us." Kurt did not slow down.

Chasing us. The phrase reminded me of something. Chasing us...somebody would be angry at me for rushing off to the hospital in the middle of the night...

"Oh my God!" I cried, remembering. "We forgot to call my father!"

I clenched for the next wave of pain. My father had insisted upon knowing exactly when I went into labor so he could fly out to the coast. For nine months he had repeated over and over that he wanted to be present at the birth of my baby. Just yesterday he had phoned, saying his bags were packed, and we were to call him as soon as labor started.

"We did not forget," Kurt said evenly, never taking his eyes off the road. "We'll call him after the baby is born, not a minute before. Remember? That's what we worked out with Paul." His lips were tight and he gunned the engine unnecessarily. I yelped.

My mind wouldn't focus; I couldn't remember what the

final decision had been. Would my father be called so he could be in the delivery room, as he demanded; or would we obey the doctor's orders that my parents not be informed until after the baby was born, with Paul taking all responsibility with my family?

The two sets of orders had gotten mixed up in my head. I held my breath as the next pain swept over me; Kurt turned sharply into the hospital parking lot and braked hard, flinging himself out his door, opening my side and lifting me out.

God bless Paul Baker, our doctor. It was he, more than anybody, who had helped me get through this pregnancy intact. Not only was he one of the best general practitioners in town and the only one willing to allow Kurt to participate in the birth itself, but he was also our best friend.

It was during my second visit to him, just weeks after we had arrived in the Bay Area, that he had asked with unfailing intuition,

"How have you been sleeping?" I stared down at the fingers tensing in my lap. In fact, I had been having nightmares which were awakening me almost nightly. I had not been aware that it showed.

"Poorly," I admitted, chagrined and also relieved that he had noticed.

"Bad dreams?" he asked matter-of-factly. I nodded.

"Would you tell me one?"

He crossed his legs and leaned back in his chair. His face remained receptive and attentive; I felt I could trust him.

"It was on a beach - in the rain," I began, the words coming out in shudders. "It's gray and cold - a wet day. But the rain isn't exactly rain..." The horror returned and I began to quiver. He waited patiently.

"It's - sort of - poisoned meat that's falling out of the sky. And everyone is running around trying to catch it and eat it. I'm the only one who knows it's poison, and I try yelling it to everyone, but nobody listens." My fingernails were digging into my thighs, and he took my hands gently and held them in his.

"Anyhow - I try to stop children from eating it, but they stuff it into their mouths and start dying...dying..."

My voice disintegrated into a sob, which I gulped back, breathing hard. He simply sat with me, saying nothing until I was calmer.

"Is there something about this pregnancy that frightens you?" he asked finally. I sighed and looked away. I had not intended to speak to him about my father, but in fifteen minutes he had found his way to the raw nerve.

"Yes," I admitted. "Um - it's just that my father, uh, keeps badgering me about being in the delivery room during the birth." Dr. Baker's eyebrows shot up. "He calls at least twice a week to remind me..."

"Does he," he began delicately, "have any reason to suspect this could be his child?" I hung my head in shame. "You don't have to answer," he informed me softly.

"It's not so simple. Of course this isn't his child, but there's been a history...of, um... I don't know what he thinks!"

"Ohh," he breathed out, his nostrils flaring in anger. "You don't have to talk about it unless you want to, but let me tell you unconditionally that no matter what he insists upon, there is no way I will *ever* let him come near you in the hospital!"

"Thank you," I breathed, hardly able to speak. Except to Kurt, I had never expressed my shame before. It felt like a betrayal, but of whom, I couldn't say. Dr. Baker leaned forward.

"Have you told him straight out that he wasn't welcome?"
"No," I confessed.
"Why?"
I shrugged. "He wouldn't hear me if I did."
"Would he hear me?"
"I have no idea. He's pretty crazy."
"May I try?"

"You'd phone him?" I asked. He nodded. The lines around his lips were white; I loved him for that. "Would you try?" I asked, feeling like a very little girl - but safe.

He called my father that day, and that evening phoned us to say that he had gotten nowhere with him.

"He's as irrational as you say," he informed us. "I don't think I've ever had a conversation like that with an adult. He simply wouldn't let me finish a sentence."

"That's dear old Dad," I said wryly. "Now you know why I couldn't just say no."

"I'd like to try one more thing, though, with your permission. I'd like someone from the hospital administration to inform him that it's against hospital rules."

"Give it a try," I suggested, "but I'm willing to bet it's the same story."

It was the same story, unfortunately, but the episode brought Paul and I and Kurt together as more than doctor and patients. We, along with his wife, Angie, became friends, and then something like family. By the sixth month of my pregnancy Paul and I were meeting twice each week - once for my regular check-up, and once to explore the subject of how emotional states affect the body's health. Using me as a guinea pig and my nightmares as material, he would observe my blood pressure, pulse rate, dilation of pupils, and the color of the tongue as I recounted my dreams. We would talk about stress and the adrenals, anxiety and the immune system. His work, seminal and radical at the time, appeared to be the flip side of my interest in how art and religion promoted states of extraordinary well-being. As collaborators we asked, in the sanctum of his office, questions few people in medicine were asking out loud. And I began to learn about the human body, and how to keep it well.

Paul was there at the Emergency Room entrance when we arrived, chatting with the night nurse.

"How'd you get here so quick?" I panted, wincing as a new contraction started.

"Slept in my clothes," he joked, with a wink at Kurt. "I figured you'd come through one of these nights."

"Sorry about our timing," said Kurt, steadying me as I leaned heavily on his arm. He steered me like a barge into the antiseptic warmth of the hospital corridor, shaking off the water that clung to his hair and beard like a wet puppy. We dripped water onto the polished floor. I held onto his arm until the contraction loosed its hold and Paul timed it on his watch.

"I wasn't doing anything tonight anyway," he teased.

"Except sleeping," I panted as the pain subsided. "I tried to convince Kurt to wait till the morning, but he wouldn't listen."

"Smart fellow, your husband," Paul declared, reaching for Kurt's pulse. "Steady as a rock," he noted, letting go of his wrist. "He'll be a good Papa."

"First, though," I joshed, talking fast before the new contraction took hold, "I've got to do the Mama part."

The Maternity Ward was silent. The two delivery rooms stood open and empty, and neither of the labor rooms had a woman in it.

"We're in luck," Paul remarked, glancing around. "We've got the place to ourselves. We can do whatever we please."

"Like tapdance?" I suggested, giddy with four a.m. wit.

"Why, yes," concurred Paul, breaking out into a leap-shuffle-ball-change routine. His eyes were bright blue and full of fun, and his wiry body nimble in blue jeans and checkered shirt. I applauded when he finished with a flourish. "Your turn," he said. Kurt folded his arms across his chest, shaking his head at our antics.

"East-Side-West-Side...," I sang, waddling from one foot to the other before attempting a high kick, "...all-around-the-town..."

My thighs turned to jelly as my womb went rock hard. Kurt reached out to catch me and I leaned into him, clenching my teeth until the pain passed.

"Another time, sweetie," advised Paul, leading me into the closest labor room. "We've got something else to do right now."

After I was installed in bed and propped up on every side with pillows, Paul came in dressed in hospital greens and informed me that the nurse on duty was not one of his favorites.

"She's a bit stodgy," he said, "but we'll work around her."

"Will she try and keep Kurt out?" I panicked. Fathers were allowed into the delivery rooms only rarely, and often only if they themselves were physicians.

"Her shift will be over soon," he assured me. "If this baby cooperates, you'll deliver with the next nurse, and she's a gem."

"But you think she will try and keep him out, right?" I grimaced, twisting to find a comfortable position.

"Oh, you mean the other doctor on the ward?" he grinned, wrinkling his nose at me and watching as the new contraction took hold. "I sent him off to get into doctor-clothes, don't you fret." As if on cue, the nurse walked briskly in.

"Hello Dr. Baker," she said professionally. "And how are we progressing here?" Reaching under the blankets before I knew what was happening, she spread my knees apart with an expert hand.

"Wait!" I yelped, shutting my legs tight. "Contraction," I lied, making a face. They waited politely, while my faked pain became a real one. While she timed it, Paul said,

"Here's the procedure: the nurse is going to take your vital signs, and then she'll check to see how far your cervix is dilated. She will always make sure you're not in the middle of a contraction, so none of this will be painful." He glanced at her for confirmation, his speech becoming more and more deliberate.

"Then," he breathed, shaking his head slowly up and

down, "she will measure your fundus to see how the baby is positioned, O.K.?" He smiled engagingly at her. Paul had either gone out of his mind, or was stalling for time. "After that, she will listen to the baby's heartbeats with the stethoscope..."

"First I'm going to get her shaved and enema'd," the nurse announced, pulling out her razor.

"Let's just begin with the vital signs," Paul suggested, patting me reassuringly on the arm. "I'll be right back."

As soon as she finished taking my blood pressure, the nurse was ready again with the razor.

"Temperature," I reminded her, sticking out my tongue. A new wave of pain took up the next few minutes. She waited until I caught my breath, and then came at me again with the razor.

"Pulse," I said, holding out my arm. Where did Paul go?

"The next nurse can do that," she replied sharply. "I've got to get you shaved and enema'd before I go off shift."

"Wait!" I croaked as the next contraction took over. She glared at me like a prizefighter sizing up his opponent, and would have attacked, I'm sure, if Kurt had not returned at that moment with Paul. They were both garbed from head to toe in green, but Kurt's suit was several sizes too large for him. He was the Jolly Green Giant with hair, holding onto his pants to keep them up. A riptide of giddiness rolled through me and I had hysterics, my whole body trembling out of control.

"These were the only ones that fit," he protested, letting go of the waistband. His pants slid right down, and I couldn't stop laughing, my teeth chattering as if I were cold.

"I thought you had to see it," grinned Paul, handing Kurt a string to loop around his waist. The nurse bustled around them, trying to take charge of an unruly situation.

"I want this girl enema'd," she announced, pulling the bed-curtains closed. Paul smiled endearingly at her, and pulled them open again.

"Let me check the heart tones first," he said mildly.

"Then I want both of you to leave," she declared, picking up a sloshy rubber bag with snake-like tubing.

"But he's my doctor!" I protested. "And he's my husband!"

"You don't want men to see you get an enema," she informed me flatly, preparing the slippery bag for business. Paul caught my eye over her shoulder and winked, pointing to his watch. Then he handed his stethoscope to Kurt.

"See if you can tell the baby's position by where the heartbeats are the loudest." Gently, he displaced the nurse and the two men bent over me. Kurt listened and his eyes grew tender. Then he gave me the stethoscope and I could hear those little birdbeats drumming, steady and sure. We held hands until the next contraction swept over me, and I clung to his hand even after it passed, suddenly scared. This was really happening.

This was serious!

"Well positioned," murmured Paul, listening to all the quadrants of my stomach. Keeping a protective hand on my belly, he smiled sweetly at the nurse who impatiently held out the enema tube like a cobra ready for the strike, and kept himself strategically placed between her and me. Then, his eyes glinting with mystery, he said, "What is rekab?"

My belly grew hard, and the strain pulled into every crevice of my body, as if I were being overtaken by a tidal wave. I panted hard.

"Doctor...," entreated the nurse, trying to get around him.

"What is rekab?" he repeated, holding his ground and folding his arms across his chest. I could barely catch my breath between contractions now.

"Rekab?" I asked, squinting at Kurt, who tapped the face of his wristwatch in reply. The nonsense word was as surreal as the sensations in my body.

"Why, it's Baker spelled backwards!" Paul declared with a grin, taking the enema bag from the nurse's arms as soon as her shift was officially over.

The delivery room was bright with light, white tile and chrome fixtures, and was still except for the swishes of the new nurse's movements.

"Hi, I'm Shirley," she said in a reassuring voice, holding my hand as she timed a long contraction. "Nice," she nodded as I blew out the last of it. She flashed me a smile which dazzled in her broad, brown face and patted my arm. "You ain't the screaming type, I take it?" she remarked, tweaking my toe companionably as she set up the stirrups. "Dr. Baker said you was one in a million, and we were going to have some fun."

"Maybe you will," I joked, panting with the oncoming pain. "This I could do without."

"You're doing fine - just fine."

Paul and Kurt came in, closing the door behind them. Draped in green caps and face masks with only their eyes showing, I hardly knew them. Blue eyes, intense and professional, gazed at me for a moment and then went down to the working end; warm brown eyes stayed by my head and grasped my hand in his. I clung to Kurt as the contractions whooshed in without letup. There was no comfortable rhythm to breathe in. This was like nothing I had ever felt before.

"Go ahead and holler if you have to," suggested Shirley, smoothing away the hair clinging to my brow. I shook my head, holding my breath. Kurt's eyes registered my pain, and I squeezed his hand as hard as I could.

"Good, good," encouraged Paul. "Pant now - don't push yet." I inhaled in the second of respite before the next huge wave took over, trying to hold it all in. Then, like drowning, everything was effaced by the white-hot rush coursing through me.

"Nice..." With a gloved finger, Paul massaged the lower edge of my perineum to keep it from tearing. "Keep panting - don't push yet - keep breathing - that's it..."

I gasped and choked with the effort of not pushing. I was a swollen seed pod in the moment before it popped; a cresting wave in the second before it tumbled into foam.

"Easy....easy..." urged Paul, his voice coming from thousands of miles away. My fingernails bit into Kurt's palm and I gripped harder, and harder. Inside me the fireball surged forward, unstoppable, searing everything within its path. I heaved, bulging with the inexorable urge to erupt.

"O.K!" cried Paul, "Now! Push your baby out!"

With relief I let go into the storm, bearing down as if bearing down was the only thing I had ever wanted to do in my life. The whole force of the universe bore down with me, spreading me wide open, wider even than exploding suns.

"That's it!" cheered Shirley, sponging my forehead. Kurt lifted my shoulders and pushed with me. By the sweat beading on his face, it could have been him propelling our baby out. Clinging to him as if he were the only thing anchoring me to the ground, I pushed my ball of fire towards the air. "Good going!" called Shirley, urging us on.

Oh God, it hurt. But there was only one way to go, and that was towards the high windwaves of mid-ocean, always forming, never breaking, never settling, never resting. But they crested, moving towards an invisible shore, again and again and again.

"Look in the mirror!" cried Paul. Cracking open a tear-blurred eye, I saw my own gaping vagina stretched impossibly wide and a black slimy mass coming forward from within me.

"Ohhhh!" I heaved, pushing with the force of all the stars and suns and planets in the universe. From my body a little head began to emerge. Oh God, my baby!

Cradling the tiny head, Paul maneuvered out the shoulders and the buttocks, and then flailing purple arms and folded legs. I felt the pressure ease. A miniature person covered with slime and wax, at the end of a twisted purple cord sucked in its first breath and gave a tinny howl. We all cheered.

Paul lifted him up for me to see.

"What kind of baby do you have?" he called.

"A boy!" I crowed in a voice grainy with excitement. I struggled to sit up as Paul laid him on my belly. Feeling his warm solid weight, I gazed at the miracle of nostrils and eyelashes, fingers and toes. I still clung to Kurt's hand hard. "Look at him!" I exclaimed over and over. I couldn't stop laughing. A minute penis shot a stream of hot urine into the air and everyone applauded.

"Oh Paul," I breathed, unable to take my eyes off my baby, "thank you."

"Wasn't Dr. Baker that did the work," laughed Shirley, dropping silver nitrate into the baby's eyes. She held out a pinky, which the baby grasped tightly. "He was just the reception committee."

"You guys did it yourselves," Paul agreed, massaging my abdomen with firm fingers. He held up an imaginary toast to Kurt and me. Our hands were still tightly locked together. "You two make a good team."

"That Papa didn't look like he'd faint even once, did he doctor?" She blew Kurt a kiss, who smiled broadly and hugged me. We both acknowledged Paul and Shirley with a thumbs-up sign; he waved back with a bloody hand and she, with a saucy wink, sashayed over to Paul and planted a kiss on his masked cheek. He pretended to swoon and we all laughed, bubbly with euphoria. Then the baby, with a great splurt, shat a stream of black mecomium onto the sterile white cloths. Kurt and I gasped with delight.

"Precocious kid," Paul remarked, examining the sticky stuff with a gloved finger. "Mecomium sometimes takes hours to come through."

"Check out these reflexes!" exclaimed Shirley, tickling the tiny bottoms of his feet.

"You've got a fine, healthy son, my friends," Paul declared. "Whenever you're ready, we can cut the cord. Kurt, will you do the honor?"

He handed Kurt the scissors. We untangled the viselike grip of our hands, and I began to cry.

"Not until you're ready," Paul said quietly.

"I'm ready," I gulped, wiping my tears on Kurt's green suit and wincing as my baby, in the space of one moment became a separate person.

We surrounded this child, four people who one generation earlier might never have found themselves on the same continent, much less the same room. And here we were now, bonded by this new baby.

"You're on your own, m'boy," whispered Paul as soon as the cut was made. His eyes, I noticed, were glistening.

I was awed by the power of this child.

In those quiet hours before dawn, the delivery room had the aura of a holy place. The baby, breathing the same air we breathed, became one of us; our little community of four had, overnight, become a community of five.

While Paul waited for the placenta to come out, Shirley brought me the baby for his first suckle. She steered my nipple towards his tiny pursed lips and with a voracious instinct he grabbed hold, clamped down and sucked.

"Aagh!" I shrieked as a strong contraction took me by surprise and a gush of blood steamed hotly out onto the sheets. The baby lost my nipple and squalled angrily in my face. Shirley laughed and placing her warm, brown fingers on my breast, guided the nipple back into his lips. Clamping, he sucked hard and my belly gave another lurch.

"That's perfect," murmured Paul, coaxing the severed umbilicus gently out of my body. "One more push - here comes the placenta!" He held the spongy, bloody mass up to the light. "It's healthy," he observed, examining it carefully. "Want to see where he's spent the last nine months?"

With the nuzzling baby in my arms, Kurt and I poked our fingers in the used-up placenta. Dark deposits had formed on the inside walls and portions of the cord had grown stiff.

"I never cease to be amazed," mused Paul, "at the way the placenta stays fresh until just before the baby is ready to be born - and then it ages quickly."

"Just in time," I commented, cuddling my son and wondering if my own mother, and her mother before her, had known this same protective instinct. Had this once been felt for me?

With my newborn at my breast, I joined for the first time every other mother in the history of the world and knew that both he and I together were in the company of every mother and child in the universe. Which meant everyone.

We were part of a multitude.

"Hello," I whispered to my child. He let go of the nipple and stared up at me hugely. For a long moment we gazed into each other's eyes, bonding. "Hello," I whispered again. "Hello."

Out in the busy corridor, we showed him off to everyone who stopped - nurses, laboring women, a harried father in jeans. They agreed that he was beautiful, extraordinary. Yes, the world had indeed been changed by his birth. I couldn't take my eyes off him; my heart, as if taken by surprise, had jerked open and my lips could not stop smiling.

"Hey, you!" I wanted to shout to all of them, "Listen: we've all been born! It's a miracle! Every single one of us - even you over there with your hands between your knees - Yes, you too!"

It was true; we were all bonded by the same amazing event, whether we realized it or not. I gazed down at the baby curled at my breast, and I could hardly believe my eyes.

The midnight storm had given way to a drizzly day and the baby - Saul Micah - came back from the nursery diapered and name-tagged, already a citizen of the world. Tucked in my warm bed I held my swaddled child and gazed at him, totally absorbed. Kurt and Paul, both exhausted, stood by my bedside and silently watched me and the baby. I wasn't tired at all.

"Why don't you both go home and get some sleep," I suggested. I sniffed the sweetness of the baby's head. "I'll be fine now." They glanced warily at each other. Kurt spoke first.

"There's still something we have to do," he said, shifting his weight uneasily. Puzzled, I looked up at his kind, worried face. The baby yawned and pursed his lips, giving a little pink-tongued smile.

"Look! I think he smiled!" I crooned, hugging him closer. Paul sat down on the edge of my bed and placed a hand on my knee. Kurt sat down next to him and simply stared at me. "Isn't he gorgeous?" I asked. Kurt's hand went out to the receiving blanket, almost as big as the whole baby.

"We've still got to call the parents," he said bluntly. For a moment I didn't know what he meant. Then I remembered - my parents. I suddenly felt very sleepy. The baby stirred, making my breasts tingle.

"I'll dial," he said, handing the receiver to me when the number started ringing. Paul's eyes narrowed as he watched my face. For the space of two rings the four of us were motionless. Then my mother answered.

"Hi Mom!" I cried, affecting a bright voice. "Guess what, we've got a..." She interrupted me in an angry voice.

"Get Kurt!"

"We've got a boy!" I persisted, my eyes wanting to close and my mind shutting down. How could my disobedience be more important than this miraculous being we had created?

"Put Kurt on!" she insisted hoarsely. I handed over the receiver; Paul took my hand and warmed it against his chest.

"Hi!" said Kurt, in the same bright tone. "We did it! It's a..." He stopped dumb and turned his back to me, his shoulders rising with tension. "When did it happen? Oh, my God..."

"What...?" I cried, reaching for the telephone while my mind slid in the other direction towards sleep. Paul sidled closer to me and the baby, as if to protect us. Still listening intently, Kurt turned and stared at us, his mind elsewhere.

"Yes, I'll tell her. No, you don't have to talk to her. What? Yeah, the baby's fine - she's fine too. Everything went well. Listen, I'll phone back in about an hour." Replacing the receiver slowly he just stood where he was, his face contracted with sorrow. He slumped down onto the bed and reached for the baby and me before speaking.

"Your father's had a heart attack," he said. "It was a bad one, but he's expected to recover." My arm tightened involuntarily around the baby, and my mind went numb.

"When?" I whispered. I didn't want to hear what I knew was coming.

"Just about when you started labor - I didn't tell your mother that."

Paul hung his head and covered his eyes, and I felt the energy drain out of my whole body. "He's in Intensive Care..." From a distance, I heard Kurt say,

"You know this isn't your fault, don't you?" but I was too groggy to respond. Anyhow, I did not know that it wasn't my fault - would never know. Sleep closed my eyes; I was suddenly too tired to even hold my baby. One of the last things I remember was seeing Paul, with the baby in his arms, leave the room. Kurt pulled a chair close to the bed and lay his head against my thigh, a warm pressure. When he left, I was not aware of it.

My father did survive that heart attack; he was, after all, only forty-five years old. And he survived the next one a few months later. He was too ill, therefore, to insist upon coming out for the birth of our next baby, Eva, fourteen months later, or the next, Abram, a year and a half after that.

It wasn't until the children were about three, two and one that my parents made their first, long-awaited trip west to California and met their three grandchildren. My father's health had been holding, as long as he took things easy, and his doctor thought a vacation might do him good.

On their third day with us, after a jolly breakfast of pancakes and blueberry syrup, we waved goodbye to Kurt as he set off for the university on his bike. It was Monday, and my first day of dealing with my parents and the children on my own without Kurt. I had scheduled a check-up appointment for the children so that Paul and my parents could meet in an uncharged, professional setting. Paul couldn't help but make a good impression, and the children were sure to be charming. And it would take up a good part of the morning.

Paul was indeed reassuring and kind, like a wise, favorite uncle to the children, who were as adorable as grandparents could wish. I was pleased with the visit and assumed my parents would be also but I was mistaken. My father refused to sit down the whole time we were there and wouldn't speak a word until we had left the office.

"You were very lucky nothing went wrong," he informed me in the parking lot. Nervously, he lit up a cigarette.

"What do you mean?" I asked, trying not to be defensive. Abram squirmed to get out of my arms, and finally won.

"That's not an experienced man," my father informed me. "He wouldn't have known enough to call a specialist if anything had gone wrong." I had almost forgotten the convoluted logic of this man's mind. Brushing the hair from my eyes, I held a Kleenex to Eva's nose.

"Blow!" I barked, regretting my tone immediately.

"You know," he went on, "my bags were packed and ready to go. I fully intended to be here."

"Yeh," I mumbled noncommittally.

"Kurt wouldn't have called in a specialist," he went on doggedly. "You're a very lucky girl that nothing went wrong." There was no polite response possible. I caught up with my mother who walked, solemnly, hand in hand with Saul.

"He did have his bags packed," she whispered to me. I simply nodded. Abram crawled between our legs, stopping to pick a cigarette butt off the tarmac and stuff it into his mouth. Grabbing him up, I probed his mouth with a finger and pulled out the wet butt; in his struggle, he landed a foot and an elbow in my ribs.

"Don't..." my mother pleaded as my father extracted a cigarette from his pack and lit up. Ignoring her, he coughed and then blew erratic smoke-rings for the children. They were entranced by the coughs as well as the puffs of smoke. He was, with his magic, the hero of the moment and they watched him wide-eyed and speechless.

But his triumph dissolved into a fit of body-wracking wheezes, and the children's eyes gleamed with fear. He hacked away as if he would spit out his heart, and I considered running upstairs to get Paul.

"Put it out!" my mother begged, her body tight as a bowstring. "I can't get him to stop smoking," she complained bitterly to me. "He chokes like this every single time he lights up. He'll kill himself!"

"My doctor's given me permission to smoke," he gasped defensively, for my information more than for hers. "It's considered better than the stress of withdrawal."

I said nothing, and after a few more heart-straining coughs he took a last, deep puff and threw the lit cigarette onto the ground, only half grinding it out. Abram made right for it. I stubbed it out all the way and kicked it out of reach, holding the baby back from pursuing it. Predictably, he fought to get out of my grasp.

"Don't!" I cried much too sharply, slapping his diapered bottom. His black eyes opened with shock and his lips curled as he dissolved into a heap of outrage, sobbing as if his heart would break. Abram's screams would not be stilled. My mother blamed it on my father. My father reached for another cigarette. Eva had to pee. Saul stood gazing dreamily into the parking lot, reading numbers off license plates. I sat on a step and rocked Abram in my arms.

"I know...I know..," I crooned, wiping up tears and drool with the hem of my sleeve, "but you can't eat cigarette butts. Sorry."

It was only ten o'clock in the morning, day three of a ten-day visit. Every one of us was ready for a nap.

"You know," my father remarked as we pulled the car into traffic, "you should be keeping your mind up."

I laughed at what I assumed was a joke after the lengthy ritual of getting all three children buckled into their car seats.

"A mind that's not used gets stagnant," he claimed. The man wasn't kidding.

"The mind is like a muscle," he went on, using the same pontificating tone that had accompanied the humiliations of my childhood, "and education is what keeps it in shape." I kept my eyes on the road and tried not to drive aggressively. When he reached for another smoke, I said with forced calm,

"Not in the car, please." My mother, in the back seat, tapped his shoulder for emphasis; reluctantly he returned the cigarette to his shirt pocket.

"Kurt," he continued, unstoppable, "is intellectually stimulated at the university every day."

"Me too," I peeped under my breath. He glanced at me significantly.

"And so are his colleagues..."

"You mean he'll be ashamed to show me off in front of the other professors?" I said meanly. "That's why I should get smart?"

"Maybe not ashamed...," he replied in a voice weighty with meaning. "But keeping yourself informed on current affairs would make it easier for you to talk to them." The depth of his offense was deflected by Abram letting out a great, smelly fart. His grandmother had hysterics. I did too.

"Peee-yew!" commented Saul, holding his nose. Shaking with laughter, I handed out small boxes of raisins and told the kids to share. Saul lined up his raisins along his thighs, one by one, counting them out; Abram stuffed a fistful into his mouth and sprayed the rest around the car and Eva, peacekeeper even at the age of two, offered raisins to Grandma, then Grandpa, and then me. For a few moments we were distracted with thank-you's.

"Just one evening class at the university," my father persisted, never knowing when to stop. "Just so that you don't make a fool of yourself altogether." He reached for his cigarette again as we pulled into our street. Already, my eyes rasped in their sockets.

Abram, I could smell, needed his diaper changed; Eva was getting restless and would soon need a nap; Saul had taken off his shoes. Kurt had a seminar until late and couldn't get home before dinner. I had to do a load of diapers or I'd be all out by tomorrow afternoon, and dinner was going to be a production.

All I wanted was to be in a quiet place, sitting by myself under a tree. My father was still admonishing me when I pulled up in front of our house, and my mother complained about the cigarette held loosely in his hand, but I lifted the kids out of their seats one by one, swept out the raisins littering the car, and picked up shoes. Abram flung a bottle of apple juice behind him, hitting Saul, who yelled. Eva and my mother got caught in the ensuing crossfire and scrambled out, slamming their door behind them.

When we were at last all out of the car, our bags and bottles and sweaters and shoes tumbled around us on the sidewalk, my father shut all the car doors and locked them. My hair was in my face and my armpits prickled with sweat. With a sigh of relief I fumbled in my pocket for the housekey, but it wasn't there. It wasn't in my bag, either.

It was, we soon discovered, dangling from the car ignition with the rest of my keys - locked in.

During those early years of marriage and children, my life was indeed a round of cooking and cleaning up messes, but what my father could not understand was my deepening friendship with Kurt and our passionate commitment to these children we had created. Not having had it himself, he could not know how much intelligent people could learn from their growing intimacy with each other, their day- by- day wonder at the unfoldment of their children. For him, family had been a failure; for us, it was an experiment in love and trust.

He was unaware that through our own development and the growing of our kids, I was able to glimpse at larger evolutions. He couldn't see me learn along with them as they took their first bandy-legged steps, lurching full tilt into bipedal exploration of the world around them.

As the children's minds sharpened and their curiosity became insatiable, I found my own boundaries expand to include them - or be included by them. We learned things from scratch, together. Their power to teach me was the power of the life-force itself. I felt it probe into rock-hard layers of myself, breaking up deep, destructive habits and setting down tentative roots in new soil. The compacted mud of old fears was eroded, bit by bit, by the root-hair tendrils of my newly discovered capacity for love.

We kept them close, those first few years, doing everything as a family and focusing almost exclusively on the welfare of the children.

Of a winter evening, as dusk trailed early into dark, I would pull the curtains closed as soon as Kurt arrived home from work, lock the doors behind him and light the lamps. With baked bread still fragrant from the oven, and onions browning slowly on the stove, the five of us would gather in our cozy kitchen and get ready for dinner. Kurt would kiss the back of my neck and tell me about his day, finally hunkering down in the middle of the kitchen floor to play Gulliver to the childrens' Lilliputians.

Ecstatic to have their Daddy home, the kids would tumble

in and out of his arms, ruddy with giggles. He would roll them around the floor, tickling and teasing and pretending to be knocked over by their mighty tackles. I, meanwhile, would add chopped garlic to the onions, cutting up tomatoes and celery and parsley, stirring them in.

"Here comes Mister Lion..." Kurt would rumble, down on all fours, his red-bearded face casting about for the closest child. Shrieking with excitement they would all scatter away from him until one, overjoyed, got swept into his embrace.

Leaning from the stove to the chopping board across their game I would scoop yoghurt into the stew, adding the fish at the last moment. Sidetracked by my bare leg straddling him, Kurt would reach up for a surreptitious tickle, for which he would get a quick toe in the ribs. Or parsley in his beard, if I was fast enough.

This was home, our life. It was safety. On the other side of the drawn curtains was the unknown night. For years, I didn't leave the house alone after dark.

Saul stood tippy-toe at the stove, sniffing.

"Mmm-mmm," he hummed, rubbing his tummy. Kurt lifted Eva into her highchair, then Abram. Saul climbed onto his chair as I brought the steaming pots to the table. Kurt wiped six dirty hands with a washcloth, tied three bibs onto three necks and poured the milk. By then, three children banged their spoons impatiently on their bowls.

"Hot, hot!" I warned, spooning fish stew onto each plate and blowing away the steam. Kurt sliced the bread and buttered it, handing it around. And then, except for the juicy noises of eating, the childrens' breaths industrious behind the smacking of their little lips, all was silence.

The ritual of dinner at the round oak table in our kitchen, which would continue unbroken for the next twenty years, was underway.

After nine o'clock I was more than ready for bed. After the childrens' bath and bedtime story, we would clean up the kitchen slowly, yawning and talking over the day until we dragged ourselves into bed. Sometimes we talked until late, sometimes were asleep almost immediately, and occasionally, when I still had the energy to read, I'd open a book that matched the level of attention I still had left. When I was exhausted but restless, only a Gothic romance would do; when I was restless but not exhausted, a Victorian novel, or a self-help book on child-rearing did the trick.

I had another category of reading as well - the 'babysitter' book. This was for when I had an uninterrupted two hours to read. In those early years, this book was Charles Darwin's *Origin of Species*. I read it paragraph by paragraph, gradually absorbing the idea of evolution as it applied to my own life. I watched myself learn things from the ground up, saw how I adapted to life with growing children, changing to match their changes.

I observed us finding our niche in the neighborhood and the playground, discovering who were our friends and where we belonged, much as the creatures had found their ecological niches in Darwin's Galapagos Islands. What he discovered in that raw, volcanic archipelago I was finding in the homely atmosphere of our house, our street, our playground.

Thinking about biological evolution, I learned a new way of looking at things; watching my children grow, I began to wonder about how consciousness evolved as well. With Paul Baker, I continued asking questions about the body and the mind, and with Kurt it came clearer to me how love fit in. Darwin, somehow, had the key and as I read slowly through the *Origin*, steadily and surely my eyes began to open.

"Plants and animals remote in the scale of nature are bound together by a web of complex relations."

While the children took an unprecedented nap together, I copied this quote from Darwin onto a file card. An ant, with tickle-feet, mounted my arm and scurried down my hand towards the sugar bowl in the middle of the kitchen table. He climbed off my thumb and unerringly found his way towards the sugar, a nomad in the desert.

That ant and me - what was the web of complex relations between us? If I were to squash him under my thumb, how would my life be affected?

Another ant followed the trail, then another, then a file of them. In moments they had the crusted sugar bowl surrounded. Cold-bloodedly, I snuffed them out. Then, with a wet napkin I wiped up the rear column marching blindly across the kitchen floor. After stuffing their entryway with a wad of paper, I sat very still in my chair and tried to sense how I had been changed by their eradication. At first I felt no different; it was just a few dozen ants, after all. No big deal for either their species or mine. But if I stayed very quiet and listened attentively, I could subtly feel their loss. Deep within, at the almost imperceptible edge of sensation, I felt something akin to loneliness.

I took a deep, shaky breath and read on:

"In the long run, the forces are so nicely balanced that the face of nature remains for long periods uniform."

A squawk from the bedroom roused me from my book, and I leapt towards the door to remove Abram before he woke the others. But I was too late. Abram, rosy and creased with sleep, had gotten a foot caught between the mattress and the springs, and he called his distress loud and clear. The whole crib creaked loudly as I extricated his foot and hauled him over the side.

"Down!" he shouted, finally waking the others. They blinked their eyes open and rolled over.

"Can we go to the park?" they demanded in voices still fuzzy with sleep.

"Sure can," I replied. I gave the *Origin of Species* a wry, mental shrug. "Diaper change, Abie, c'mere. Saul, go to the potty - yes, Eva, you can bring your doll."

For the next half hour I changed diapers, gathered sweaters, put on shoes, poured juice, filled a backpack, located buckets and shovels and searched for my keys. On the way out, the kids toppled the toy basket by the door.

"Out!" I commanded, herding them through the door before anything else went over. Slamming the door behind me, I carried the stroller down the porch steps, remembered I hadn't locked the back door and unlocked the door again. In my whirlwind way through the house this time, I grabbed my Darwin from the kitchen table, saved my place with a paper napkin and plopped it into my backpack with the rest of the stuff.

The high-pitched clamor of kids at play guided us towards the park. Overhead, seagulls cawed and circled, diving down for the brown-bag prey they had learned to come inland to find.

Saul rattled the gate latch, threw it open and raced away to join his friends playing ankle-deep in mud by the drinking fountain. From the gate, they looked like just any bunch of kids in dirty overalls, but I knew them to be Kevin, Jenny, Aaron and Joshua - the mud crowd. Saul tugged off his shoes and jumped in. I tried not to wince. Braking the stroller by the chain-link fence, I set Eva and Abram loose with their buckets and shovels. They made right for the sandbox.

The sun had burned through the early haze and the air was bright with warmth. Every swing and slide was busy with a child, and the mothers sat chatting or reading around the sandbox area.

Some days I joined them; some days, like today, I sat apart and read. After greeting my friends, I moved on to an empty bench at the far end of the playground - but someone got there before me.

"Hi bird," I said softly, hoping she would stay. A seagull sat perched on the armrest, alternately preening and watching for signs of dropped food. I took a cautious step closer; she ignored me. And another. As I reached the bench, she spread her wings and lifted easily into the air.

I kept her in sight, distinguishing her from the other gulls until they had crossed flight paths one time too many; I could no longer separate her from the rest.

"Mommy!" called Eva from the sandbox. In the welter of children's shouts, I responded to my child's voice immediately. She waved her shovel at me, a grinning toffee-head in yellow overalls amidst others of approximately the same size and shape. "Wanna slide!" she hollered. If a careless giant were to enter the park this minute, he could snuff her out with his finger as I had dispatched the column of ants on my kitchen table.

My daughter!

I ran all the way to the sandbox.

"Watch me!" she demanded, clambering up the steel ladder on sturdy little legs. On top, she centered herself and stood looking out, triumphant. Then she sat and whizzed down, much faster than she expected. I caught her before she landed on the ground. "I slide!" she shrieked, still catching her breath.

"Me too!" whooped Abram, jackknifing to a stand and making for the ladder at a baby toddle. His face was lit with determination, but Eva overtook him and started up the ladder ahead of him. "Meeee..." he wailed, attacking the steps again.

"Let's try one more your size," I suggested, disentangling him from the steel steps and carrying him over to the kiddie slide.

"No!" he screamed in protest, flipping out of my grasp as Eva came plummeting down the big slide. "Wanna go Eva slide!"

"Little slide," I insisted, carrying him back again.

"Nooo!" Three times he escaped; three times I carried him back. At last he condescended to stay on the tamer slide, riding an erratic course to the bottom, his arms spread like Victory, his face tilted to the sky.

Above, a gull skimmed upon a current of air, its wings

spread like arms and head focused down. Abie pointed a chubby finger.

"Bird," he declared.

"*Squ-eee!*" said the gull. Abram shrieked in response. The gull's wings flicked with the wind and the gull swooped down, landing on the chain-link fence. Abram bumped off the slide and picked himself up, arms spread wide for balance. The gull lifted off, tucked its legs under and took to the air. Abram stumbled back to the kiddie slide and started to climb.

"Swing me, Mommy!" cried Eva, finished with the slide. She charged towards an empty swing, dodging the occupied ones like an expert. I put her in it, pulled the swing backwards and let it go with a push.

"Wheee!" she sang, her fine hair streaming behind her. Shifting her weight, she bent her legs forward and back, gathering momentum.

"Don't push me, Mommy," she called, breathless. "I do it myself." I stood to the side and made funny faces at her as she swung by. Giggling and pumping, she propelled herself higher and higher, as if she were flying. Leaning backwards, she gazed up at the sky.

Above, a seagull soared, at play with the wind. It dipped and it coasted, at home in thin air. Eva spread her arms, also flying, but the swing lost its momentum. Impatient, she shifted forward again and began to pump ferociously. Her chubby legs bent and they straightened; slowly, the swing rose higher and higher.

The seagull glided effortlessly, its wings cushioned by air. Resting, it rode the currents; resting, it rode the wind.

Back at the bench I opened my Darwin and read:

"Almost every part of every organic being is so beautifully related to its complex conditions of life..."

"Hi there." Adrienne, the mother of Kevin and Jenny of the mud-crowd, joined me on the bench. "If dirty is attractive, then filthy is magnificent, right?" We laughed, observing our progeny in the mud puddle.

"What's the point of mud unless you get it in your hair and up your nostrils?" I agreed.

"Not to mention both eardrums and your vagina," she added, sitting down next to me. I closed the Darwin.

"I think it's warm enough to just hose them down when we get home," she said as Kevin aimed a full bucket of water at their little red wagon. Saul scooped up a handful of mud and added it to the top of a growing mound. Jenny patted it down and sculpted battlements while Joshua and Aaron dug a moat around the drinking fountain.

"It does look like fun, though," I mused.

"Maybe we should try it sometime," she suggested.

"Sure - why not? We could go up north to the mudbaths and see how it feels to be covered with the stuff!"

"And invite the men?" she added archly, taking out her knitting. We chuckled at the idea, watching as a gull lit softly on the grass and stilted towards my backpack. Pretending innocence, it looked every which way before making a pounce on an opened box of graham crackers. Three others swooped down to join it.

"Let's wait and see what they do," I suggested as Adrienne made a move to shoo them off. The gulls edged backwards towards the crackers, glancing from side to side before making stabs at the box with quick bills.

"Cheeky," commented Adrienne as a gull extricated a wrapped packet and began to peck at the paper. Another gull landed, bickering with the others over the booty. They dragged the package onto the grass, shoved each other aside and finally tore open a hole in the wrapping. Screeching, they all dived in.

"Birds! Birds!" cried Abram, waddling full tilt towards the fray. Other children came running over as gulls fluttered down, clattering and jabbering around the crackers. One gull escaped with a whole square, and another gave it chase. Banking and turning, it swallowed the cracker down whole, and landed again on the grass to try once more.

Hooting with one-year-old machismo, Abram charged into the squabbling gulls, who scattered and then landed again boldly, making grabs for the crumbs.

"Can we have a cookie?" asked Jenny, mud dripping from her chin. Adrienne handed around an unpilfered box of Saltines, which the children reached and pushed for, just like the gulls.

"One for Laurie, too?" asked Eva, holding out a sandy palm. Clutching her gift, she ran back to the sandbox where Laurie was swinging from the bars.

The mud-crowd hung around, besplattered, until the last of the crackers was gone, and then charged back to their mud mound and silted moat. Sweeping up the crumbs, we tossed them onto the grass for the gulls. Descending, they pecked away busily - just like the kids - and when they flew away, not a single crumb was left.

My copy of Darwin didn't come along with us to the mountains that summer, but almost everything else in the house did. For a one-week camping vacation, we crammed the car with food, diapers, clothes for all weathers and a borrowed army tent that neither of us knew how to put up.

A week in the woods was my idea, not Kurt's. He was skeptical about any vacation that took this much work, especially if it was in the wilderness, but I was convinced that once we were in the woods, surrounded by towering granite and clear mountain streams, he would be won over.

I hadn't counted on the effects of five hours in the car with three restless kids, however. By the time we reached the place it was early twilight and everyone was grumpy, even though our campsite was beautiful and serene and smelled of resin and sun-warmed rock. I stood and stretched, rejoicing in the sounds of birds and the muted burble of the nearby stream.

"Don't you love it?" I exclaimed, trying to drum up some enthusiasm. The kids revived and responded, tossing pinecones and hiding behind trees, but Kurt was not to be easily placated.

"Let's get this damn tent up before there's no light to see by," he muttered. He pulled down the tailgate of the car with more force than was necessary. Not an auspicious beginning. I organized the children into a game of picking up the pinecones from where we would sleep.

"It's not a *damn* tent," I told him as he dragged the poles and canvas out of our borrowed tent, grumbling. "I'll help you," I said pleasantly, determined not to get into a fight on our first-time-ever camping trip.

"And how do you propose to put this thing together?" he asked sarcastically. He *was* determined to get into a fight. Realistically, there was no way at all that he and I, equally inexperienced in the woods, could put up a tent in the dark.

"How about tomorrow?" I finally suggested. Night was coming on fast. We needed a fire, some food - not a tent.

"Hand me a pole, please," he said, ignoring my suggestion. I handed him a pole. "I don't want the kids soaked in a mountain storm in the middle of the night," he mumbled, feeling the ground for a flat space in the dimming light. "Where's the flashlight?"

I found the flashlight, and also a sandwich for each of the kids. This was going to take awhile.

"How about over here?" I paced out an area surrounded by pines and outlined it with the flashlight.

"Too close to the woods," he considered, choosing ground closer to the car, that was hummocky with roots.

"Too close to the car," I objected, suddenly wanting to call the whole venture off. I was close to tears. Why had I assumed that my New -York- City- Mathematics- Professor- husband, would want to be in the wilderness as much as I did? He was a city boy, as he often reminded me, and not a man whose mind was easily changed.

We finally reached a compromise, but Kurt wasn't happy. He lit the Coleman lantern and dragged out the rest of the tent cloths. The children picked stones and pinecones from the site. When the first star showed solitary and pristine in the deepening sky, I pointed it out to the kids. Nothing would ever induce me to sleep in a tent on this cloudless night.

We shook out the canvas, grunting under its weight and regarded it skeptically. Neither of us had any idea what to do next.

"Pole," Kurt said. My impulse was to hide it behind my back; I handed him the pole without expression. "Alright - this seems to fit in here..." He tucked the pole into a flap in the canvas. "Here we go!"

Grunting, he raised the pole, lifting yards of heavy canvas off the ground. The kids, with the healthy abandon of children who have been cooped up too long, chased each other around the campsite, tripping over a trailing edge of the canvas and almost toppling the whole thing.

"Off!" shouted Kurt, sending them off to the safer environs of the car.

If he caused *my* children to feel timid in the woods, I would never speak to him again!

"Should I do the other one?" I snapped, fumbling through yards of smelly canvas to find the second flap. If we had to do this nonsense anyway, we might as well get it done quickly. I searched in the dark, unable to find a second flap, and finally only pretended. Kurt knew immediately.

"Come hold this one," he said crossly. "I'll find it." I swallowed an argument about the joys of sleeping under the stars.

Like tightrope walkers crossing a single high-wire, we carefully traded places. I hung onto the first pole while Kurt got tangled in the other end of the canvas. In the sky, new stars appeared and blinked steadily over the darkening silhouettes of the mountains.

"We've got to get it from underneath," he declared, ducking under the fabric at his end. I began to feel a fit of the giggles coming on. This would not end well. I got very serious with my corner of the tent.

"Get underneath!" he demanded.

"I *am* underneath!" I shot back. The hot, mildewed tent lay heavy on my back. No way was I going to sleep in this thing. "What do you want me to do now?" I could not keep the derision out of my voice.

"Just hang onto it," he spit out. "Don't let it go no matter what I do."

"And just what are you proposing to do?" This was no time to tease.

"Thanks a lot," he retorted, tugging at his end which made my end sway precariously. "Where the hell's the hole?"

No longer able to hold it in, I burst into laughter which he, for a moment, joined. The whole tent shook like weighty jello. Then he turned serious.

"I can't see a damned thing!" He was not going to admit levity into this operation.

"Why don't we wait until morning?" I tried again. I was about to suffocate under all that canvas.

"And do what tonight?" he shouted, unbalancing his end of the tent so that my pole slipped out from under me, dragging yards of collapsing canvas with it.

We were both buried. I clawed my way out, hysterical. A floundering hump in the canvas marked Kurt's position and roaring with laughter I pulled at the canvas while he fought his way out. He was not in a good mood.

"What's so funny?" he snorted, kicking away a mass of fabric still caught on his boot. Giddily I kicked at the canvas too, hooting with merriment.

"What're you guys doing?" Eva asked reasonably. This redoubled my laughter and I collapsed onto the pile of tenting in a heap.

"We don't know!" I cried, catching her as she jumped in on top of me. The boys leapt in too, rolling in the tangled folds of canvas and whooping with the game. We were all berserk!

"OFF YOU GUYS!" Kurt shouted in a tone that had to be obeyed.

"Why, Daddy?" asked Saul, completely buried in canvas. He asked why to everything these days.

"Because that's where we're going to sleep, that's why!"

"Not me," I whispered, in a voice that only Eva, who lay splayed across my lap, could hear.

"Me too!" she squealed at the top of her lungs. In the dark, I winced.

"Me too! Me too!" chanted Saul and Abram in rhythm, jumping up and down on top of the tenting. Kurt threw down his pole and stalked away. Abram ran after him, tripping over the canvas and set up a wail that echoed off the walls of the canyon. Eva and Saul fought over who got to have my lap and I tossed them off, grabbing up Abram, whose lip was bloodied.

Under a tree, away from the malevolent tent I sat down on the ground with all three children crowded on my lap and rocked them sadly. My husband had disappeared into the night and I was out in the wilds where I had always wanted to be. Except that now I didn't want to be here. Least of all with him.

I gazed up at the stars, blinking back tears. I was quite sober now.

A sickle moon sat like a yellow cradle above the dark towers of granite. I breathed in shakily, loving the deep, embracing darkness. Here, where the land stretched for miles unsullied by human civilization, was where I felt at home. For me, the city moved at too fast a pace, was too noisy with motors.

For Kurt, though, it was the city that felt like home; wilderness was unpredictable, unfamiliar. So we were different - nothing wrong with that. We knew that when we married. But how could I be married to someone who wanted to put up a tent between himself and the night sky?

"Everyone's going to sleep out tonight," I announced quietly.

"Yayy!" shouted the children.

"Ssshhh," I admonished. I lay out three small sleeping bags on the crumbled tenting.

"Which one's mine?" asked Eva gleefully, pulling off her shoes. Child of my heart.

"Eva in the middle, Saul on this side, Abie on that side." I held Abram's bag open and he dove in headfirst. I hauled him out and changed his diaper. The others giggled and squirmed cozily into their bags, loving the adventure.

"Where's Daddy?" asked Saul.

"I'm right here," Kurt said briefly, coming out of the dark. He pumped up the Coleman which hissed and burned brightly again. We did not look at each other. I walked past him to the car, took out my sleeping bag and went to the far end of the campsite, close to the woods. He could make his own arrangements; sleep in the car, if that's what he wanted.

Unlacing my boots, I pulled them off and unzipped my jeans. I crept into my sleeping bag, pretending to ignore Kurt's movements. He pumped up the lantern again, checked on the kids, slammed shut the tailgate of the car. Then he rummaged through the food chest. I could hear him chewing.

The lantern flared, sputtered and faded out. We were covered by night. I realized I had forgotten to eat, and suddenly felt hungry. The childrens' whispers and giggles punctuated the darkness until they, too, were quieted by the night. Only the stars, and Kurt and I, were awake.

In the dark, he made his way to the edge of the woods where I lay. He put down his sleeping bag alongside mine on the tarp.

"I'm sorry," he murmured, kneeling to take off his shoes. I turned away from him, a million words crowding my throat. I said nothing. He handed me an apple and some cheese, and I began to cry.

"It's not going to rain," I blurted out.

"It probably won't," he admitted. "Want to zip our bags together?"

"No!" I would not let my anger be deflected by his sweetness. "I want to let you know how much I need to sleep on real earth with wind in my face, and to walk where concrete hasn't suffocated the ground - and how you've spoiled it all, and I'll never, never go to the woods with you again!"

He said nothing.

"And it's not the Hell going to rain!"

"There's a shooting star," he said.

"I don't care."

He laughed, then stifled it. "I'm sorry," he repeated. "But storms come up in the mountains unexpectedly, you know that."

"Maybe they do, and maybe we'll even get wet, but so what? That's the whole point of coming, to rough it a little. I don't want to have a picnic under a tree - I want to live in the woods!"

"I know that's what you want - I'm just not used to it."

"But neither am I!" I wailed. "It's just that you don't even want to try it out, and I've been wanting to do it for my whole life!"

"I don't mind being in the woods," he said quietly, "it's just sleeping in the woods that gives me the creeps..." His voice faded as if remembering other days. A child, fleeing from Nazis, hiding out in dense forests...

I reached for him, and pulled him down, burrowing into his shoulder. I felt him soften and we both cried a little.

"Let's put up the tent first thing in the morning," I

whispered after awhile. Fumbling in the dark, we zipped our sleeping bags together.

"O.K," he agreed, "and if it rains tonight, we'll cram the kids into the car and get wet. I bet we'll love it." I stifled my giggles in the mat of his beard.

At dawn I was wide awake, waiting for him to stir. But he slept through the flutterings of the morning birds and the brightening of the air. The sun rose, striking the granite and warming it to pink, and then gold. I began growing restless when the breeze riffled the pines, and I crept out of our shared bag and tip-toed over to check on the children.

Abram's eyes sprang right open, and he giggled. Soon all three were chattering like the birds, inching around the campsite still encased in sleeping bags. Like drunken inchworms they bumped into each other, their peals of laughter ringing through the canyon and bouncing off trees.

Kurt got up sleepily and started a fire in the firepit.

"Lookit me, Daddy!" they squealed, bunching and flinging themselves at each other. He smiled, continuing to nurse the fizzling fire until he got it started with pinecones. I changed diapers, laced up sneakers, combed mulch out of hair, snapped up overalls. Breakfast and erecting the tent took up the rest of the morning.

Breakfast was mostly cold, and the tent was a sagging, lopsided affair, but we had survived our first night in the woods. By the time we got everything out of the car, sorted out all our food, clothes and sleeping bags, the kids were clamoring to go swimming, Kurt and I were ready for a nap, and it was almost time for lunch.

The trail to the stream was a cushion of Irish-green moss, still dewy in the shade. Trees rose like cathedral columns towards the sun, which sent rays of muted light into the dense coolness of the forest floor.

I breathed in the rich, tangy perfume and did a quick, happy two-step on the trail.

"You really love this, don't you?" Kurt regarded me with his crinkly smile, planting a little kiss on my forehead. Abram squirmed in the kiddie-pack on his back, and the other two ran on ahead.

"I love it!" I exclaimed, calming Abram before he got his feet caught beneath him. Kurt shook his head in amazement, looking around him.

"But you really don't love it, do you?" I challenged, running a hand along the rough bark of a Jeffrey pine. He considered for awhile.

"I can't say I do," he admitted, "but then I can't say I don't, either."

We heard the bubbling of the stream long before it came into view. As we rounded the last bend of the trail, the soft roar of the water became a loud roar as the trees gave way to open sky and the sunny jumble of the bouldery bank. The children whooped and made for the rocks; Abram yelled to get down, scrambling after the others to the water's edge. At the edge of the stream we knelt, freezing our fingers in the snowmelt and christening each other with ice-cold droplets.

"Can we go swimming?" asked Saul, tugging off his sneakers. Eva's overalls were already bunched around her ankles, and she tripped into a sit on the gravelly bank. Abram fumbled ineffectually with shoelaces, and Saul, still talking, was inaudible behind the tee-shirt he wrestled over his head.

"Isn't it too cold?" I remarked. Kurt, as excited as the kids, was already rolling up his pant legs and pulling off Abram's shirt.

"Hey kids!" he shouted above the roar of the water, "is it too cold for you?" In chorus they answered, "NO!"

"Look Mommy, we're in the water," chattered Eva, goosebumps rising on her silky body.

"Too cold for me," I shivered, unpinning Abram's diaper and handing him over to Kurt. They all waded in, and three pairs of lips were instantly blue. But their dark eyes shone and they slapped at the flowing stream with delight.

"They're so beautiful," I commented to Kurt as our naked children played at the shallow edge of the stream, their bottoms rosy.

"I told you we were a good team," he joked. "Aren't you glad you married me?"

"I'm glad," I agreed, kissing the inside of his wrist. "Even if you're not so good at putting up tents."

Eva splashed out of the water, a smooth stone clutched in her fist. Her red-blonde hair dripped watery tendrils about her neck, and her tender flesh dimpled with every move.

"It's for you, Mommy," she said proudly, nuzzling me wetly before slogging back to the others.

"I'm not a complete dud in the woods, though," Kurt claimed with a grin. "You should see me skip rocks."

"You learned on the Hudson River pier," I teased.

"Yup. Practiced with flattened beer cans. Hey kids, lookit this!" Hunkering down to their level, Kurt tossed a small, flat stone over the surface of the stream. It bounced four times before it went under. Saul was mesmerized.

"Hold it sideways, like this," Kurt explained, wedging a stone between Saul's thumb and forefinger, and flinging another one out to demonstrate. Like a Florentine cherub, Saul hauled backwards, letting go of his stone. It skipped once.

"Good first try!"

Eva chose her stone carefully, got into position, wiggled her bottom and tossed wildly. The stone went right under.

"Good first try!"

Encouraged, they both searched the bank for flat rocks while Abram brought up a fistful of pebbles and broadcast them like seeds upon the water.

I ambled off sleepily to a nearby boulder and stretched full out in the sun. Eva's gift stone I tucked into my shirt pocket, against my heart. It pulsed gently up and down with my breaths. The stream tumbled hypnotically in the sunheat around riverrocks and swarms of gnats zigzagged just above its spray. A breeze blew, scudding clouds through the tops of pines and riffling needles. Kurt bent, tossed and straightened; Eva twisted and flopped; Abram threw pebbles; Saul jumped up and down.

Everything was in motion; nothing stayed still. Feeling dizzy, I shut my eyes and colors continued to flash back and forth. Beneath me, the very rocks seemed to be breathing. And the stream continued to flow, coursing over and over its inexorable way to the sea.

It was like being part of a huge dance, where everything in the world - rocks and trees and streams and people - were all doing their steps. The sun's dance was on the grand scale; the stone's dance, smaller. The water danced fast and the earth's dance was slow. And every part of me was in motion, dancing, from my molecules and cells pulsing to the begetting of the next generation. So what if I hadn't become a dancer; the dance was going on anyhow, following the pushes and pulls of the universe. I turned over, feeling hot rock against my skin.

Saul was catching on; his stone skipped two times, and he tried again for three. Eva tossed overhand, content with a single plunk and Abie continued to dredge the bottom for pebbles.

We all did what came naturally, following a path of least resistance, it seemed. The stream ran through its bed; the winds rose and sank with the sun's heat. Home was where you found it, whoever you were. For a tree, it was the soil; for a bird, it was a tree; for a mite, it was a bird; for all of us together, it was the whole, glorious world!

When we died, we crumbled back into the earth and atmosphere, making soil and potential substance for all the generations of everythings to come. Evolution was circular;

everything was gained and nothing ever lost. How reassuring.

I grasped Eva's stone, held it to my cheek and said a prayer of gratitude for my family - the big family - and fell asleep in the sun.

The weather continued fine and we never needed to sleep in the tent. Each morning we hiked to the stream, walked back to the campground for lunch and a nap, and went exploring in the afternoons. After dark, we huddled cozily around the campfire eating a supper of hotdogs and soot-flecked cocoa, and listened to Kurt's made-up stories about three tigers in the woods who were amazingly like Saul, Eva and Abram.

"...They ran and ran until they got to the river, but - it was flooding! But they jumped in anyway, and dragged the baby tiger across by his tail, and were almost all the way to the opposite bank, when..." Wide-eyed, the children huddled closer, breathless with suspense,"... when the middle tiger lost her hold on the little one's tail!"

"Then what happened?" Saul was the one who loved danger.

"Then a friendly otter came along, and rescued the baby, pulling him up onto the bank where the others found him all safe and dry." Kurt lowered his voice mysteriously. "They had never been on this side of the river before, so they went exploring through jungles and forests, holding onto each others' tails so they wouldn't get lost. And then, they came to a high cliff..."

"Oooo!" squealed Saul, "With a cave in it, right?"

"How did you know?" Kurt replied, astounded.

"What was there - a monster?"

"Not a monster, but a very strange light, which went on and off and came from the far other end..." Eva sucked in her breath and clutched at my thigh. "So they went in, step...by step...by step..."

"And the light went out!" shouted Saul.

"*Daddy* tell," said Abram, pulling his thumb out of his mouth to make his declaration.

The beam of a powerful searchlight interrupted the story at this point, followed by a burly Park Ranger.

"Sorry to disturb you folks," he apologized, squatting down alongside Saul. "But we've got a child lost in these woods, and we're rounding up all the able-bodied men in the canyon." Kurt rose in a single motion and brushed off the seat of his pants. We both glanced out at the inky darkness beyond the circle of our firelight. The moon was barely more than a football in the sky.

"Real sorry to break up your cozy campfire, kids. Sorry, maa'm. We'll supply the searchlights, sir." In only moments, he and Kurt were gone, the night and the forest closing in behind them. I dropped another log on the fire to keep us company. The kids and I snuggled closer and I tried to continue telling the story.

But my heart wasn't in it and the children quickly lost interest. Not only could I not dream up plots the way Kurt could, but my story was about a lost tiger, alone in the woods, tiny beneath huge, tall trees. She was cold and lost and couldn't find her Mommy. She had fallen down a ravine, and there were prickle bushes and it was night...

No, no. She kept walking, that was it - she kept walking, farther and farther away from where everybody was looking for her, but she was so small, and it was so dark that nobody could find her...

I was trembling, imagining myself the mother as well as the child. Right this minute she was picturing her baby broken and bleeding in the night; cold, hungry, afraid...

"Let's go find other people!" I decided, jumping up suddenly. Holding hands, with only a flashlight to light our way, we set out towards the bathrooms in the center of the campground.

People had begun to gather around points of light - campfires, Coleman lanterns, the public bathroom. We joined the first circle around a campfire and were taken in right away by the women and children there.

"The Rangers know what they're doing," said one woman, handing out cookies to all the kids. "I remember when there was a kid lost for two days..."

"Stay where we can see you!" another mother admonished all the children.

"How far do you think she could get in the dark...how old is she?"

"Did your husband go...?"

"Has anyone seen the mother...?"

"How old are your kids? Which ones are yours...?"

Bonded by our shared concern, we spoke to each other like old friends - or extended family. Our children seemed to belong to all of us collectively.

From the woods came the echo of mens' voices and we saw the crisscrossing of many searchlights. The voices grew fainter as the men fanned out.

"They've got the mother in the Rangers' Station..."

"This is the second time my husband's been in a search party..." This woman's arms were wrapped around a child who stood pressed against her legs.

"How do they manage not to get lost themselves?" I asked. Would a search party have to go out to find the searchers?

"They do it in lines," someone explained. "They go ten abreast, and then another ten. I don't think they've ever lost a man," she chuckled. We all glanced around to count children.

"Anyone want some cocoa - kids?" offered the lady of the campfire. They all nodded shyly. From far away came the gruff shouts of men signalling to one another.

"They'll find her," another woman said confidently. Somebody else offered coffee; another produced a bag of potato chips. I suggested we cook up a potluck stew for the men when they returned.

"Good idea. I've got canned hash to start it off.."
"I'll put in celery and a package of hot dogs.."
"I've got macaroni..."
"I've got a pot of beans on..."
"I'll watch the kids while you go get your stuff. Can someone help me build up the fire?"

An hour ago we had been strangers; now we were neighbors. The kids' job was to look for twigs and pinecones while their mothers cooked up a communal stew and their fathers searched for a lost child. Like a real community we shared our resources, bonded by our common need. We took the hands of any child who strayed and guided him back to the firelight.

In short order, a spicy stew bubbled on the firepit. The children learned each others' names and the women got to know about each others' lives. I was chatting with a woman whose son had taken a liking to Saul, when the cry that the child had been found echoed through the woods. With tears of relief, we threw our arms around each other and hugged every child in sight. The children, catching the joy, were ecstatic.

Jugs of coffee appeared, and paper plates and mugs. When the men, dirt-streaked and grinning, appeared, we greeted them as returning heroes. Everyone was an automatic friend and it was everyone's reunion, not only the lost child's with her family. With pride, we introduced our husbands to each other, and dished out the stew. The kids whooped around the campfire as the men ate and we listened to their accounts of the search. Each one told his version; each one described the darkness of the backcountry; each one expressed admiration for the little girl; each one praised the efforts of the Rangers. We replenished the fire with logs, dished out more stew and repeated the story again as new people joined our group. It was the best party I had ever been to in my life.

Kurt lifted a tired Abram onto his shoulders as we said our goodnights. The children were drooping, but I could have stayed there all night. Finally, we hugged, exchanged telephone numbers in the city and went back to our separate campsites to put the children to sleep.

Snuggled in our sleeping bag later, Kurt told me his story again.

"The woods had the same kind of darkness I remember from that time in Czechoslovakia," he confessed. "I freaked at first. But then all I could think about was that kid. It could have been ours."

"Thank God they found her," I murmured, cuddling against him and breathing in his smell of resin and woodsmoke. "How did it feel when you knew she was safe?"

"The relief was incredible, and then all I wanted was to get back to you and the kids." We held each other tightly beneath a sky mobbed with stars and as I sank into sleep, I couldn't remember what it ever felt like to be lonely.

Simone phoned from New York as soon as we returned home.

"You'd better get here quick," she said. "Dad's not going to last the week."

My father, just two weeks short of his fiftieth birthday was in the hospital with another coronary. "They're letting him come home today, but I think he's a goner," she informed us.

It was one week before Saul was to start kindergarten, but we parcelled the children out with neighbors, packed a suitcase and took the night flight to New York. My father himself greeted us at the door, his face ashen and swollen with drugs, his eyes scared.

"People are dying who have never died before," he quipped, leaning against the doorpost in a contrived gesture of ease. I took his hand as he gave way to a fit of coughing, and he let me take most of his weight. Kurt steadied us both and maneuvered us inside where, my father's grip still in mine, I lowered him onto the sofa. I banished a flicker of resentment that the hand I held was his, and not Saul's on his first day of school.

"That's the way he's been talking," my mother complained, giving Kurt and me a kiss. She stood by anxiously as he labored for breath on the sofa.

"The doctor told him to take it easy, but he's been pacing back and forth like a caged animal!" Simone was right - he had very little left.

"He's trying to die, that's why," whispered Simone after my mother left the room. Her arms were crossed over her chest and her eyes were hard with horror.

"Where's Nate?" My brother had not put in an appearance yet.

"He stays away most of the time," Simone replied, "or sits in the garage and plays his guitar until it drives everyone nuts. Even me!" Kurt, with a glance towards me, went out to find Nate.

"He's really trying to kill himself!" Simone told me. "That's why I called you to come. Wait till you see him run up and down the stairs trying to have a heart attack!"

"I don't want to see it."

"You probably won't have much choice," she fumed. "And the two of them together just break my heart. This morning Mother said to him, 'Die already, if that's what you want!'"

"And what did he say?" My heart had already gone into hiding deep in my belly.

"He mumbled something about when he was good and ready."

During the next two days my father's pallor grew waxen and his breathing deteriorated to labored wheezing. Each morning, he dressed in full suit and tie and then paced up and down the stairs, muttering to himself and smoking cigarette after cigarette. My mother followed him up and down the stairs, begging him to stop. Daily, we called the doctor who daily told us not to worry.

"For pity's sake," Kurt told him, "don't tell me not to

worry. You can speak candidly to me about his condition - I'm his son-in-law."

"I don't care who you are," replied the doctor coldly, "my patient has instructed me not to give out any information about his condition to either family or business associates."

"I've never heard of anything like this!" I cried on the other phone. "I'm his daughter..." But the New York City heart specialist had hung up.

On our third day home, in the thick air of the house, my father choked on a breath, arched his back and grabbed at his chest. My mother screamed for Kurt, who dialed for an ambulance and then went to my father, feeling for a pulse. It was weak, but there. Simone stood in the doorway, transfixed, and I stayed by my mother. In the garage, my brother kept playing the same chords over and over.

The ambulance sped out of our neighborhood, sirens blaring and red lights flashing. Everyone stood on their porches, hands over their mouths. Kurt rode in the ambulance with my mother, and Simone, Nate and I took the family car. All the way to the hospital we told each other corny jokes, actually enjoying being together again, just the three of us, after so many years.

By evening, my father was dead.

"But the doctor said not to worry..." whispered my mother, not believing the news. "I knew he was sick, but I never expected it was this bad..." We sat for two hours, stunned. My brother was in shock; my sister exasperated with their denial; and my mother kept saying the same thing over and over again.

"He was too young...People don't die of heart attacks at fifty... The doctor kept telling me not to worry..."

When we drove home very late at night, all the papers had been signed and Kurt had begun arrangements for the funeral. In the cafeteria, we ate potato chips and drank black coffee, numb.

Except for Kurt, none of us knew how to behave in the face of death. We were waiting, I suppose, for permission to see the body, but it never came. At last, we gave up and went home. I, for one, was relieved. In the car going home Kurt drove, and the only words spoken were one knock-knock joke told by Nate, at which nobody but my sister laughed.

    We were ushered into the funeral parlor by an undertaker in black, his face powdered the color of death. The door slid open on oiled hinges and we were shown into a dimly lit room with deep, sound-muffling carpets and discreetly placed armchairs and sofas. When the family was inside, he cleared his throat and bowed his way out, shutting the door noiselessly behind him.

    Kurt walked my mother to a wing-backed chair and sat her down slowly. Simone and Nate stood frozen by the door, unwilling to come all the way in. I also stopped, my neck taut and every muscle in my back hard as wood. I sensed a ghost.

    "Where is he?" cried my mother hoarsely, rising from her chair to locate the casket. It lay in a half-hidden alcove at the far end of the room, and letting go of the chair arm she tilted unsteadily towards it.

    Beneath the satin lining of the open cover, my father's profile was just visible from across the room. She gazed down at him like a mother watching over her sleeping babe.

    Kurt slowly joined her, then Nate, then me. Simone held back, turning away from the coffin and stalking over to the brocade drapery on the other side of the room. Her hands clenched, she stared at the wall. I had to will my feet to move forward, to keep my eyes open, to breathe. At the edge of the casket, I had to force myself to look down.

    He lay there as if asleep, in a blue-serge suit and a white silk tie. His face had been rouged and his lips forcibly puckered into an expression that had not been his in life. He looked oddly unfamiliar, as if his particular features had been given to somebody else. This stranger, who looked something like my father, was a man of no pathos, no bravado, no history. I hardly recognized him.

Smoothed out by the embalmer he appeared not peaceful but trivialized. Scented by their perfumes he belonged to them, not me. Even in death I couldn't claim a father.

The door opened to admit Lucky and his wife Lily. Teddicoo followed behind them, then Sollie and his wife. I hadn't seen any of them in years, and I ran to Lucky and burrowed gladly in his arms. And Teddiecoo! And Sollie! They all rumpled my hair as if I were still a kid, muttering gruff, uneasy condolences and avoiding looking in the direction of the coffin.

"How *are* you?" I kept asking, hugging them with delight and wanting to know all their latest news. By the time I started reminiscing with Teddiecoo, ("Hey! I'm Ted now!"), sorrow was simply not on my mind.

The stream of mourners soon appeared at the door, their expressions hovering between grief and fear as they came in to present themselves to the family - and the corpse. Here were people I hadn't seen since I left Brooklyn: neighbors, business associates, distant family. They offered their condolences with faces pinched, eyes downcast. My father was so young, so young. Next time, it could be them...

"It's so hard to lose a father, darling," said our old dentist. He never called me darling before. I nodded and grabbed his arm, recalling long-ago cavities and asking about his kids.

The Antonellis - the undertaker and the prostitute - looked properly bereaved, but I noticed him taking in the ambience of the room, comparing it with his own.

"It's <u>great</u> to see you!" I gushed, hugging each of them in turn. "You may not believe it, but I think of you often!"

"Such a young man..." he murmured, but she gave me a wink.

"You've slimmed down, you look gorgeous," she

whispered throatily in my ear.

I was having a wonderful time! Here was my past parading before me, my father's last gift to me.

"Hi!" I greeted an old neighbor. "How is Harriet? She must be in college by now..." Flushed with feeling, I wanted to know everything about everybody. "Did Bobby become a fireman like he wanted to? He's studying Physics - no!"

"Thanks God he got to know his grandchildren. How are the children, Marta?" They tried to look mournful.

"I've got pictures!" I exclaimed, running over to Kurt and excitedly grabbing the wallet out of his pocket. "This is Saul - yes, named after my uncle; and this is Eva, and that's the baby, Abram."

"Oh, they're beautiful..." they all admired, telling me with pride about the diplomas, grandchildren, good jobs in their families. I hugged everyone, no matter who, loving their make-up, their beehive hair-dos, their pencil moustaches for the first time in my life. Lily sidled up to me, smiling, and followed close behind as I flitted from one person to another. Having fun, I gave her a hug too, giggling.

"Remember when Ruthie taught me to shave my legs?" I recalled, all but squealing with nostalgia when I saw Ruthie's mother in the crowd, "and you, I remember, once brought chocolate bunnies!" I exclaimed, throwing my arms around the neck of the accountant.

Lily just shadowed me, with Lucky close behind, and when I declared,

"Oh Delores, what a beautiful young woman you've grown into!" and finally burst into tears, my throat erupting like an abscess, they caught me in their arms and lowered me onto a couch while I wept. I sobbed into Lily's neck, then crumpled onto Lucky's lap. He handed me a clean handkerchief, still warm from his pocket and I soaked it through in minutes. For a whole childhood of not crying, I now cried. Sobbed. I didn't even try to stop.

Lucky and Kurt traded places, and it was Kurt's familiar

arms that held me. I could weep to my heart's content, with Lily gently patting my hair.

"It's hard, it's hard," she kept murmuring. "Cry it out, go ahead."

But as I wept, I knew that I wasn't crying only for my father, I was crying for all of us - for everyone whose life was left unlived. It was for my crippled grandmother and my frightened mother; for my abused sister and my repressed brother. It was for every moment that could have been used, but had not been because of fear.

I blew my nose and laughed out loud at the noise. Then I wept again. I mourned the loss of all the goodness and intelligence we didn't share with each other, all the laughter we could have had. Crying, I understood that every one of us was trying to work up the courage to love, and that very struggle bonded us together, whether we wore our hair in lacquered beehives or had it plaited down our backs in a long braid.

I came up for air, blurry and swollen. A sound somewhere between a burble and a giggle escaped my throat.

"That's better," said Lily, smoothing my hair. The side of her dress was wet with my tears. Kurt took my hand and laced my fingers through his.

"Where's Aunt Sadie?" I asked, wiping my eyes with the back of my fist to see more clearly. She didn't seem to be in the room. Lily looked around.

"The Antonellis were supposed to bring her," she said. "But they're here..."

On a neighboring divan, my mother leaned towards the Rabbi.

"Death is part of life," I heard him intone. "The Lord giveth and the Lord taketh away." He looked as frightened as anyone in the room. I sighed and clutched Kurt's hand tightly.

A wailing cry, rising into a shriek came through the walls from the next room. I would know that voice anywhere.

"It's Aunt Sadie," I said urgently. Kurt, Lily and I all jumped off the couch at once and made for the door. Lucky and Sollie followed close on our heels.

"Get your dirty hands off me!" she screamed out in the hallway, fighting off the undertaker who tried to remove her from the next room. She pushed her way back into the room and all five of us barged in after her. "Leave me be!" A crowd of white-faced mourners stood by in shock, as she tore out of the man's grip and tottered back towards that family's dear departed.

"Help us," we grimly beseeched the horrified crowd. Sollie stalked from one direction, Lucky from another. Kurt's position was in the middle and Lily and I tried to get her attention.

"It's Marta, Aunt Sadie," I cajoled, creeping up behind her. "It's me and Lily."

"Mom, it's Lily. You're in the wrong room, Mom," she said softly. "We're disturbing these people - we're over in the next room, Mom." Aunt Sadie wheeled around, her pocketbook flinging like a weapon.

"C'mon to the next room with us," I coaxed, creeping closer.

"*Oy*, Marta!" she screeched, clutching me like a drowning woman. With one hand she tore at her hair, with the other pressed me to her bosom, screaming in my ear. The men gathered round us and nudged us, like a single bundle, towards the door. "Where is he? He's not dead!"

"In here," we grunted as we propelled her in the right direction. Lucky opened the door and we shouldered her in. Much as she must have done the first time, she threw up her arms at the sight of the coffin, opened her mouth and let out an ear-splitting shriek.

Everybody in the room froze in place. Family members bowed their heads, neighbors felt sorry for us and business associates openly gawked. A flush of shame crept up my mother's neck. The Rabbi looked poised for escape.

Lurching forward stiffly, Aunt Sadie made her way like a sleepwalker towards my father. Lucky and Sollie rushed behind her, ready to intervene, but she outran them and flung herself, pocketbook and all, into the open casket. Even her sons stopped in mid-stride.

"Come back!" she screeched, lifting my father into a sitting position. His head lolled coyly on her shoulder. "You can't die!" she cried in a falsetto that sent shivers down every spine, rocking him in her arms until his carefully puckered lips parted slightly. "C'mon back so you can drive me home!"

"I can't stand this!" my mother cried out. "Get her out of here!"

Suddenly everyone leapt into action: Lucky and Sollie grabbed her from behind; Teddiecoo prepared a cage with chairs in the corner; Kurt took over my mother, and Nate and Simone huddled together in a corner of the room, fish-belly white. The Rabbi sprinted for the door and escaped neatly; I considered following him.

As most of the others did. Taking their opportunity, they left.

I couldn't blame them, but whether I liked it or not, this was my family. Furious with Aunt Sadie, who yet again and in weird cahoots with my father, spoiled yet another important event in my life, I walked deliberately across the uncrowded room to the casket where my father lay dead. Standing by myself at his side, I looked down.

He lay there in his fancy clothes, a strange guest at his own party. It wasn't like him to stay in a corner by himself, not breathing. Normally he would be embarrassing me roundly by this time with his bad jokes and pontifications, but all he was doing now was lying still. I stared at him as if to will him back to life.

"You can get up now," I told him in my mind. "The joke's over. You can stop holding your breath - I've learned the lesson." He didn't move a muscle.

"Really," I persisted. "Things can be different now. If you come back, we'll try life the *real* way, not that crippled version where fear shaped us into craziness. This time we'll take our meaning from real things. This time we'll taste the air for truth!"

Not a blink. Maybe I was being too poetic.

"Look," I tried again. "Love is so obvious - how could we have missed it?" He was playing hard to get.

"For God's sake, you're hardly fifty! You've got a whole life ahead of you!" He wasn't convinced. I had to try another tack.

"Listen, if I die at fifty, then I've only got twenty-three years left. That's not fair. Give me a better chance than that!" I waited. Nothing.

"O.K. Father, if that's your attitude, then I can't change your mind. But let me tell you one thing: I want to dance. I've always wanted to dance. Did you know that? Well, if I've only got twenty-three years left, then I want to spend them dancing. How do you like them apples?"

Did I apprehend a wink? I scrutinized his face for something more.

"Father, I'd like to know that I have your blessing." Was that the smallest nod of the head? Did I see a slight lifting of a finger?

"You mean you will give me your blessing? You won't consider me ridiculous?" He didn't answer, but I thought I felt a 'Yes'.

Something also felt off; smelled off. The air purifier in the bottom of the coffin had run out. It was time to go home.

I gazed down at him, wanting a sign. Something real. I had to know he wouldn't think I was a fool. My whole body was tense, my legs stiff. I shrugged my shoulders to relieve the strain and bent my knees slightly. A rhythm, like a slow dirge, began in my head.

Dum dum dadum Dum dum dadum Dum dum dadum

My right foot rotated outwards, and my right shoulder followed.

Dum dum dadum   Dum dum dadum   Dum dum dadum

 Left heel, swivel, right wrist, bend. Tilt of the head, slight twist of the torso, dadum.
 Weight on one knee, turn the hips, dadum. Too subtly to be seen, dadum.
 To anyone watching, I'm just walking slowly.
 Dum dum dadum.
 But my knees bend, my feet turn, dadum.
 Away from the coffin, dadum.
 Back to Kurt, yes, dadum.
 Step, step, dadum. Heel-toe knee, dadum.

I am dancing for my father.

Yes, pause and step
Yes, pause and step
Yes, pause and step.

5

GOSPEL SONG

Throat Chakra - Thyroid Gland

*The communicating voice;
expression in language, song and art;
the urge to connect and be heard.*

My voice rang strained and hollow in my ears; I was much too nervous. Putting down my notes so that the shaking of my hands was less apparent, I began speaking extemporaneously to the psychiatric staff of the hospital. Not one doctor would look at me directly.

The psychiatrists sat scattered around the conference room, their faces professionally non-committal behind the swirl of their cigarette smoke. Only Sonya, the head nurse of the Psychiatric Unit and my one real ally on the staff, seemed to be listening. I cleared my throat and addressed them more forcefully.

"Many patients," I declared, "have gotten so wound up in their heads that they've lost all contact with their bodies. The work I am doing with them is an attempt to bring mind and body back together again."

They shifted in their seats; some examined their fingernails.

"If you consider that psychological health involves a reasonable balance of all the aspects of a person, then it stands to reason that the body should be specifically addressed at some phase of the therapeutic process." A few doctors raised their eyes at that, but most stared into their styrofoam coffee cups.

It was Sonya's suggestion that I present the ideas behind my work at the weekly meeting of the psychiatric staff. Although I had been in the Psychiatric Unit for the past six months, most of the doctors had no idea what I was doing there. To those who noticed at all, I was an exercise teacher, the bumps-and-grinds lady. The others, for all I knew, may have thought I was some other doctor's patient.

But although I had been hired to do exercises with the

patients, in fact my work was considerably more than that. And now that I was getting remarkable results with several patients, I felt a need to consult with the doctors and request their help. Paul Baker warned me that they might not be overly receptive to that.

"My work," I continued, "is based on the premise that the emotional and psychological traumas of a person's life tend to imprint in the body as tight muscles, shortened tendons, elevated blood pressure - and so on." I noted a glint of attention from some of the younger residents and Dr. Elmer, not one of my favorites, observed me closely out of smoke-slitted eyes. I detected some amusement.

"So I use very gentle movements to help release those held muscles - like this." I swung my arm softly back and forth. "Invariably what happens is that as the muscles start to release, the unconscious material that had gotten locked in them begins to come up into consciousness."

A few more faces perked into attention.

"Then I encourage the patient to let it out."

"How?" barked a senior resident from the back of the room, eyeing me skeptically.

"Various ways. Often, it starts as crying, so I do the obvious; I pull out a hanky, put my arms around them, let them cry or talk. It depends on the patient."

"What do you do when it starts as anger?" someone asked. They now all eyed me closely, wondering, I suppose, how I had managed to not get myself killed by this time.

"I try to get the anger discharged safely, like jumping up and down, or yelling, or punching pillows - or even just stamping hard." I began to demonstrate, but then thought better of it.

"How long do you spend with a patient?" one doctor asked.

"As long as I have to. Some can only concentrate for a few minutes, others will take as much time as you can give them. With some, I can work in groups; others need to work alone - I play it by ear." I smiled, encouraged as they began to sit up and take interest.

They would have been embarrassed to realize how much like the patients they were in receiving what I had to offer. Wary at first, even rude, but then gradually giving way to curiosity and finally, trust. I hoped, with the doctors, trust.

Feeling more confident, my voice became clearer. I could speak more quietly now; I had their attention.

"Many of the patients are afraid to move at all, as you know. With them I start very small - it may be nothing but a slow walk around the room." I took a few deliberate steps back and forth. "Or maybe just making a fist and opening it up. Then once they've made some kind of movement, even if it's this minimal, I remind them to breathe."

Everyone in the room took in a breath, looked around sheepishly, and tittered.

"Most of us hold our breath most of the time," I observed, taking a deep breath. There was a rustle as they did too, readjusting their chairs and crossing and uncrossing their legs.

"Once the movement is started," I went on, "then I simply encourage it to continue. For example, say they've begun with a hand..." I demonstrated, clenching a fist, rotating my wrist and arm and then shoulder, finally shaking everything out gently. "Try it," I suggested, "and don't forget to breathe."

Again there was a collective breath, and laughter. Stiffly at first, they shook out their hands and arms and then more vigorously.

"Breathe," I called out. Dr. Elmer swung both arms over his head in a grand gesture, looking at me for approval. I ignored him. As a group, these doctors were as tight and self-conscious as any patients I had encountered on the ward. Sonya, rolling her shoulders forward and back, caught my eye and winked.

"The goal of all of this, of course, is to eventually lead the patient into some form of self-expression. Although it rarely gets into actual dancing with most of them, that's what I'm trying to get at."

Eyes began again to grow guarded. I hurried to explain. "The point is to make it safe for them to express what they're feeling, however I can get them to do it."

"So how is that so different from what we're all trying to do?" one doctor asked.

"The fact is that many people simply can't," I replied. "Their heads are too scrambled, they are so blocked they don't even know how they feel. Getting the body into movement is like a lubricant for the mind." He looked wary. "It has the effect of venting energy that's stuck, clearing away cobwebs, waking up stuff that's gone dead or is hurting so bad they can't see past it..." He pursed his lips, skeptical.

"Once the body starts to loosen," I declared, "I've found that the feelings and the psyche also start to loosen. Then," I charged on, taking my chances," once a person starts to loosen up, they can be shown how to transform their pain into something beautiful - they can make art out of it!"

A few eyebrows lifted; other faces went smooth and blank. I was losing some; had I gained others? I decided to go for broke.

"I think people get sick when they feel unloved and unlovable - when they feel worthless." I tried to tone down the passion in my voice, but couldn't. "If they can experience themselves as beautiful, and therefore worthy of being loved, then I think they can get better!"

One doctor got up and slipped out of the room; others glanced down at their wristwatches. Sonya loyally sat still, her full attention on what I was saying.

"Nobody's ever *really* listened to them," I tossed out

rakishly, as long as they were half out the door anyway. "What I am doing is encouraging them to express the best of themselves, and then listening to them with everything I've got."

"What about Joanie Maynard - have you worked with her?" Dr. Elmer challenged. Joanie was his patient and had been hospitalized for almost a year. She'd not spoken a word since a week after she arrived.

"Yes," I replied quietly.

"Did you get anywhere with her?" He cupped his chin in one hand provocatively.

"Yes."

The room suddenly was silent and no one else got up to leave. Nobody on the staff could get anywhere with Joanie, even though she was having shock treatments two times a week.

Sonya's eyes cheered me on. It was, in fact, because of the headway I'd made with Joanie that Sonya urged me to present the work I was doing at the weekly staff conference. "Tell them," she urged.

"Well," I began, nervous again, "she's been crying for about three weeks now, and I've gotten her to dance a few times..."

"Is she talking?" barked the senior resident.

"Not talking, but if you've noticed, she has begun drawing. She makes sketches of the other patients that are remarkable..." The doctors glanced guiltily at each other, observing that the others hadn't noticed Joanie sketching either.

"...when she thinks nobody's watching," I added, softening the blow.

"Well, why didn't you tell someone?" Dr. Elmer. Too sharply, I shot back,

"That's what I'm doing now!"

He did not respond.

"With Joanie, as you know, it's a matter of convincing her every day that she deserves to breathe the air or eat breakfast." There were a few begrudging nods.

"How were you planning to continue with her?" a doctor asked. I glanced quickly at Sonya.

"Actually, I was hoping to ask you the same question," I smiled. "The truth is that I'm getting in over my head - not only with Joanie, but with other patients as well. I need to do this work in conjunction with you, not separate from you."

I felt their withdrawal slide through the room like the passage of an eel. I had no choice but to ignore it.

"I frankly need your help. As I encourage Joanie to draw as well as dance, I will need to check in with you to make sure I'm not going too fast with her, or doing something counter-productive to her treatment."

Most of the doctors and nurses and social workers studied the floor or their wristwatches. One shrugged apologetically and extricated himself from the conference chair; others followed his lead, draining the last dregs of their coffee and leaning over for their briefcases. Already, they were in transition for their next appointments. A few smiled at me, nodded before they left or wished me luck. Others didn't bother.

Dismissed, as it were, I sat down and gathered up my notes, dismayed by their rudeness. Sonya came over and put a reassuring hand on my arm.

"Nice job," she said. "I think it went over well. Gotta run. I'll see you later on the ward."

"Very interesting." called out a young intern as he left. "Good luck with it."

"Thanks," I called to his retreating back, wondering if he was one I could call on for help. Even those who smiled as they left did not offer to work with me; only Dr. Elmer stayed around to talk.

"Let's have coffee," he offered.

"Sure," I replied hesitantly. "I can't right now, though." Of all the doctors in the Unit, he was the one I would have chosen last.

"Tomorrow at ten?" He pulled out his appointment book and wrote it down before I had agreed to the time.

This man was used to calling the shots.

"I know what you mean about dancing," he remarked, revealing small teeth and a wide expanse of gums as he smiled. His dark, wavy hair came to a point at the nape of his neck and his eyes were a bright, startling green. "I'd like to hear what you have to say about Joanie." He gave a conspiratorial grin. "Tomorrow at ten, then, in the cafeteria?"

With a debonair wave of the hand, he swung out the doorway without waiting for a response.

After lunch, the Common Room of the Psychiatric Unit was nearly deserted. A lone figure, Tyrone, lay slumped on the couch in the corner fast asleep. A frenetic fly buzzed angles above him, landing fitfully upon his dangling hand. He twitched it away.

Joanie huddled in a wing-backed armchair, her knees hugging her chest and her pale blue eyes staring vacantly ahead. Her fine-boned features were pinched, as if she would erase them from her face altogether if she could, and her listless yellow hair hung slackly to her shoulders.

The air hung heavy, dust motes visible as smoke. The walls seemed to exude the sour stench of generations of lost souls who had sat thus in this room, tainting the air with their fear. It was a wonder anybody ever recovered in this place. I sauntered across the room and sat on a chair near Joanie's. She didn't turn her head.

The ward, closed off from the rest of the hospital by locked doors and sealed windows, was more a carpeted cage than the livingroom it was designed to resemble. A wall of thick, institutional glass enclosed the nurses' station from the rest of the ward, and on the bare walls only fingerprint smudges, hand high, offered adornment.

A forlorn sweater hung from the arm of a chair and one well-thumbed magazine sat upon a scarred table. Otherwise, the Common Room was empty, the other patients either being up at

Occupational Therapy or asleep in their beds.

Tyrone snuffled and shifted his position. The fly went frantic. A nurse glanced up from her charts, then bent back to her work. Tyrone's mouth gaped open in sleep, spittle dribbling from his lower lip. Joanie remained remote; when a fly landed on her forehead she blinked, but did not brush it away.

My first days of work on the psychiatric ward had been something of a shock. I had applied for the job of Recreational Specialist and had been hired as an Exercise Therapist. What either of those titles meant, I had no idea, but I had intended to experiment with my own fledgling technique of dance improvisation as healing and to work it into the program in my own way. What I had not counted on was the extent to which the patients had been drugged.

The ward was a scary place. People were medicated into a dullness that unfocussed their eyes and made their minds fuzzy. They paced like frantic beasts; they twitched and babbled, their bodies bursting with excess energy for which they had no outlet. Others, overwhelmed by events too confusing to fathom, sat stoned like lumps of comatose flesh. In whimpers or roars, they each seemed to be crying, "What's going on here?"

Into this scene of fear and confusion the doctors made darting forays, like minnows in a tidepool. They would rush in, make contact, check a chart and prescribe a drug, and rush out again as fast as they could. They seemed to be as frenetic as the patients. Unlike the patients, however, they did not acknowledge that anything was wrong with them.

During my first weeks in the Unit, I wasn't sure on which side of the glass enclosure I belonged. On the patient side was honest desperation and some very courageous personal battles; on the medical side, mostly the unacknowledged variety. It was after a small initiation administered to me by a patient - which I unqualifiedly flunked - that I opted for the inmate side of the glass.

"Hey you!" a young woman accosted me as I arrived in

the morning. She was disheveled, her skin gray and her speech slurred. "Don't I look like Death warmed over?"

"Not at all!" I lied brightly, placing an encouraging hand on her shoulder. She brushed me away contemptuously, her lips curling with disdain. Then turning to her fellow patients, she said,

"See? I told you she was just like the others."

For the rest of the day, I ached with the rebuke and vowed never to make the same mistake again. In fact, I soon came to appreciate leaving the *sane* world outside for the stark honesty of the *insane* world of the Unit. The inmate community was like an oasis of truth-telling in a desert of denial. The outside world dissembled in a thousand ways; the inside world, on the inmate side of the glass, tended not to.

So after a few weeks, I threw in my lot with the patients and walked boldly into their midst. The staff found it worrisome, but I didn't care. From that time on, my work with them flourished; from that day, my love for them grew.

Joanie sat curled up in a corner of the armchair like a wounded bird. Cupped in the palm of her hand was a scrap of paper on which she sketched the sleeping Tyrone. With a few swift strokes she caught the angle of his body, the lay of his arm, the slackness of his expression.

She looked like a hurt creature hiding in dry grasses, camouflaged by the pallid surroundings of the Common Room. Her fragile face, brittle and pinched, held a pair of eyes with little light. Except when she glanced up at Tyrone. She sat hunched over her drawing but when she noticed me, she crumpled up the picture and jammed it into her pocket. I got up and left the room.

Poor baby. And only nineteen years old. One year ago, after a panicky abortion resulting from her first sexual encounter, she had tried hard to die. Having been raised in a strict Catholic family, she'd been too afraid to tell her parents, but did confess the deed to a parish priest somewhere in the city. He had, apparently, confirmed that she was evil and she, in her innocence, had believed him. Her mortified response had been to swallow a full can of latex paint. Fortunately, she was found in time to pump her stomach free of the poison, and from the Emergency Room she had been sent upstairs to Psychiatry.

At first, she had been willing to talk about her experience, but after a single visit from her outraged family she went silent and refused to speak another word. That had been a year ago.

With me she had at first been characteristically unresponsive, but after a few weeks she let me massage her tight shoulders, and would clench and unclench her fists at my request. Rubbing her hands gently, I would chat casually with her about things I'd seen: a flock of birds over the bay, a funny incident at the supermarket. Sometimes a bit of color came into her cheeks; once she even smiled. Then one day she began, tentatively, to move.

Within a week she was spreading her arms, rotating her head and taking a few hesitant steps. It was after she had done her first small dance that she broke down and cried in my arms.

And her sketches got bolder. She was able, with a few deft strokes, to conjure up the essence of the other inmates by reproducing the angry curve of a shoulder or the longing held in an arm. Through her drawings she seemed to have found a way to express comfort to her fellow sufferers - not by approaching them directly, but by feeling with them their own agonies.

But once she had completed a picture, she would savagely crumple it up and stuff it into the bathroom trash can. Later, I would slip into the bathroom to retrieve the wadded-up bits of paper and painstakingly smooth them out to add to the growing stack I kept at home. If she knew I was doing this, she never let on. But, in fact, it was after I rescued her first picture from the trash that she let me coax her into her first, timid dance.

Tyrone awoke with a start as the other patients trooped in

noisily from Occupational Therapy. Dazed, he glanced around frowning and then fell back again onto the cushions. Joanie hastily crammed her drawing into a pocket and squeezed both hands between her thighs.

"Let's go, everybody," encouraged the orderly, herding the patients into the ward and locking the double doors behind them. They shuffled, stomped, tiptoed and dragged in, some morose, some timid, some laughing. They were dressed in everything from torn jeans to chiffon dresses and business suits; they were housewives and hippies, Asians, Caucasians, and Blacks, long-haired and short-haired, messy and neat. They were a cross-section of everyone in the city, bonded now by their illness. Their voices created a sudden babble in the quiet ward; in a surge, they gravitated towards the public telephone in the corridor.

The telephone provided a lifeline to the outside world. Here it was that the patients kept contact with family and friends, receiving encouragement as they could - or renewing the frustrations that had put them here in the first place. They crowded around the phone, gradually settling upon an arbitrary line-up and chatting with each other while waiting their turns.

For some reason, these outgoing calls mesmerized Joanie. She, of course, never used the phone herself, but each day she crept up close and crouched against the wall to listen to the others talk. Tilting her head with concentration, as if to remember how it was done, she would pay close attention to everyone's whisperings and mumblings and then creep away to settle unblinkingly in an armchair. The others never chased her away.

A new patient joined the line - an older woman, corseted and well dressed, who fidgeted with her pearls while the others used the phone. Nervously, she picked imaginary lint off the sleeve of her dress and patted her white curls. The first few days were always the hardest; I took a place behind her on the line.

"Hullo," I said. She had no way of knowing I was not a fellow patient. "Have you just come?"

She nodded furtively, glancing about to avoid meeting my eyes. She pursed her rouged lips in and out, clasping her hands tightly together.

"That's a pretty pin," I commented, pointing to her cameo brooch. She drew back. I smiled reassuringly.

"I'm leaving this place tonight," she declared in a vehement whisper. "They've made a mistake - put me on the wrong floor! Did you ever hear of anything so ridiculous?"

"Really?"

"I'm calling my lawyer right now!" she exclaimed indignantly. "I'll sue!" Her voice rose alarmingly and her chin began to tremble. I considered leading her off to the bathroom and letting her stamp and kick against the noisy tiles to blow off some of her rage. "I'll sue! *I'll sue!*" I nodded a signal to the orderly who stood by, watchful.

"Of course," I murmured as the orderly sauntered over to join us. She calmed down in his steadying presence and regained her dignity with difficulty, resuming in a more normal voice,

"As soon as I can get to my lawyer, he'll take care of this stupid business! What's taking them so long...?"

The peace was shattered only moments later, anyhow. Sounds of a melee on the other side of the double doors were followed by indignant yells as the doors crashed open to admit a voluminous Black woman draped in a long, flowered dress and bright tasselled shawls. Emerging onto the ward she stopped short, quivered with fury, and surveyed the scene like a great African Queen.

"No!" she roared. Spinning on her heel, she shouldered her way back through the double doors. The orderlies charged after her, scuffling with her and muscling her back onto the ward. This time they locked the double doors behind them.

"These *niggers*..." sniffed the lady by my side; but she was trembling. The others on the telephone line pressed against the wall, alert, some pale, others primed for excitement. I went deliberately calm and kept an eye on the frightened ones. Joanie crouched beneath the phone, her arms clasped around her knees and her eyes glazed.

"No!" the newcomer spit out again, tossing the two men away from her like matchsticks. "No! No!"

Sunlight glinted off the dark halo of her hair and she lifted her face and arms upward, as if supplicating the heavens. She held us all spellbound by her monumental presence.

"NO!" The sound rumbled up from her belly and burst into the room in a single syllable of despair. The whole ward seemed to vibrate. From the nurses' station an emergency call went out to the other units of the hospital, and two nurses, hypodermics at the ready, inched their way towards the woman. The orderlies closed in, tense and alert.

"NOOOO-O!" She shook her head violently back and forth, her brow beaded with sweat. A golden shawl fell to the ground unheeded.

"NOOOOOO-O!" she bellowed again. Help poured in from all over the hospital and in moments the furious woman was surrounded. White-coated people stalked her in a wide circle, intent. Her eyes widened as she saw herself trapped and her roar of rage started up from her innards, gathered steam in her chest and emerged from her mouth as her feet stomped out a dance on the floor:

"NNNOOOOOOOOOO!"

Her predators spiralled in closer, their circle growing tighter and more lethal as, with needles filled with Thorazine, they drew in on their target. Wild-eyed, she made one last attempt at escape, flinging herself at the double doors and swiping the syringe out of a nurse's upheld hand.

"I SAID NOO!" she hollered. Her pinky, in transit, caught

on the nurse's hooped earring, and pulling violently to release her finger, she ripped the earring clear through the woman's earlobe.

Screaming, the nurse grabbed onto her head and ran while the others, en masse, made a lunge for the crazed woman. Holding her down on the floor, they injected her with a double dose of Thorazine and restrained her with one of her own shawls.

Still, she struggled amazingly to her feet and spun around, facing down the person who had plunged the needle into her arm. One by one she glared at her captors, breathing heavily. They drew back, not breaking their ranks. The Thorazine would take effect shortly. They glared back at her.

The ward, for a moment, was silent. Every eye was fixed on the African Queen. As the injection took, she gave a hoarse moan, like air leaking out of a tire, and slumped into the waiting arms of the orderlies. Beaten.

A wheeze escaped from her lips and her eyelids drooped, covering her eyes' cries of anguish. The room echoed from her shouts; at the telephone we stood frozen in place. Then the emergency helpers filed out one by one, the orderlies prepared her a bed and the nurses went back to their stations.

The episode was over. It had taken six minutes.

Verona Smith, during the next week, sat facing the wall in a corner of the T.V. room, doped into a stupor with tranquilizers. She kept the television set on low, as if for company, but didn't watch it. The other patients avoided the T.V. room, leaving her to sit in there alone hour after hour, rocking back and forth and humming a deep, monotonous drone to herself.

The story was that she had just lost her man. He had taken an overdose of heroin and had come crawling to her doorstep in an agony of delirium to die in her arms. As Sonya told it, Verona had carried his body into the house, grabbed up a kitchen knife and gone rampaging through the streets for the local drug dealer.

Out on the avenue they found her kicking savagely at people, breaking windows and stabbing wildly at the air around her. Except for the Pastor of her church, nobody dared get near her. He had tried, for hours, to try and talk her back into reason, but she would not be moved. Murder was on her mind; her man had been done in.

"Vengeance is mine, saith the Lord!" she had ranted over and over. She was too deranged to leave alone and too violent to leave with friends. Finally, they brought her in to the hospital.

In the Unit, she was kept heavily sedated for days. With dark, brooding eyes and slack lips she sat like a dark mound in the shadows of the T.V. room, and she rocked. And moaned. And hummed. After a week, as if sensing that it was now safe, others began to come in to watch T.V. and even sit deliberately alongside her. She didn't say yes and she didn't say no. She just rocked, and hummed. Sitting in the corner, her face to the wall, she just kept her own counsel and rocked.

The door to the T.V. room was open and Verona sat on the floor, facing the wall. I knocked softly, Joanie by my side.

"May we join you?" I asked. She nodded without looking around. Joanie hung back, but when I held out a hand she followed me in. "We want to do a little exercise," I explained. "Do you mind if we close the door for some privacy?" She nodded again, and reached out to switch off the T.V. set.

"It's O.K. to leave it on," I said. She shrugged. Her powerful arms hung slack by her sides and she stared down at the carpeted floor.

"If you want to do this with us, you're welcome to," I informed her. She shifted her body even closer to the wall. Joanie remained by the couch, passive. I longed for a window to open; the place was stagnant with cigarette smoke and disinfectant. Verona didn't respond.

"Let's start lying down," I suggested to Joanie, clearing a space by the sofa. She lay there like a bewildered child and gave me her hand. That in itself was progress. I took it and massaged her palm gently. Verona glanced over, her breaths loud and wheezy in contrast to Joanie's barely audible birdbreaths. "Can you squeeze my hand?" I asked, giving a bit of pressure. After awhile a response came, but with little force behind it.

"A bit stronger now," I encouraged, gripping her hand tighter. Something stirred in her, but she didn't know where in her body to place the effort. She gave a grunt and her fingers twitched without coordination.

"That's better," I said, discouraged that we had to start from scratch every time. The shock treatments seemed to wipe out all trace of memory. "Now, take a good deep breath and try again."

This time her grip had some strength and surprised by it, she clung hard to my hand until her whole body shook with the effort.

"Good," I breathed. "Now, when you feel you can't hold on a second longer, then let go suddenly." With a great expulsion of breath she let go, flushed and panting. "Good. Now rest."

Verona turned her head and watched the proceedings with suspicious interest. Joanie's frail chest rose and fell as she took in the lifeless air of the T.V. room. Verona eyed her bemusedly, then turned back to the wall to resume her relentless rocking.

"Let's do the other side now, Joanie," I said, taking her other hand.

During the course of the next half hour, every part of her body had been coaxed into motion. Color came into her face, her breathing became less shallow and tears had begun to flow. Verona now watched with unfeigned curiosity.

"What you gonna do now?" she asked in a hoarse whisper. It was the first time she had spoken since her dramatic entrance a week earlier.

"Wait and see," I replied, helping Joanie to an unsteady

stand. "We could use some music - could you see if there's anything playing on the T.V.?" For a moment, she lifted her eyebrows sardonically but then fiddled the dials until she found a rock band in concert. For a few bars she just listened and then she snapped her fingers to the beat, her whole body starting to sway. Joanie clung to my hand and stared hard at the reviving Verona.

"Great! Let's start with the arms, Joanie. I'll do it with you." Tentatively, she lifted a wrist limply, then shook it out. I rolled my shoulders and slowly extended one arm to demonstrate. She followed my lead. At first her movements were stiff and jerky, but by the end of the number she was stretching her arms above her head, bending her neck from side to side and tilting her face upwards.

Verona watched like a hawk. Her shoulders rippled suggestively, and in her ample lap her fingers snapped to the beat.

"That girl sure can dance!" she muttered loud enough for Joanie to hear. Joanie flushed.

"Let's add the feet and the legs now," I suggested. I bent my knees, spread my arms and kicked to one side. Joanie followed, hesitantly at first but then more boldly, thrusting out a hip and raising a knee. She kicked to the front and brought it back; kicked again and brought it back. Her movements were still weak, but her rhythm was perfect. Verona and I exchanged a glance of admiration. With her eyes closed, Joanie tossed back her head and let her arms lift, her feet stepping to the band's beat and her face suffused with color.

"Dance, girl," Verona whispered, tears glistening in the corners of her dark eyes. She shook her head back and forth, wiping away her tears with the back of her hand.

Joanie, unself-conscious now, twisted from side to side, then bent over to sweep the floor with her hair. Uncurling slowly, she let her arms lift and reached out with immense longing towards the four walls. Her face was soft, alive.

When the song ended she lost her balance and stumbled

backwards against the couch. The spell was broken. Her eyes flung open, startled and vulnerable, and her body went suddenly limp.

I caught her and gently swung her around as the next piece of music started up.

"It's O.K. to lose your balance," I declared, stumbling against the couch as she had done and turning it into a leggy movement. "When you make a mistake, you don't have to give up the whole dance." She refused to budge. Verona took it in, thoughtful.

"She's right, honey," she murmured. "You were doing real good. No need to quit just because you take a little tumble." Joanie hung her head and two fat tears spilled down her cheeks. Verona and I both extended our arms, surrounding Joanie as she collapsed into sobs on the floor. We all three rocked together in time to the music.

"Poor kid," muttered Verona after awhile, her whole being radiating compassion.

"Yeah," I whispered, covering Joanie with my sweater as she drifted into a doze. Verona unwound her shawl and laid it over the sleeping girl. We sat on either side of her, whispering.

"She don't talk?" Verona asked.

"Not for a year," I replied. She shook her head piteously.

"Poor kid. She must be hurting real bad."

"I think so." I agreed. "A lot of people around here are hurting real bad." She heaved in a huge sigh as if her body would crack under such hurting, and lowered her eyes. The band's announcer made a speech and the audience applauded.

"But she's still a baby," Verona remarked when the show faded out.

"Too young to hurt so bad - you're right. How old are you?" She snickered, chipping away at her flaking nailpolish.

"Old enough to know better," she finally quipped. "How about you?"

"Thirty- three next month," I replied without hedging. She sighed.

"I'm going on thirty," she declared after some consideration. "Thirty and in some pretty bad trouble already, Lord a-mercy." For some moments she gazed at the sleeping Joanie and then she abruptly changed the subject.

"What's this stuff you doing here?" she asked, waving her hand around the T.V. room. "They pay you to do this?"

"They pay me to do exercise," I admitted, amazed at her perception. "This is the way I like to do exercise."

"Bet they don't pay you much."

"You're right," I admitted. "I do it because it's work that I love." She whistled softly between her teeth.

"Me, I wouldn't come near this hellhole if they hadn't dragged me here." She snorted angrily. "They crazy in here, girl," she informed me confidentially. We both burst into laughter, covering our mouths so as not to awaken Joanie.

"Not you," she amended. "Not every single body here, being fair. It's just we paining real, real bad..." She sucked in a deep wavery breath and let it out in a low humming. "I guess some of us just gone off our head cause it hurts so much." She waited for my response.

"It's true," I agreed simply.

"Out there," she gestured in the direction of the glass-enclosure," some of them are really nuts." She watched closely for my reaction, testing me for truth. The fact that I agreed with her didn't make it easier for me to respond.

"I think many of them are hurting real bad too," I remarked, "and they don't quite understand that all of us are in the same boat. You understand what I'm saying?"

"They're too dumb to know it," she spat right out.

"Too scared, maybe," I countered.

"But they get to go out of here at the end of the day..." she wailed.

"You will too - as soon as you get yourself together." She sighed and stared down at her hands.

"Poor kid," she muttered, gazing again at Joanie.

"We can help her," I suggested in as low and offhand a manner as I could produce.

"Who's *we*?" This woman was quick.

"You and me, for example."

I raised my eyes to her, dead serious. She turned it immediately into a joke.

"You want me to dance around with her when nobody's looking?" She flashed a wicked, white-toothed grin and slapped at her thigh.

"Why not?" I shot back, raising the ante. She blew out a rumble of sound and shook her head.

"No, not dance," I persisted, serious again. "You see, she thinks she's shit. She just needs to be told as much as possible that she's good. Like when you said how you liked her dancing. It'll help - I swear it'll help."

"I know just how she feels," she admitted, her voice cracking into a sob. She buried her face in her hands and I shimmied over to her, taking her into my arms and rocking her back and forth until she cried herself out.

I met Dr. Elmer the next day for one of our periodic consultations in the cafeteria. Although I came newly hopeful to each of our sessions, I tended, by the end of the conversation, to be reduced to a drained and wary silence. He rang false to me, like a note slightly off key, and the effort of listening wore me down.

But he was the only doctor who would talk to me. The others kept a polite distance, dashing onto elevators or into their cubicles when they saw me coming. So I stuck with Dr. Elmer, framing my questions to him carefully so I could pick up information I was not privy to otherwise. Given the smallest encouragement - or no encouragement at all - he would launch into discussions about diagnoses and Freudian theory, much of which was actually interesting to me and I could often ask him to refer the theory to specific patients, like Joanie Maynard. In all, it was better than nothing, so I kept coming.

He leaned across the table with a smile that didn't quite extend all the way to his green eyes.

"You spent a lot of time with Joanie and Verona yesterday?" he began, cradling his briarwood pipe. He sucked on the pipe until a haze of pungent smoke wreathed him, making him seem almost attractive. Except for the sardonic twist of his lips, in his smart tweed jacket and his dramatic coloring he was almost a handsome man. I nodded casually and speared crumbs from the table with my index finger. "Anything to report?"

Instinctively, I drew back. Report - like a spy? Taking a delicate bite of my bun I concentrated on chewing for a few moments.

"No," I replied at last. He caressed his pipe, regarding it like a genie's magic lamp.

"Are you sure...?" his voice insinuated. I was Desdemona receiving the oily inuendos of a wily Iago. This was playacting. Then he flashed me a practiced, charming smile. "Nothing at all?" he added in a voice that would melt butter. In my mind, safely out of his reach, was the vision of Joanie's ecstatic dance and Verona's warm compassion. I would never tell.

"We watched some T.V. together, talked to Verona a bit..." So far, the truth.

"Yes," he coaxed, leaning forward to emerge from his smoke-cloud. I gazed around the room, wishing I hadn't agreed to meet with him today.

"So, what's Verona like?"

"I rather like her," I replied. "She's smart, she's got a heart of gold and seems basically solid."

"I'll say she's solid," he laughed. I didn't laugh with him.

"She's a real person, is what I meant. She's gutsy and feisty and very, very kind. And what's more," I added, "I don't think she's crazy."

"Just out of her wits."

"Scared out of her wits..." He sucked on his pipe thoughtfully - posing, I thought.

"She knows she's scared out of her wits - that's the difference. I mean, she's got the courage to admit she's scared - she's willing to grapple with being scared..." I was leaning across the table, pleading with him to understand. But the more passionate I became, the more supercilious his expression. He assumed a pose of the experienced doctor, calm and in charge.

"Did she and Joanie do any - interacting?" he asked, interrupting me.

"No!" I lied, much too strongly. It was none of his dirty business! He puffed absorbedly on his pipe for several moments and then changed his demeanor radically, like an actor changing scenes. He emerged from the smoke like a warm, confiding friend.

The transformation made me blink.

The man wasn't much of a psychiatrist, but he appeared to be one hell of an actor. I had to ask Paul Baker about him. Meanwhile, my lips were sealed. What was happening between Joanie and Verona was so delicate, so potentially dangerous that I wanted to be very cautious. If the doctors - all except this chameleon of a Dr. Elmer - were too busy to consult with me, then I would work with Joanie and Verona by myself. I would never betray these women, no matter what.

He appraised me with a studied look of wisdom and warm humor. I didn't trust it for a minute, and kept my expression non-committal.

"Let's do the following," he said with confidentiality, as if we had always worked as a team. "I'd like you to keep an eye on them over the next few days..."

"No," I breathed out, too astonished to speak. His eyebrows lifted. "No."

It was no wonder Joanie stopped talking to this man. I would too.

He drew in a deep breath, closed his eyes and presented me his profile. I was reminded of John Barrymore. Pipe in hand, he turned his face towards me slowly, the timing perfect, and fixed those green eyes deliberately on me, now a Master Magician. It was amazing - this man was a consummate actor. It was not Dr. Elmer who sat across the table from me, but some medieval wizard! With sudden inspiration, I blurted out,

"Have you ever been an actor?" As soon as the words were out of my mouth, I could have bitten my tongue. He'd never let me get away with this. But instead of a sarcastic put-down, he stopped the charade and stared at me with genuine surprise. It was the first authentic expression I remembered seeing on his face.

"Yes!" he replied. "How did you know?" Now it was my turn to be surprised. "The theater is my first love." The smile he showed me was sincere.

"Have you done much acting?"

"Yes - quite a bit. Before I went to Med School."

He fumbled with the matchbook in his hand. I recognized my own restless longings to be a dancer in him. We had something in common, after all.

"Why'd you give it up?" I asked. He sighed.

"My father was a doctor..." He glanced up at me and smiled half-bitterly. "When Papa's a doctor, first son doesn't become an actor - he goes to Medical School." His lips were tight and he turned the matchbook over and over in his fingers.

"So you had no choice...?"

"Nope. Not with *my* father." He puffed aggressively at his pipe.

"I understand," I began. "I always wanted to be a danc-"

"It's a hell of a long haul to internship when you'd rather be on the stage." he muttered bitterly. "But, you take it year by year, and by the time you look up to breathe ten years have gone by, and there's no turning back." His eyes were pained; there was no superciliousness around his lips now.

"You get older, too," I added with a sigh, "and then it's too late to start over."

"Right," he breathed.

"I've been there too," I began. "As a kid I had my heart set on..."

"Acting is my real gift," he interrupted. Had he even heard me? "My acting career was just getting started. It was the best time in my life." He cupped his chin in his hand and looked right past me. I might as well not have been there.

"Say you could leave medicine and go back to acting - would you do it?" I asked. The pain crinkling the corners of his eyes I assessed as real.

"In a minute," he replied urgently. He gripped his pipe, nostrils flaring.

"Are you good enough?" I asked, nervy.

"Yes," he replied without hesitation. "I was born to act."

"I know just what you mean," I exclaimed. "I feel the same way about choreography." He ignored the hint, lost in his own thoughts; I would not try again. Instead, I asked,

"What made you choose Psychiatry?" He regarded me openly, as if wondering about my motives for asking.

"You want the truth?" he began slyly. I nodded. "O.K., here it is." His face took on the mien of a storyteller about to tell a tall tale.

A mask for the truth, I immediately decided.

"While I was interning on the Psych ward, I fell in love with a patient." He dared me to believe him; every shift of his expression was designed to indicate fiction. But I sensed he was telling the truth. I followed the game, pretending to play it too.

"So," I whispered, "if you couldn't do Greek tragedy on the stage, you could do it in real life, right?"

For a moment he looked flustered. Then he recovered.

"Yes. The night was dark and stormy. I was alone on duty..." He lowered his voice mysteriously, "...when from out of a room floated a woman in white..."

"Who was very beautiful - and troubled..." I added, for him.

"Very beautiful and troubled," he repeated, his eyes unable to mask his genuine anguish. He stared into the middle distance. I almost reached out a hand to him. For the first time since I had met him, I liked Dr. Elmer. He shook himself out of his reveries, his game of truth - disguised - by - art having backfired. Then he glared at me, brows drawn.

"I've got to go," he said curtly, glancing at his wristwatch. "Keep an eye on those two, would you?" Knocking tobacco embers out of his pipe into his coffee cup, he stood up and stretched, looking at his watch again. The moment of truth was over. He avoided my eyes.

"I've got to go too," I said, not adding that I would indeed keep my eye on them, but not for his benefit. I took a last bite of my bun and stood up. Pocketing his pipe, he gave me a cursory wave and strode away, disappearing down the long hospital corridor at almost a run.

During the next weeks, the growing bond between Joanie and Verona became increasingly apparent to everyone, staff and patients alike. Joanie, still mute, was rarely found very far from Verona, who talked enough for both of them. They made a complementary pair - one pale and insubstantial, the other full-blown as a ripe, juicy plum. It was as if each drew essence from the other, attempting to strike a balance in their exchange.

The doctors and nurses began to take serious notice. The women's progress was watched from every corner of the ward, discussed in every conference room. The whole staff appeared to have a stake in the outcome.

Now, since I was known to work with them, I was in demand. I was invited to lunches; seminar doors opened to me; doctors greeted me cordially - if I would talk. But my lips were sealed. My job was Exercise Therapist, not informer. When I had to talk to someone, I talked to Sonya, or Paul Baker - confidentially. With the others, I was discretion itself.

What was happening between Joanie and Verona was still very delicate, and new. In my opinion, the psychiatrists were too heavy-handed to touch what had begun to develop between the two women. Although I lacked the doctors' training and experience, I trusted my own intuition more than I trusted any professional in the Unit. If they had responded to my initial requests for assistance, it could have been be different. But they hadn't. Now I would continue with these two women in my own way, and consult with Paul when I needed help.

Outwardly, I presented a polite demeanor to the staff, but I kept my own counsel and stayed out of their way as much as I could. If, in the end, this all resolved itself well and they were still interested, I'd tell them how I had proceeded. If not, then God help us all, especially Joanie and Verona. But it felt right. What was growing, after all, was love.

I came in that Sunday, like any visitor to the ward. I wanted some time with Joanie and Verona without the regular staff looking over my shoulder and without the weekday schedule of groups to interrupt us. Furthermore, the day was gloomy with rain, the kids were all busy with their friends and Kurt had a meeting to go to. After a long talk on the phone with Paul about what was going on with the two women, I realized that the people I most wished to be with were Joanie and Verona. So when breakfast was over, I went over to the hospital to see them.

"Forget about the doctors," Paul had advised me. "It's the patients you want to focus on. I suspect Verona is your way in - don't ask me how. But if you really listen to her, I think you'll know how to proceed. She's the strong one in the bunch."

"Stronger than most of your colleagues, my dear," I said drily.

"No doubt," he laughed. "Don't be so hard on them - they've got a difficult job to do. Don't forget, they've got to get along with *you*!"

"Whose side are you on anyway?"

"Everyone's," he said seriously. And before hanging up, he had reminded me, in a throaty singsong, "Verona is the waaa-aaay!"

The Common Room was stuffy with forced heat, and grim. Rain scatted against the windowpanes which steamed up on the insides, closing the ward in still more. The outside world might not have existed at all.

Patients lay slumped on chairs and couches, too drugged to even be restless. Sunday nurses, safely behind the glass, filled out charts and occasionally peered into the ward. But nothing much was happening. I came in, stepping around prone bodies as if I were walking amongst stones - or corpses. Nobody budged.

Except for Verona. She pranced up and down the hallway, flamboyantly dressed in a flowered *muu-muu,* bright yellow hat and stiletto heels. She paced back and forth, snapping her fingers and muttering to herself like a firecracker about to go off. Her black hair bristled out from under her hat like a dark halo, setting off the feverish sparkle of her eyes.

Even Joanie kept away from her. I found her hunched in a corner of the T.V. room sketching Tyrone and Chester, who played an aimless game of gin rummy on the couch. A basketball game, without sound, was in progress on the screen and was glanced at from time to time by the card players.

"Who's winning?" I asked. Tyrone focussed with difficulty on the screen and then slurred,

"Celts." A lanky player rose gracefully into the air, a basketball poised on his fingertips, and dropped the ball easily into the basket. The crowd rose and roared silently in the stands. The ball was stolen by a player on the other team who dribbled it smoothly to the other court.

"Nice play," I commented. A grunt of assent from the card players who seemed unable to even look up. Were they always so heavily sedated on the weekends?

Verona's bulk shadowed the doorway. She loomed over the T.V. room like a giant, predatory bird, her eyes flashing dangerously.

"Gentlemen," she intoned in a deep, steady voice untouched by drugs. She had probably held the tranquilizer under her tongue, and then spit it out. Had she gotten Joanie to spit hers out too? "We gonna have church now." Fixing her gaze first on Tyrone and then on Chester, her cheekbones seemed to rise over her ruby-painted lips like miniature wings.

"Gentlemen," she repeated, enunciating slowly, "you welcome to stay for church..." She paused, regarding each man with a deliberate stare, "...or you be welcome to *LEAVE!*"

Her last word emerged like a sustained organ note, and the men gathered up their cards faster than I thought they were capable of moving.

"Whoooo-ee!" she whooped after they had ducked out. Her whole body shook with mirth and with a gloved finger she delicately wiped a tear out of the corner of each eye. Joanie watched her unsmiling, her pencil still poised and her legs tucked beneath her.

'Verona is the way,' Paul had said, and if he were wrong then from this moment on Joanie and I were in trouble, for Verona shut the door behind her and dragged over an armchair to hold it closed. Then she turned to Joanie and me in triumph.

"Now!" she exclaimed in a dramatic whisper, "we gonna have us some church!"

She smiled magnanimously at us, blotting her brow with a white silk handkerchief. The two of us, I realized, were virtually her captives.

On the screen the players trotted, passing the ball from one man to the other. For a moment, Verona stared distractedly at the game and then she strode to the back of the television set, gripping it like a pulpit. Leaning forward, she welcomed us to worship, eyes closed she swayed, humming a hymn between each word she spoke.

"Sisters and friends of Jesus...hummm...this is the day the Lord has made! Hmmm-nmmm...Let us be glad - and rejoice in it! Hallelujah!" She beamed at her congregation of two. "Say it with me, sisters!"

"Let us be glad and rejoice in it," I repeated in a small voice. Joanie, of course, remained mute.

"Yes Lord, let us be glad, indeed, and rejoice in it! Amen."

"A-men," I breathed, barely audibly.

"Say it like you mean it, girl," she chided.

"A-men!" I repeated, louder. Verona wrinkled her nose at me encouragingly and raised her arms over her head, waving them in the air.

"Yes Lord Jesus, we thank you for this day you have made!" She clapped her hands and bobbed her head up and down. "Thank you sweet Jesus!"

Joanie sat still as death, but alert. I flashed her a reassuring smile.

"We having church, yes we are..." Verona intoned, arms up and head bent. "That's alright..." She waved a hand in the air like a giant windshield wiper in a hard rain. Hesitantly, I lifted my hand and waved it also.

"That's al-*right!*" she exclaimed.

"Al-*right!*..." I copied, glancing at Joanie, who regarded me with a hint of amusement. I winked at her with more confidence than I felt.

Verona knelt and leaned her forehead against the edge of the T.V., praying. The players jogged with the ball, shot for a basket, and missed. The crowd gesticulated wildly.

"Dearest God..." she crooned, "give us clean hearts and a praying spirit, Lord... help us...help us to say YES!"

"Yes!" I echoed.

"And dear Jesus, help us to love one another - yeah - so we may do Thy work..." She gave a shuddering sigh. "We be lost, my Jesus...so lost, my Lord. We have strayed from your holy bosom, Lord, and we're lost...we lost...yeah."

"Yeah..."

"We need your help, we need your holy face a-shining on us, oh Jesus, so we can find our way through the darkness...yes we do!"

"Yes we do!" I echoed, stronger now.

"And my sweet Jesus, I pray you will help my Levi - he was weak, but Lord, he was blind. Help him to see, sweet Jesus! Help him to see!"

"A-men!" I prayed with her, waving my hand while she hummed and wept for her man.

"And help everyone, Jesus - all the folks I know, cause I belongs to them and we belongs to You! Bless us, Lord. Bless us."

"Bless us, Lord."

Gazing up, she prayed to the acoustic tiles for all the poor, all the sick, all the shut-ins. Warming to her prayer, she included the nurses, the doctors, the orderlies. Then her voice dropped, and in a caressing singsong she prayed for Joanie. Joanie gripped the arms of her chair and froze.

"A-men!" I sang softly.

"And Marta, help her Jesus..." Taken by surprise, I waved my arm in the air along with her.

"A-men, Jesus," she breathed, swaying. "That's alright, girl - you got the spirit. Just keep the faith. Jesus loves you..." She turned again to Joanie.

"Bless this child, my Lord," she intoned gently. Joanie stared at the basketball game. "We know your eye is on the sparrow, Lord. We know that there don't be even one tiny sparrow you don't see. We know you watching all of us, Jesus. Help this little bird, my Lord, oh, help her...."

Blowing out her rising heat, she stamped and clapped her hands over her head, startling both Joanie and me.

"We know You here, Lord! We know You here, Lord! We know You here!" Stamping hard, she panted with emotion and pointed a finger at Joanie.

"Jesus Loves Us!" she shouted. "There ain't no*body* that ain't some*body!*"

She clutched onto the T.V. for support, entranced and unsteady on her feet. She flung her head, pupils dilated, forwards and back, sending a spray of perspiration into the room. I mentally calculated how to get Joanie out of there if I had to.

"JESUS! JESUS!" she sobbed, pulling her hat off her head. Hanging onto the T.V. she stamped convulsively, screaming, "JESUS! JESUS! JESUS! JESUS!"

"Oh God!" I cried involuntarily.

"YES! GOD!" she shouted orgiastically. "JESUS IS GOD! PRAISE HIM! PRAISE HIM! HELP US JESUS. HELP US DEAR JESUS!"

Verona was out of control. Joanie lowered her feet carefully onto the floor, terrified. I had to get her out of there. Verona bucked and quivered, shrieking JESUS!, her eyes rolling white in their sockets.

Oh God. I had actually encouraged this. The doctors were right; I didn't know what I was doing! My stomach gave a lurch of panic.

"*Verona is the waa-ayy!*" Paul had sung. Could I trust that he was right? Paul's instincts, over the years, had always been sound. Anyhow, I didn't have much choice at this point. Joanie and I were locked in this room with her for the duration.

"Al-right!" I called, waving my arm in the air. "Help us, Jesus." A calm settled over me. It would be alright.

Verona, like a raging storm breaking into gusts of rain,

slowed down to a sobbing and the sobbing ebbed to gasps which loosened gradually into long sighs of release. Her grasp on the T.V. relaxed and her eyes shone like newly washed windows. It was going to be alright.

"Yes, Jesus!" she breathed ecstatically. "You heard my prayer, yes Jesus." Striking the television softly with her fists, she repeated,

"Yes Lord, You listen to prayer. Yes Lord, I am Your child. Yes Lord, I am Your servant. Yes Lord, I love Your Jesus. Yes Lord, I *loves* Your Jesus!"

Radiant, she stepped out from behind the set and lifted her arms in blessing. Smiling benevolently at the basketball players, she stepped over to Joanie, who cowered in her chair. She stood tall, gazing upwards at a brighter world. Assured by a vision neither Joanie nor I could see, she breathed in deeply, expanding her bosom and opening her lips with the first note of her song.

"OOOOOOOhhhhhhh...." She shook her head slowly, listening closely to her sound. When she came to the end of her breath, she closed her lips as if she were kissing the air around her.

"Take my hand.....Precious Lord.....mmmm-mmmm" She tasted her words, savoring them like rich cream.

Lead me on....Let me stand..."

The words were half sung, half whispered, and filled the room with faith, suffering, prayer.

"Through the storm...through the night
Lead me on...to the Light..."

She sobbed out each phrase, cutting them off with the tip of her tongue. I felt the storm, the dark night. Felt myself guided towards hope...

"Take my hand...Precious Lord!
Lead me on!"

Tears coursed down her cheeks and she held her fists triumphantly out to the sides. Her faith bubbled up from the depths of herself, her undertones and overtones spilling over like waters from a Holy well.

It was hard to keep back my tears. Joanie, transfixed, stared at her friend with shining eyes and flushed cheeks. On the screen the lanky payers loped off the court, slapping each others hands and throwing comradely arms about each other.

"Amazing Grace....How sweet the Sound.."

She rolled into the hymn right away, embellishing each tone with musical curlicues. Rising precipitously into her highest range, she poured down into a rich pool of belly notes, sobbing out triplets of longing over and over until her breath ran out.

"That saved....a wretch....like ME!"

She attacked the line with breaths and whispers, letting each note run its full course. Her song came up from the mud and rose into the air, through tears and struggle, towards hope and faith and Love.

"Was blind...but now...I SEE!"

Breathless, she pushed all the way through, glowing, to the Light. She encompassed lovingness with her whole, monumental being, as if she were wrapped in the mantle of it. Her body quivered with its enormity - the vastness of the truth she was expressing. She spread her arms, hot and trembling, and reached for Joanie, who rose easily from her chair and moved unhesitatingly into Verona's embrace. Verona enclosed her, holding her safe. Together, they swayed; pale crescent against the dark of the moon, a moving circle of dark and light.

Joanie clutched at Verona as at a lifeline, sobbing hysterically into the haven of her bosom. She shook with the desperation of the trial she had endured and Verona steadied her, crooning softly, praising the Lord. Locked together like pieces of a puzzle, their healing was catalyzed - each for each.

A sharp rapping at the door. Stopped by the armchair, the doorknob turned futilely and my heart dropped. Preoccupied, neither Joanie nor Verona heard the intrusion. I leapt for the armchair and sat down hard, leaning back against the door. My heart pounded wildly; I dug in my heels for good measure.

"What's going on in there?"

"It's alright," I said through the keyhole. "We'll be out shortly."

The two women remained oblivious. The game had resumed; a ball whooshed through the basket as the fans rose to their feet.

"What?" came the voice. "Open the door!" The rapping persisted.

"Not now!" I hissed through the keyhole. How to explain miracles to a strange nurse?

"Yes, now!" she commanded. I could hear others gathering to help. I sat tight. This could cost me my job, but I made the sacrifice in a second. Verona murmured comfort and Joanie sobbed like an abandoned child rescued at last.

"Thanks to Jesus, you be al-right. Yes, you came through the dark and you now walk in the Light - thanks Jesus. Thanks Jesus..."

Joanie gulped, then coughed.

She was trying to speak!

Just a little while longer, Jesus... I heard myself pray. Don't let them call the hospital emergency squad, Jesus. I waved my hand in the air for emphasis.

"Say it, honey," urged Verona softly. "Jesus loves you. I love you. You safe now, darlin'...you can say it."

"Nmn...ghhh-" croaked Joanie in a voice unused to sound.

"You just say it, child. Jesus loves you. I love you. Marta loves you. We all love you. You safe now..." She kept up the murmur like a ground bass drone upon which a melody could sing itself out. I continued to grip the floor with my heels, listening anxiously to the scuffle and voices on the other side of the door.

"Take your time, honey. We in no hurry..."

Little did Verona realize."Take your time and say whatever is in your heart. We listening. Jesus listens to His angels..."

"I..." Joanie cracked out a syllable. Stunned by her own sound, she buried her head in Verona's lap and pulled her knees convulsively into a foetal position. Patient, Verona kept rocking.

"You're alright. You're alright. Take your time..."

"I..." Joanie tried again, and stopped. Verona, in her wisdom, did not push her.

"Under....ugh...mattress...," she croaked, her consonants slurred by disuse. Neither Verona nor I moved a muscle.

"Under the mattress...," Verona hummed softly, "yes Lord, under the mattress..." She rocked Joanie in a steady rhythm.

"BBroken..." Joanie blurted out. "B-broken bottle." She burrowed deeper into Verona's lap. My fingers went numb with the news. For how long had she wanted to take her life? Verona never even blinked.

"A broken bottle under your mattress..." she repeated in a matter-of-fact singsong. A sharp look from her told me not to make a move. "You alright, honey. You safe, now. Yes, thanks to Jesus, you safe under His wing, Yes you are, you are..."

"TAKE....IT....AWAY...!" Joanie spit out each word like ripping scabs off a wound. Her self-hatred filled the room like a putrid fume. Verona held her close.

"That's right, honey, no more broken glass, thanks to Jesus. Once you was blind, but now you see. Thanks Jesus, you don't need it anymore. Take the glass away - yes. You was lost, but now you're found. Amazing Grace, you're found! Thanks Jesus, you alright now. Thanks Jesus. Thanks Jesus!"

Not until the shift was over and the nursing staff gone could we slip out of the T.V. room. The basketball game had given way to a quiz show, and I spirited the two women out and into the bathroom. Then, trembling, I went to Joanie's room, closed the door behind me, and removed the shards of glass from underneath her mattress. Stuffing the lethal slivers into my purse, I sauntered out onto the ward with studied casualness and then fled, leaving by the back stairs. Knees buckling, I ran breathless through the parking lot and out onto the street where I mingled with the crowds. Nobody followed.

I stopped looking over my shoulder only when I was several blocks away. My breathing slowly returned to normal. The air, after the rain, smelled fresh and the sidewalks steamed with their particular wet-sidewalk perfume. At a municipal trash can, I dumped my deadly cargo and covered it over with newspapers.

Then I hitched my purse up onto my shoulder, took a deep breath and turned towards home.

****

Joanie Maynard was released from the hospital two months later. She attended Medical School, specializing in Pediactrics.

Verona Smith left the hospital three weeks later. She works now as an organist for a Baptist Church.

I was dismissed from my position the next day.

6

MEDITATION AND VARIATIONS

Brow Chakra - Pituitary Gland

*The seeing eye;
clear perception;
understanding and mental development;
becoming one's own teacher.*

Taken from my Journal:

January 26, 1977
Although it's been two years since I was in the Galapagos, the islands still appear in my dreams. Last night's dream took place on the beach at the cape on Fernandina Island, and was about a man Kurt and I met about a year ago at Adrienne's house.

She had invited us and some other friends to dinner to meet this man and his wife. It seems he had recently been installed as the head meditation teacher of a local ashram after its old Oriental Master had died. She said that he and I had ideas in common and that we'd like each other.

Actually, he had made a rather powerful impression on me. He was tall and raw-boned - a kind of Paul Bunyan type - who wore jeans and a flannel shirt and had a shaved head. I remember his head gleaming starkly in the candlelight at the dinner table, and sensed that he was well aware of the impression he made. Anyhow, it had been hard to take my eyes off him all evening.

In fact, had he not been quite so self-consciously brilliant, I might have been more interested in finding out about his ashram. His ideas were arresting, and many of them struck home but he was just a bit *too* charming, and dropped *too* many names for my taste; I didn't quite trust him.

Even so, something passed between us that evening. It was as if we were both lone wolves pretending to be sheep and had surprised each other in neutral territory. Saying goodnight, we exchanged pleasantries and he gave Kurt and me a copy of the Old Master's essays. Then he and I exchanged the wary glance of two solitary creatures. That was all. We haven't seen him since.

Now, a year later, he appears in my dream.

He is coming towards me on the beach at Fernandina, dressed in robes.

"Remember this!" he says, reciting a short poem about a green horse and a white horse. Then he bows, and walks on. I realize I've already forgotten the poem.

Behind the cove, he meets up with me again.

"Remember <u>this</u>, he says, reciting the next three lines of the poem. Then he bows and leaves again. I say the lines over and over to myself, but I forget the last line anyhow. Then the first line slips away. All I can remember is part of the middle line

...the green horse and the white horse....

I woke up in a sweat, understanding for the first time that I have never known how to use my talents well. I could have remembered three easy lines of poetry, but I didn't know how to. Maybe that's what meditation is all about - to learn how to use your best effort. If that's what he teaches, then perhaps I could stand to try and learn it.

By morning, I knew something profound had happened during the night and that I had to take a step. And since it was this guy who appeared in the dream, I suppose that's the right place for me to start.

I called his ashram and asked for an interview with him. Then I sat down on a cushion out in the garage and tried to meditate with my legs crossed. All I got out of it were aching ankles.

March 19

After seven weeks of waiting, I finally had the interview, and God help me, I'm a practicing student!

A black-robed monk led me into the ashram at five in the morning, and showed me into a silent vestibule with round, black cushions lined up like lilypads in the dark. After giving me instructions on how to bow and enter the Teacher's study, he left me there to wait for the Teacher to ring his bell for me.

My heart was racing. It was hard to sit still although I was supposed to be meditating while I waited. A gong reverberated through the building and the sound of voices chanting rose from the Meditation Hall below. I was thrilled. Then came the *ding* of his bell.

I bowed inside the room, which was dim and musky with incense, and went to sit on the cushion just opposite him. He sat still as a stone dressed in robes, but I recognized him right away. Would he remember me?

Above his head was a photograph of hills reflected in a pond. It struck just the right note, and for a second I looked at it instead of at him.

"Hi," he whispered, smiling. He remembered me. His eyes weren't lone-wolf eyes now. We both grinned. "It's nice to see you here."

"Thanks," I stammered, "I want to be a student."

"Why?" His eyes were piercing, and I had no choice but to tell the absolute truth. For some reason I felt relieved, and blurted out,

"Because I suspect myself of mediocrity and don't want to live even another day like this!" I found myself trembling. I hadn't anticipated getting so passionate - or so honest. He regarded me kindly.

"How old are you?"

"Almost thirty-eight."

"And I remember you have children...?"

"Three." He cocked his head skeptically as if children were not an asset to the practice. "But they're teenagers - they're not babies anymore. I mean..."

"Three..." he murmured.

"I've worked out a possible schedule," I hurried on. "I could come for the morning sittings three times a week, and the evening sittings twice..." He shook his head and picked up a polished wood staff that lay in his lap. Then he appeared to fall asleep. My heart pounded with disappointment.

"No," he said finally. Tears brimmed in my eyes. "That's too much disruption for the family." The only sound in the room was of our two breaths. "I'd like to try something different with you. You'll be our experiment. I'd like you to meditate at home every day, before the kids get up, preferably. Can you do that?" I nodded eagerly. "Then I'd like you to attend the student lectures every Wednesday night, and see me for an interview once a month. Can you do that?"

"Of course," I breathed.

"Normally, we like the students to be part of the practicing community, but in your case I'll make an exception. You're clearly ready to make the commitment." I felt happy beyond reckoning. "Will you come to your first student lecture this Wednesday?"

"Yes, yes," I replied, bowing. He bowed to me too. I couldn't stop smiling. It was only after I got home that I realized I had totally forgotten to tell him my dream about the white horse and the green horse.

March 24

Last night was the lecture. When I stepped into the Meditation Hall I found a room filled with people dressed in black robes, their heads either shaved or cropped close to the scalp. Most of them looked to be about twenty five. With my long braid and bright red shawl, I felt like an aging gypsy. I sat way in the back.

The place, however, pleases me greatly. It's spare and

simple in design, with light woods and clean, open lines. I felt calmed by the simplicity and quietness of it all.

The Teacher made his appearance after about twenty minutes of meditation. My legs, by then, were numb. Then everyone chanted, and they lit incense and rang bells, and I had to rest my legs again. The others sat still through the whole ceremony.

He took his place on the platform, sitting down on his cushion slowly and deliberately, as if with every move he was saying, "Watch me."

I watched. He crossed his legs, draped his robes, straightened his spine with mindful attention. The care that he took filled me with gratitude. This is what I have come for.

His lecture was about the value of meditating.

"It's the ordinary things we have to learn how to do," he said. "Walking, breathing, sitting. You know - the easy stuff." Everyone laughed.

"We have to be willing to be a beginner at every moment. Forget what you think you know. Start from scratch all the time. Keep going back to being a beginner..."

The lecture took a different turn. Was it my imagination that he located me in the crowd before he spoke?

"We have to learn how to train the aural memory to concentrate and remember precisely what we've heard, as a means of enlarging our awareness." He gazed around the room and, I swear, his eyes rested on me.

"For example, if I were to come up to you and recite a short poem to you, could you remember it?" I stared, astounded. Had I told him the dream? I'm sure I didn't.

"I won't do it," he chuckled at the students' nervous snickers, "but that's the quality of attention we're trying to cultivate." Everyone sat up straighter.

"Wake up!" he declared sternly. "That's what you have to learn. Pay attention! Open your eyes!"

The lecture was over. Everybody bowed. When I put my palms together, every cell in my body was committed to consciousness. I had come to the right place, and my heart was full. If only Kurt would do this too, then it would be perfect. He, however, had been suspicious of this man from the night we met him.

"Are there questions?" he asked. The room was still. Again, he seemed to be looking at me. I heard myself speak.

"What about dreams...?" I began awkwardly. From where I sat, it looked like he was holding back a gleeful grin.

"Can everyone hear her?" I spoke louder.

"I am wondering about how we learn in the dream state." My heart was thumping. I hadn't intended to bring this up until the next interview - certainly not in public. His eyes were twinkling.

"That's an enormously fascinating subject, isn't it?" he remarked by way of reply. "Why do you ask the question?" I was tongue-tied.

"Don't get caught by tricks of the mind," he declared sternly. "They are not the point of meditative practice. We are simply learning how to pay attention. Everything follows our ability to pay attention. That's all for tonight."

I sat still with the others, my mind in a dither, while he did his bows and strode out of the Hall.

April 10

I've set up a little makeshift altar in the garage and cleared a space to meditate every morning. On an orange-crate shrine I've put my spiral shell, the two bits of mosaic from Ravenna, Eva's stone from the river and the knob of chalky bone from Fernandina.

Every morning, as early as I can pry myself away from Kurt's warm body, (but not nearly so early as my fellow students at the ashram), I roll out of bed and go to the garage.

There, I light a stick of incense, bow to my bits-and-pieces altar, and sit down to meditate.

Day by day, I am making this time and space mine. With painful knees and cluttered mind, I struggle for clarity. The garage is dark and musty and filled with stored stuff, but it's slowly taking on the feel of a sacred space.

The Teacher was right; sitting still is not easy. I drift into daydreams after a few minutes. At my second interview he told me that I had a good grasp of the principles of the teaching, but that at the practice I was like an infant. He's right, of course. I can't seem to concentrate for more than two seconds at a time!

"Real freedom," he said, "is the ability to do nothing, as well as to do whatever you want. If your mind wanders despite you, then it's clear you aren't free."

Sometimes, though, my legs hurt so much I wonder if I'm not too old to be a beginner. The tendons in my ankles burn and my knees feel like they're going to snap with the strain- sometimes after only ten minutes. One of these days, I'll stretch out those ligaments; one of these mornings, I'll sit for a whole hour without moving. And then, when I stagger in for breakfast with red ankles and the kids ask me why I'm doing this to myself, I may even be able to answer them.

June 8

Being a beginner evokes some painful memories of childhood. As a kid, I was so numb that much of what I learned hit and melted right away, like snow on wet pavement. Everything I know - from the multiplication table to playing the flute - had to be learned later on.

When I started learning the flute I was seventeen, and all the other kids in the class were eight. My first dancing lessons, after my father's death, were at twenty-eight, while everyone else was sixteen and had been studying since they were ten. And now, nearing forty, I find myself in an ashram with troubled twenty-five year olds.

I wonder now about the significance of this pattern in my life. Even as a child, I sat on the curb and watched the other kids play. Half in and half out of things. The fact is - I don't really belong in the ashram. No more than I belonged in the beginning flute class, or the ballet class. I'm older than the others, and just picking up techniques so I can go out and do it by myself.

My kinship here, however, is with the Teacher. I'm not sure what it is, but the two of us seem to be connected. That hint of recognition I felt at Adrienne's is still there. He feels it too, I think. There are too many coincidences between us. Here's the latest - it starts with a dream:

I'm wandering through a crowded bazaar in India. It's monsoon season and the street is ankle-deep in water. The Teacher is there too, striding through the mobs of people. His face is alert and his movements are free.

"Watch how I walk through the world," he says as he passes by me.

Then yesterday at his public lecture - which is open to people in the community - he talked about a trip to Asia he made. His topic was how we should move through the ordinary paces of our lives. I had no idea he'd recently been to India.

Describing the crowded marketplaces in India, he said

"How do we make our way through life? Watch the way a Master walks through an ordinary marketplace..."

I don't know what to make of these coincidences. I'd like to ask him, but he's leaving for an extended trip and there won't be any interviews for awhile.

July 30

When I went shopping today, I lost my place on the fish line because, when my turn came, I forgot what I had come for. This has been happening a lot lately - I get fixated on some little detail, and lose all sense of what I'm about.

MEDITATION AND VARIATIONS

I wish I could ask the Teacher about this, but he's still gone. I can't seem to shift from this inner concentration I'm developing through meditation, to functioning on the ordinary, everyday level. I'm sure it's all part of the process, but it would be good to have some help. Kurt, I must say, isn't too pleased with this turn of events. He can't see how all this sitting and staring at a wall is helping me at all.

In any case, I was mesmerized by the fishman's skill at slicing filets off the bone. What effortless, deft fingers he had! At fish, the man was a Master. When my turn came, I was so rapt with watching him that I got flustered and forgot what I wanted to order. Then I got embarrassed, and slunk out of the line without buying anything.

For the rest of the day, I've been depressed. There's nothing I do as well as that man cuts up fish, or Kurt does mathematics. If only I'd started dancing as a kid - I think I could have been that good a choreographer. But it's too late now; I'm just the older lady in the back of the class.

"Why are you so edgy?" Kurt asked over dinner. I told him. "But you're raising three healthy kids and you've got a husband who still lusts after you," he teased. "What's the problem?"

What *is* my problem? All I know is that it goes deep. It has something to do with feeling like an imposter. I dabble with the flute; I do undirected research on the evolution of consciousness; I meet with Paul Baker from time to time to discuss body-mind problems; I sit cross-legged for forty minutes every morning. But what is *My* real work?

To myself, I am a dancer who doesn't dance. I think of myself as a choreographer but I have never choreographed a dance in my life!

In other words, I'm a phony. Phony, phony phony!

I am a woman approaching forty who has always wanted to do one thing, and who has done everything *but* that.

The fact is, I'm wasting my gifts, my time and my life. And that, my dear husband, is my problem.

And the only one who understands this particular dilemma is the Teacher. I suspect he even shares it in some way.

I've seen the lone wolf in him again - as if he whiffed a scent of something very important to him, and wished to be elsewhere but was trapped.

That's why, even though he goes on long trips, and still drops names right and left, I think he's the right teacher for me.

September 18

I've just gotten back from an intensive meditation retreat at the retreat center in the country. It was seven long days of sitting, chanting, silence and pain. Now it's over.

There were about thirty of us, all silent and focussing inward, trying to still our restless minds. We got up at three-thirty every morning and sat crosslegged until ten at night. I alternately shook with pain, or fell asleep on my cushion. I've never done anything so hard in all my life, but I wouldn't have missed it for the world.

I did laughably badly. I fidgeted for seven days straight. Just because I can finally sit still for an hour a day, doesn't mean I can sit still for sixteen hours a day, seven days a week!

Even so, the experience was remarkable. I feel very quiet now, and delicate. I am reluctant to speak or even write, but I want to record the quality of that silence so that when I lose the calm, I can look back and remember.

In the quiet of the night, the Hall where we both sat and slept is fragrant and mysterious. We file around the altar on bare feet, walking mindfully to our places with only the altar candles to guide us. The gong marks the beginning of the first meditation period, and by four in the morning we are sitting in the dark, legs crossed, spines straight.

Every single motion is made with ritual slowness. The fingers are held just so, the bows must be perfect, every step must be mindful.

As the day wears on, the sun makes its transit from one end of the Hall to the other, and the shadows change their slant. When the wind blows in from the sea, we hear surf; when it blows from the land, we hear cars. A cough from across the Hall is felt on the skin and the taste of hot oatmeal in the morning is a revelation.

The first day, for me, was a shock of pain and fatigue. My mind spun with protest. What the Hell was I doing here?

I dreamed up mischief: I'd knock over the altar candles and start a fire; I'd escape into the woods after the first break.

Gradually, though, I calmed down. Day and night began to flow together. Time was sitting, walking, chanting, bowing. Space was four walls of polished wood. The world consisted of thirty black-robed students, the Teacher's daily lectures and the interior of my head - a jumbled can of worms.

The Teacher's talks were the only words I heard spoken all week, and they entered me like light-tipped arrows.

"Look to your pain," he repeated over and over. We were reminded at four in the morning, and he whispered it urgently after the last sitting at night. In my aching body and hurting heart, I felt its truth. Look to my pain. Once the tears began to flow, they wouldn't stop.

It must have been after the fourth day that the hallucinations began. My father's face appeared on the wall in front of me and wouldn't go away. Even when I closed my eyes he was there, sneering, mocking, laughing at me.

At first I was scared out of my wits. I wanted to go to the Teacher for help, but that day he hardly came into the Hall. His cushion sat empty up on the platform hour after hour. I didn't know what to do.

For two days I dealt with the terror on my own, but then I

felt my confidence slipping. My father was hounding me every minute and the Teacher, I felt, had abandoned us all. I had no choice, I thought, but to go out and find him, so during a break I walked by his house - out of bounds for us, of course. As I approached, I heard laughter and the chinking glasses of a party in full swing. The Teacher's voice called out to someone in the garden, then more laughter.

Instinctively, I dropped to a crouch behind his hedge and then ran, in a rage, back to the Hall. I flung myself back onto my cushion, stinging with betrayal. Fueled by shock, I stared down my father on the wall until he disappeared. With another burst of effort, I cleared my mind of what I had witnessed and reached for stillness. From that moment, my intensive meditation began.

During the final two days, my anger resolved into an emotion more delicate as something prickly inside me cracked open, revealing a tender core inside. I became aware of the gentle wash of all of us breathing together. It merged softly with the silence and I understood that one day all our breaths would, indeed, be stilled.

That evening, the Teacher arrived for his talk and apologized for his absence, saying he had been called to perform a funeral. I swallowed my disbelief. Then he gave a lecture on the subject of tenderness and mutuality, expressing gratitude to all of us for our sincere efforts. He asked us to be grateful to each other, as well. All my misgivings evaporated.

"Can you hear us all breathing?" he asked dramatically. The Hall pulsed with our breaths. "We are in this together - breathing and dying, breathing and dying..." The stillness was profound enough to register the twitch of a tired muscle.

Later, I bowed to the altar and then to my sleeping mat. It was like bowing to myself. I could have bowed and bowed. When I turned to bow to the student across the Hall, the Teacher was standing there facing me, his palms raised. We bowed deeply to each other. In the candlelight, I detected his lone wolf look; he was sniffing, curious. He bowed again, and with the slightest indication of a smile, he left the Hall.

November 14

I went over to the ashram retreat center this weekend to help with sandbagging. They're expecting some winter flooding, so the whole community was asked to work on filling sandbags for lining the stream. It was a good chance for me to meet some of the students more informally, and also to be outdoors at that gorgeous place instead of inside facing a wall.

They set up in the dunes behind the beach, and our tasks were handed out amidst stacks of burlap, twine, shovels and wooden loading frames. A whole mob was there - students, friends, beachcombers, locals. We dug sand, filled burlap bags, sewed them closed and hauled them into the gully from whence they got carted away to the stream. It was amazingly orderly and good natured and I felt glad to be part of such a community.

In the afternoon I did stitching, sitting out of the wind behind a sandune with a woman named Maria. Her husband has been the ashram's photographer for years, although neither she nor he have been students since the Old Master died. We had a lot to talk about, especially as I learned that she, also, has three teenagers.

"Don't you think he looks lonely?" Maria observed, gesturing towards a rise where the Teacher furiously shovelled sand by himself. Everyone else was working in pairs.

"I'll join him," I suggested, handing her my needle and twine. "It looks like the others are too scared to." I grabbed a free shovel, greeted him with a smile and dug in. I tossed when he pitched; he tossed when I pitched. Our rhythm was perfect, and the bag was filled in moments. I grabbed a corner to help him haul it down into the gully.

"I'll do it," he said shortly, lifting the sandbag onto his

shoulder. Then he staggered under its weight into the gully while I fitted the next bag onto the frame. I was sort of amused, but also annoyed that he couldn't do the job like everybody else.

We filled four sandbags together, and he hoisted all four onto his shoulders while I stood there and waited. He showed signs of flagging - they must have weighed one-hundred pounds apiece - and I wondered how long he could keep it up. I considered disappearing discreetly in order not to witness his eventual collapse, but the lunch-bell saved him. Mid-load, he dropped his shovel and stalked away without so much as a by-your-leave.

Rude? Macho? Just plain dumb?

In any case, it's not attractive. But he's so good when he's teaching! I can't put it together. Is it possible to trust a teacher, and dislike the man?

Maria introduced me to her husband Tony, a hefty Italian guy with a bushy beard and a huge smile, his neck festooned with cameras.

"Smile, ladies!" he cried when we approached him, aiming his camera at us. Maria made a face and he took the picture anyway. When I heard his Brooklyn accent, I told him I came from Flatbush. It was old home week after that. We compared childhood notes, reminisced about Coney Island, giggled about our elementary schools. In twenty minutes, it was as if we had known each other forever.

I asked him about his work, and he said that he loved exploring the line between illusion and reality. That reminded me of the haunting photograph of hills reflected in a pond which hung in the Teacher's study, and I asked if that was his.

"Yes it is," he replied in his Brooklyn rumble. "Like it?"

"I certainly do," I said warmly. In fact, I was fascinated by it, because in the dim light of the Teacher's study, I could never make out exactly what I was looking at.

"Why?" he asked. He watched me intently.

"Well," I began, not knowing how to describe the sensation it gave me. "It's as if you took a picture of something that was there, but wasn't *really* there - it's hard to explain." He slapped his knee, gleeful.

"She's got it!" he crowed. "Say more."

"I've only seen it in a dark room, you realize..."

"Sure. Say!"

"Well, it's as if the picture was of the shape between things, rather than the things themselves."

"Try - the reflection of the shape between things..." he prodded, grinning.

"That's right!" I exclaimed.

"You bet your bottom dollar that's right!" he laughed, his cameras jiggling. "Hey, Maria - I like your new friend. She understands my pictures. Listen, hey, c'mon over to my studio and I'll give you a copy - O.K.?"

November 23

Tony showed me the photograph at close range in his studio today. What a treasure! It's a picture of the shape of sky between two hills, reflected in a pond, but what it appears to be, at first glance, is a single white mountain. The impact is one of authentic confusion.

"First I see the white mountain," I observed, staring at it, "then I see that it's really two hills, upside down - and then if I keep looking, I can see the hills and the mountain at the same time."

"And then maybe you get that the world is full of ambiguity, right?" he finished for me.

"Something like that," I agreed with a laugh.

His work is superb. I saw stacks and stacks of photographs taken of ordinary things, but caught with the glancing eye - pebbles, peeling paint, vegetables. You don't know, at first, what you're looking at: you think it's an orange, but it's a naked pregnant belly; you think it's a landscape, but it's the pebbles by the curb, close-up.

"Hey," he said, after we had talked for an hour, "let's do a book together!"

Just like that.

"C'mon." I protested. Tony is an impulsive man.

"Hell, we're both from Brooklyn, we understand each other, you're good with words - it'll be terrific!"

So, it seems to be in the works. We're talking about exploring the difference between what can be seen by the human eye, and what is actually there. So we'll deal with perspective, light and shade, transitions and boundaries, scale, definitions. In other words, we'll look at familiar things in ways they're not usually seen. I think it's a great idea.

As I left, he presented me with my own print of the hills-in-the-pond photograph. I hugged it to me. Then, as an afterthought, he handed me another print - one of the Old Master. It's the same as one that hangs in the Teacher's study.

"Thank you - what a marvellous face he had."

"Does he look like he's watching you?" Tony teased, gazing down at the enigmatic face.

"He does," I agreed, slightly disturbed by the portrait.

"Well, he is!" laughed Tony.

"What do you mean?"

"Oh, you'll see," he drawled, showing me to the door.

As I write, the two photographs are propped up before me. The hills, as always, put me into a dreamy state of mind. The Old Master, despite where I put him, seems to be watching me. It's eerie. I'm not sure what to make of it.

December 3
Last night's dream:

We're moving into an old Victorian which hasn't been lived in for years. The stairs are broken, the floors are foul, the kitchen is filthy with grime and grease.

I'm in the hallway surrounded by our boxes, and the doorbell rings. I have to crawl over dusty cartons to answer it. It's the Teacher. He's got a suitcase in hand, as if he's come to stay for awhile.

But I'm completely unprepared. He's testing me, I know. I'm completely flustered by the mess and filth he has found me in. I invite him to lunch, even though I know there is no food in the house. He accepts.

In the refrigerator I find some stuff left over from the last people: a melon, overripe and watery; a lemon, rancid and green.

December 16
Last night's dream:

The Teacher is giving me the ashram's most advanced test. I have to walk through the clubhouse of the Bronx Zoo at midnight. It is the most scary place in the whole city.

The Teacher meets me there just before midnight. The rules are that I am to open the door, walk through the room slowly, and leave by the opposite door. He won't tell me what I'll find inside.

I open the door, scared out of my mind. I'm quaking. Inside, the air is choking, like smoke. Ghostly smudges pluck at me, and wail like women in anguish. My legs are so heavy they will barely move, and my arms are stuck to my sides. I feel the ghosts' terror, and it permeates me like putrid water. My pores are clogging with their despair. I need to vomit.

Desperate, I drag myself through this quicksand towards the other door. I pull myself blindly, choking, getting weaker every minute. I can't make it. The test is too hard.

My hand hits the doorknob. With my last breath, I turn it and fall *out into the fresh night air. I lay there, too weak to move.*

The Teacher comes out of the darkness and sits beside me.

"Now that you've seen my ghosts," he says, "I can show you my pictures."

December 23
Last night's dream:

The family is spending a lazy Sunday morning. Everyone's still in pajamas, the remains of breakfast are all over the kitchen table and my flute is lying keys down in a pile of crumbs.

There's a knock on the front door. It's the Teacher. Of course. I'm furious that he's going to catch me in such sloth again. But I have no choice. I invite him in. The others scatter to get dressed, but I have to entertain him in my nightgown, hoping he won't notice my flute lying on the kitchen table.

These three dreams seem to go together, as if they're trying to tell me something. In each one, the Teacher is giving me a test, but it occurs to me they may be more about him than they are about me. Is he asking me for help?

If so, the message I get is that I'm in too much of my own mess to really offer any. My heart suddenly goes out to him.

December 31
Happy New Year, world.

February 16, 1978
Tony and I have named our book *Margin of Vision*. I'm pleased with the title. We have a work schedule that will include

photographing all over the place in the next few months. We want to do a whole series at the hills-and-pond site near the retreat center, and a series on snakes, and some aerial shots taken from a helicopter. Tony's got a taste for the outlandish - me too!

Hurrah!

March 1

I've moved the portrait of the Old Master from my desk to my altar out in the garage. I could have sworn he smiled when I put him there.

For weeks, it seemed as if he were trying to catch my attention. Weird. Once I thought I detected a wink; a few times I could swear I was hearing his voice. This morning it was clear that he belonged out in the garage where I do meditation.

His eyes appear to have crinkled up with pleasure. It's as if he were saying,

It certainly took you long enough to catch on. Now pay attention to me! I've got things to teach you.

March 10

At this morning's interview with the Teacher, it felt sort of homey to be sitting in the same room as the Old Master and the hills-and-pond picture, as if I were amongst friends, not so much an outsider.

I told the Teacher about working with Tony on *Margin of Vision*.

"We want to examine the subtle interactions between what the eyes see, and what's actually there," I said.

"Interesting," he returned. "You realize that that's what our practice is all about?"

"I think so. I'm quite fascinated by the problem of

understanding the more delicate aspects of the world, the stuff that's not so easy to put your finger on." He smiled. I considered mentioning my lifelong desire to dance, but thought better of it. Another time, perhaps.

"Tony is an excellent man to work with," he said. "We've been good friends for years." I nodded, but noted to myself that Tony had been strangely silent on the subject of the Teacher. I'll have to ask him why.

Our conversation wound around all over the place, from the connections between inner and outer reality, to ways in which art coincided with spiritual practice. Whatever else can be said about this man, he's a damn sharp guy. I thoroughly enjoyed our talk, and hardly noticed when the dawn had brightened into morning. By that time, I had told him in detail about the structure of the book, and our plans for photographing it.

Just before leaving, I told him about my three dreams. He listened with narrowed eyes. I would have stopped when I saw his expression, but I had already gone too far.

"I guess many students have dreams in which you figure," I suggested. He barely shrugged.

"What do you think they mean?" he asked in hardly a whisper.

"Well, either you were testing me, or I was testing myself, or...," I hesitated, and then just spoke it, "...or you were coming to me for something."

The whole place seemed to pulse around us. He said nothing.

"Thank you," I mumbled, bowing, getting off my cushion and out of there as quickly as I could. I didn't look at him.

But as I was putting on my shoes in the vestibule, I noticed that although there were four students waiting for their interviews, he didn't ring his bell.

March 19

The Meditation Hall was packed yesterday for the public

lecture. I came late, and had to squeeze in at the back of the Hall.

He talked on the subject of 'Seeing'. In fact he more or less reproduced my last interview with him. There was one crucial point, however, in which he departed from the original. He announced the lecture by saying that a student had come to him and asked, "What is the difference between what I can see, and what is actually there?"

"My response to the student was..." he said, and then went on to repeat our conversation! Giving himself all of my lines, too!

I was shocked by the misrepresentation, and then wondered if I shouldn't feel flattered instead. But no! I feel used! Why couldn't he have said the truth, which was that he *discussed* the subject with a student? He plagiarized me!

At the end of the lecture he answered questions, in excellent form. The crowd warmed to him, as they always do. He had everyone (except me) in the palm of his hand. While everyone was gazing at him with adoration he played it for all he was worth, and recited a poem.

> *True friendship transcends alienation and intimacy.*
> *Between meeting and not meeting, there is no difference.*
> *On the old plum tree*
> *The southern branch owns the whole Spring,*
> *As does the northern branch.*

A beautiful poem, I must say. He looked around the room, smiling.

"True friendship...," he began again in a dramatic whisper. His eyes raked the crowd, and damned if they didn't rest on me. "...transcends alienation and...?" He let the unfinished sentence hang in the air.

"Can you complete the poem, Marta?"

"Intimacy," I mumbled. People turned to see who I was. "Between meeting and not meeting, there is no difference."

"The rest?" He was smiling as if there was nothing but true

love between us.

"On the old plum tree the southern branch owns the whole spring, and so does the northern branch." I finished out of breath.

"Thank you," he said, almost grinning. He then addressed all the rest of his remarks exclusively to the other side of the room.

I was steaming. What kind of game is he playing? I stayed around for tea, lurking in the corner by the windows. He came in, caught my eye, came straight across the room towards me and stopped short at the group of people standing just in front of me. He greeted every one of them enthusiastically, and totally ignored me. It was masterful; he's much too good at it, and that bodes no good. And worse, I was probably the only one in the place who noticed!

March 20

I woke up this morning burning with rage. There is a difference between alienation and intimacy, damn it!

I want to rip off his pretentious robes and scream at him! How dare he treat me that way! The teachings that *he teaches* forbid it!

I can't decide whether he is doing this deliberately, or whether he's unconscious. In one case, he's cruel; in the other case, he's ignorant. In either case, he desperately needs a teacher himself!

Kurt says I should leave. He never trusted the guy in the first place. But I can't leave until I figure out what's going on, even though Kurt and I are beginning to have fights on the subject.

April 16

I've been keeping away from the ashram partly because I'm still so angry, and partly to keep peace with Kurt. Anyhow, the kids have been needing more attention than I've been giving them, so it was a necessary respite.

We all went to a dance concert last night, of a local group of young dancers. I watched them dance with a longing that was painful. I want to be young and supple and well-trained! I still want, more than anything, to dance! And I'm too old.

When we left, I felt like a dog slinking away with its tail between its legs. I sulked all night, even though we brought ice cream home, and the kids made the most ornate sundaes I've ever seen. Every muscle in me is twitching to do what those young dancers did last night.

June 4

The inevitable has happened. I'm leaving the ashram. The Teacher has blown his cover, and I'm sick to my stomach. Yuck.

Tony and I went on a photographing jaunt near the retreat center yesterday, at the hill-and-pond site. The place was dewy and peaceful in the early morning - so quiet we could hear droplets fall back onto the pond from birds' wings when they took off - and we hiked up and down the hills. Tony lugged his cameras, I carried the tripod. He pointed out how the changing light created different patterns in the landscape, took pictures of dew-dotted spiderwebs hanging from tree branches.

It's a pleasure following him around when he's working. Invariably, I don't see something until he shows it to me, and then I can't see it any other way: a shape echoed in a close-up bush and a faraway hill, a configuration of diagonal shadows across the countryside.

He's an easy person to be with. We gabbed about growing up in Brooklyn, about being in long-term marriages, about being students at the ashram. I asked him about his friendship with the Teacher.

"Oh, in the old days, we were buddies," he said, "before he got elevated." He grinned wryly. "Power's no good for nobody."

"But the Old Master must have really loved him to have chosen him," I remarked.

"Oh, he did. He treated him like a spiritual son." We hiked in silence for awhile.

"So how come you're not a student anymore?" I asked. He didn't reply until we were halfway down the hill.

"Let's just say I had had enough," was all he would say.

When we finally made our way down to the gate of the retreat center, we were surprised to find ourselves interrupting a formal ceremony. The students were filing out of the Meditation Hall one by one to the sound of the big gong and the Teacher was dressed to kill in silken brown robes. He just about jumped when he saw me and Tony.

"What the Hell are you doing here?" he hissed as he passed us. Tony put his arm protectively around me, but the damage was already done. I just stared disbelievingly, wondering why every student within earshot didn't just throw off his robe and leave. But not one student did. They kept their hands folded and their heads lowered. The ninnies.

"We're here for lunch!" Tony called after him brightly, breaking every rule in the book. I flinched as the Teacher scowled darkly at him over his shoulder.

When the last gong had rung and the students dispersed into groups, the Teacher came over to us with murder in his eyes.

"You didn't tell us you were coming," he said, completely ignoring me. "You can stay for lunch, but can we trust you to leave something over for the others?"

I gasped, but Tony replied lightly,

"No problem if you still serve rabbit food." This conversation didn't jibe with the sight of disciples in black with righteously bowed heads - shaved heads, no less.

"Let's go," I muttered to Tony, reaching for the tripod.

"We're staying for lunch," Tony muttered back through clenched teeth. The three of us were squared off and the disciples stood around like so many bald mannikins waiting for their Master's orders. I wanted to kick them.

"I'm not," I announced, turning on my heel. At that moment the Teacher switched from dark to light, and burst into laughter as if we had both fallen for his merry prank.

"Of course you're invited for lunch," he said warmly, throwing an affectionate arm around Tony. "Please come as my guests." He still had not acknowledged my presence.

"That's better," declared Tony, dragging me along with him towards the dining room.

Lunch tasted toxic; I could barely swallow. Before the salad, I got up and left.

"I'm going for a walk," I told Tony, slipping out as fast as I could and running all the way down to the beach. I took the trail up the cliff and walked until I was out of breath. Tony finally caught up with me, sweaty and panting.

"Listen," he puffed, pulling me to a stop. "He gets that way sometimes. It doesn't mean anything - we're old friends, really."

"It means plenty," I retorted angrily, "and I'm not going to sit around and take it. The guy's supposed to be a spiritual teacher, for God's sake, and he can't even be civil to an old friend!"

"Sure, sure. "

"And those dopey students all stand around like trained jackasses!" I shrieked, "and he treats me as if I were invisible!"

"That's one of his tricks," he explained, "but he only does it to people who threaten him. You should be flattered."

"What have I done to threaten him?" I wailed.

"It's not what you've done - it's who you are."

"What - a middle-aged housewife learning how to meditate?" He laughed and took my arm, steering me back on the trail, explaining that the Teacher had always been uneasy around women, especially women who knew their own minds.

"It's news to me that I know my own mind," I said drily.

"But you've got presence and, if I may say so, you've got power. He'll never forgive you for that."

"Well in that case, I'll just get out of here as fast as I can and never come back," I retorted. "It's shades of my father all over again - how in the world did I walk into this when I've spent so many years running away from it?"

"Fate, my friend," Tony grinned. "Hey, watch out," he warned as we approached the Meditation Hall and the Teacher came striding from around the barn, his robes swishing silkily about his ankles. He smiled broadly at us - or rather at Tony, for his eyes managed to not quite include me - and motioned to a bench beneath the cedar trees.

"I'm sorry about what happened before," he said - to Tony. "I had no idea you were coming. We're rather strict about people letting us know when they're going to be on that road. One of these days there's going to be an accident, so we try to be very careful."

Bullshit. I kept my expression neutral.

"What are you up to, anyway?" The Teacher asked - Tony.

"We're shooting some pictures for a book we're doing," he replied. "It's a book about vision and illusion, that kind of stuff."

"Tell me about it," the Teacher said warmly, leaning towards his friend and effectively excluding me from the conversation. He gave no indication that he and I had talked extensively about this project, nor that he had even given a whole lecture based on my ideas. His *chutzpah* took my breath away, and I got up and stalked away. Apparently unnoticed.

Out of sight behind a giant cedar, I leaned against the tree and gazed up into the branches. Tears blurred my eyes. I wanted out. Now.

Moments later I heard an awful grunt.

"Bastard!" grunted Tony, pummelling the Teacher with

both fists. The two men were locked in a terrible embrace, pounding each other hard, one in silk robes, the other in a sweaty tee-shirt. If my eyes hadn't seen it, I would not have believed the scene.

"Scared I'll make you sit an intensive again?" puffed the Teacher, defending himself against Tony's fists.

"You fucking phony!" grunted Tony, punching out furiously.

"Jealous 'cause you couldn't take the grind - ooof!"

"Married to prove you weren't gay - uuggh!"

The insults cuts closer and closer to the bone. I didn't want to hear it.

"Cut it out, you guys!" I yelled in the voice I used to use in the playground. "Just quit it!"

Panting, they pulled apart, fists clenched like kids in a schoolyard. They both broke into sheepish laughter, and hugged, breathing hard. I wasn't amused.

"Not as quick on the draw as you used to be," needled the Teacher, brushing himself off.

"You're putting on some weight yourself," grinned Tony. "We've been wrestling for years," he informed me and the cedars and any birds who might be listening. None of us was convinced.

The Teacher sat down again on the bench and fingered his bracelet of unmatched beads, handing it over to Tony to look at.

"What's this - skulls?" The bracelet was made of miniature ivory skulls, painstakingly carved.

"Found off the coast of Ireland," explained the Teacher in his best 'teacher' manner. "They're shrunken Celtic heads, from an ancient civilization of cannibal-priests..." Tony's nostrils flared. In a moment they'd be at it again. I just wanted to get away from both of them.

"Well," said the Teacher, rising, having had the last word. "I'd better get back to work." Taking the bracelet from Tony, he dropped it into my lap. "Enjoy the rest of your day here, and be careful going back. Next time, do let us know when you're coming down." With a slap on Tony's shoulder he strode off, leaving me with his Death's heads. The bastard.

"You forgot something," I called after him. He ignored me. I caught up with him at the door to the Meditation Hall and gave him back his beads. He turned swiftly, his face dark and mean, and snatched the bracelet out of my hand without acknowledging me. Then he rushed into the Hall, not looking back.

June 5

I'm exhausted, as if I'd run a marathon and come in last. I've been deeply betrayed by someone I went to for guidance. I feel the same as when I was a child betrayed by my father, the person I was supposed to be able to trust. What horrifies me is that I walked right into it this time with my eyes open. Does that mean I can't trust my own judgement next time?

Kurt, of course, has wanted me out of there for over a year. The whole thing has smelt fishy to him from the beginning. Now he's relieved I've finally seen the light and am leaving the ashram. As for me, my heart is broken.

I sat for a long time this morning, feeling awful. Just as I was about to get up, a voice in my head said

There's a teacher behind every bush. Even the bushes are teachers.

It was weird. When I went to bow at my little altar, I swear the Old Master smiled.

Out in the garden, the rosebushes looked particularly vivid this morning. They're studded with blooms. One bud, still sheathed in green, was just starting to open.

"*Even the bushes are teachers*," he said.

The rosebush?

Today I'll sit by the rosebush and watch the bud blossom.

June 6

It took all day for the bud to become a flower. It unfurled little bit by little bit - with hours of waiting in between. I sat there all day and most of the time nothing happened. Every once in a while I'd see a teensy little shrug, barely noticeable. But by the end of the day, lo and behold, there was a rose!

"*Even the bushes are teachers,*" he said. He's right. Today I learned about patience. Things go in slow motion, without much drama. A lot of waiting and watching. But in the end, there's a flower!

I already feel better.

June 7

Since I'm now without a teacher, I've taken a bunch of books out of the library from different religious traditions to dip into. Today I was reading the Blue Cliff Records from the Zen tradition and it's full of little nonsense stories. I read story after story, not knowing what to make of them, but then I got to the following lines, and suddenly everything began to make sense:

"*If you don't have iron eyes or brass eyes, you'll probably be confused. Those with the same disease sympathize with each other. The two men are buried in the same hole.*

You've got nostrils, but you've lost your mouth."

All at once, like a glass that's been filled too high with water and suddenly brims over, I understood what the stories all meant. All at once I got the point of the teachings, of the meditation, of everything! I could hardly believe I'd never gotten it before, because it seems so simple.

The point is that we can see the nostrils, we can see the mouth, but we tend to miss the whole face. We see the pieces of reality, but we don't know how to perceive it whole. And perceiving it whole means you have to be willing to look differently, more intuitively. And when you do that, then everything appears different.

In the light of the larger view, all the individual things have meaning in terms of the larger picture. Then you can see that everything is connected, that everything is part of the same whole thing.

Of course, oh, of course!

I feel ecstatic. Suddenly, the world has opened up its boundaries. Everything fits. Suddenly, everything makes a kind of glorious sense. How could I not have seen it before?

Of course, oh, of course!

I want to bow in gratitude to everything - to the rose, to the book of crazy stories, to Kurt, to my children, to the whole world - and oddly enough, to the Teacher. If I hadn't been pushed to this edge, I might never have learned all this.

When I meditated this evening, I received a hint of a message. I think I already knew it, though.

Stay, it said.

I don't think Kurt will be very pleased.

June 8

Kurt was not pleased. In fact, he was furious. We had a stony argument in bed, and fell asleep carefully not touching. This was my dream:

I'm waiting at the Ashram for the Teacher's lecture. He is hours late. At last, a roll of drums announces his arrival. Instead of him, though, a troupe of trained dogs comes in jumping through hoops.

I decide to leave, but then there's a trumpet fanfare. A circle of adorable children comes on, tossing flowers and dancing.

Angry, I turn to leave again, but this time a choir of angels sings to announce his presence. I can hardly believe the extent of his arrogance. He comes in carried in a palanquin encrusted with jewels, in golden robes and golden scepter.

"This isn't for me!" I cry, pushing through the crowds to get out. At the ashram doors, I turn around one last time and see his profile through the palanquin, and it is 'hollow with loneliness.'

I can't get that look of sadness out of my mind. He is hollow with loneliness. Defeated, I turn around and go back into the Hall. I can't leave now.

June 9

I thought things couldn't get more bizarre, but they have. Tony just phoned.

"The Meditation Hall's gone," he announced. "At the beach."

"Sure, Tony."

"I'm not kidding you," he insisted. "It's smashed to pieces. Remember the big cedar, just where we were sitting...?"

"And fighting?"

"Yeah," he laughed. "That one - well it fell over last night."

"Tony..." I wasn't in the mood for practical jokes.

"You aren't listening," he chided, "I'm telling you that the Hall is smashed to smithereens, knocked off its foundation, blotto, smasho, wrecked. You hear me now?"

"You're not kidding, are you?" I started to listen hard.

"You're damn tootin' I'm not kidding. Broke the pipes, too. The place is completely flooded - cushions are floating and everything!" He sounded positively gleeful.

"How is the Teacher?" I heard myself cry, clutching the receiver hard.

"Nobody was hurt. They were all in there when it happened, but everyone got out safely. Don't worry."

"How did it happen?" My mouth was dry as dust.

"Nobody's got a clue. They're speculating about shallow roots, and earthquakes - but they-don't-know-what-we know..."

"Tony, you're not saying..." We both broke into nervous giggles.

"As long as there isn't a better explanation..." he sang. "Maria thinks it's a riot and long overdue. She says it's the Old Master punishing him."

"Would he have done such a thing?"

"Wouldn't put it past him. Listen, the stone figure on the altar's busted in three pieces..."

I'm scared. I went right out to the garage to sit. This is a more dangerous scene than I had imagined. I should get out and never come back. But something still holds me...

June 10

I was fidgety when I meditated this morning. I think I've gotten in over my head and I'm not sure what to do next. A message came through, however.

You can learn compassion <u>from</u> him by learning compassion <u>for</u> him - it said. That seems to mean I ought to stay for awhile.

June 26

Kurt was vehemently opposed to my going to the public lecture today but when I insisted on going, he came along. He followed me around like a bodyguard. If this whole business weren't so scary, I think I'd find it funny.

Anyhow, probably half the city was there, everyone with a theory on how the disaster happened. We all waited for the real scoop from the lips of the Great Man. I was very curious to hear how he would handle it. Tony and Maria had stayed away, which meant that only Kurt and I knew a different version of the story from the Teacher's.

But the Teacher is a foxier fellow that I had even imagined. He gave an entrancing lecture about how the development of a disciple is like the unfolding of a rose - and he never once mentioned the accident.

"Did you talk to him?" Kurt hissed in my ear at the parable of the rose.

"No!" I shot back, offended. "He's a mind reader. I've told you so."

The talk, however, was a command performance. He captured everyone's attention within a few moments, and nobody gave a thought to the destroyed Hall anymore. It was like watching a master magician at work, and I was both impressed and horrified.

He spoke eloquently about beauty and truth. Holding up a long-stemmed rose, he demonstrated what it meant to unfold towards the gorgeous reality of *'just here, just now,'* using himself as our model.

His smile was inscrutable, his face was transformed. He held the rose lightly, emanating wisdom, love and human perfection.

I got a stomach ache and I could feel Kurt ready to explode beside me. We were in the presence of an evil genius; he had everyone, except us, in thrall.

We stayed for the question- and- answer period, even though Kurt wanted to slam out of there immediately.

Someone asked about trust and he answered that none of us can hide from one another anyhow, so trust might as well be implicit.

What was he talking about?

"If nobody can hide then we might as well all come out of hiding," he claimed. "We might as well all trust each other. Why not?"

Kurt nudged me, but I was trying to make out what the guy really meant. Everyone soaked that one in and nobody asked about the accident. Somebody had to.

"The accident at the retreat center," I blurted out, not thinking my question through. "Do you think it was karmic?" Kurt groaned beneath his breath.

"What do you think?" the Teacher shot back. His eyes narrowed like a fighter whose opponent has made a foolish move.

"I asked you," I rejoined defiantly, losing ground. He nodded coldly, and proceeded to deliver a text-book lecture on the subject of Karma which took up all the rest of the time. He never mentioned the accident.

He won the round. Kurt was furious with me and I felt like a dope. We didn't say a word to each other all the way home.

June 28

I'm confused. If a person - the Teacher, for example - can say all the right things, and say them eloquently and clearly, but seems to live according to a different standard, what is the status of his knowledge?

Kurt's answer is blunt: "He doesn't know what the Hell he's talking about."

To me it's not quite so simple. I think there is more than one way of knowing things - body knowledge, mind knowledge, heart knowledge, spirit knowledge - and people are good at either one or the other, but rarely all at once. The Teacher is a mind-knower, and a brilliant one, but his heart's totally undeveloped and his spirit doesn't have a clue. So he's a bit like a runaway brain, and doesn't even know it.

Nor do his students. That's what's so frightening.

I just don't feel I can leave without warning the others. I'm not sure why I feel it's my responsibility, but they're all so young and so vulnerable. There was a message for me when I sat this morning, one of these messages that seems to be coming from the Old Master's picture. It was:

Earn his trust by being absolutely trustworthy.

It took me by surprise, and I felt a spreading sensation of warmth all through me. My sense was that I had to learn how to love him before I left.

"Is that it?" I asked. In the quiet I thought I heard,

You're catching on.

October 11

It's been months since my last interview. Kurt, of course, just wants me to let it go, but I keep getting messages to the contrary. So I phoned the ashram and was told that my name was no longer on the list. Then they said the Teacher wasn't seeing people. Then they reneged and said I could see him this morning.

Before I left, my mind was a nest of bees. I went out into the garden and picked some late roses - for inspiration. When I bent over to sniff them, I heard,

Wait. No matter how long.

This only made sense to me after I had sat cross-legged outside his study for an hour -and- a- half. The other students had all come, seen him, and gone.

Wait... the message had said. I would wait and hopefully

understand why later. An hour later my bladder began to twinge. Concentration was impossible; I wanted to throttle him.

...no matter how long.

I recrossed my legs, figuring that if I had to pee, so did he. If a contest of bladders was what he wanted, a contest of bladders he would get! I almost dissolved into a fit of nervous giggles at the thought, but then I grew calm. I had to do this well.

Straightening my spine, I entered into a quiet state in which neither knees nor bladder offered any resistance. For how long I sat that way, I don't know. At last came the *ding* of his bell, and I calmly stood and entered his study.

He looked a wreck, lumpy and purple. His eyes appeared to be swollen shut. The man was sick. I felt him flinch as I took my place on the cushion, as if he were waiting for my tirade. But that was not what I'd come for.

"I've been asking the question, Who am I?" I began softly. "I'm starting to realize that the answer involves getting past the prism of my own personality." One eye opened a crack.

"I understand it to mean that I've got to take in the world directly and in its entirety. Ultimately, the whole world must be in everything I do, everything I see." I sat in silence. "That's all I have to say".

Both of us were breathing heavily, and it was the only sound in the room.

"That is the correct focus," he said hoarsely. "Take it to your new teacher." He opened his swollen eyes, glaring. He looked as if he hadn't slept in weeks.

"I'm not changing teachers," I declared in a firm whisper, standing up and leaving the room quickly.

He sat there, stunned. After waiting for two- and- a- half hours, my interview was over in less than three minutes.

December 31

Adrienne and I took our annual New Year's walk in the hills. The air was tangy with winter weeds and the ground squished beneath our boots. We talked about the children and the high school scene, and we talked about our mutual friend, the Teacher. . She was mystified by my stories of what went on at the ashram.

"Listen, I don't want to talk about him," I complained. "That whole business is on my mind too much."

"Have you been dancing?" she asked, by way of changing the subject.

"One class a week," I replied, "but I wish I could do more."

"Then why don't you?"

"It's just too painful - either I want to do it all the way or not do it at all, and there's no way I can do it all the way."

"Why not?"

"What do you mean, why not? I'm getting on forty, Adrienne- people don't become dancers at the age of forty!"

"That sounds like an excuse," she declared, regarding me sideways. "Nobody says you have to be a prima ballerina - but that's no reason for you not to do what you've always wanted to do. I think you should give yourself, say, two months of trying it out. Just take all the classes you want, go to concerts, see what's out there. Then, if it really doesn't work, at least you'll know you've tried."

"Sounds reasonable," I admitted, "but I'm so out of shape..."

"And there's no time like the present to get in shape. Listen, why don't we both go on diets together...?"

She convinced me to give it a go. It is, after all, a new year. I'm terrified, and a bit embarrassed. Kurt just shrugged when I told him. First the ashram, now this. I suspect he thinks I'm out of my mind.

But oh, I want to dance...

February 8, 1979

The Teacher is running scared. He flies from here to Europe; from Europe to the east coast; from the east coast to Japan; then he's back here for an intensive, and off again somewhere.

Interviews and lectures have, of course, been put on hold. In fact, everything, except his gallivanting with *'important people'* has been put on hold. I call it the 'Fancy Friends Syndrome.'

I feel like a hypocrite even pretending to be part of this community.

> *When you love him, you may leave.-* That's the message I got.
> "But how can I love him?" I wailed.
> *Between you and him there is no difference.*
> That was the reply.

April 17

Watching the Teacher sink into a morass of ambition and self-deception, I learn something about humility and honesty. He is teaching me whether he means to or not, although I must say, it's a tiring and disheartening process.

> *Watch out!* I hear when my attention wavers.
> *Stay soft. Stay firm.*
> How can I be soft and strong at the same time?
>
> *Balance,* I am told.

April 19

I bless Adrienne daily. Her push was the one I needed. I'm

dancing four times a week now, and when I dance I'm the person I'm supposed to be. It's like being able to breathe out after a lifetime of holding my breath in. This is what I was born for!

I'm enrolled in two classes which both meet twice a week: one in improvisation and the other in choreography. I couldn't be happier. My muscles have begun to loosen and my joints are becoming limber. Moving through the space of the room - even though I'm by far the oldest in both classes - is more to me than dancing, it's <u>Living</u>! It's feasting after famine. It's coming home.

April 21

Margin of Vision is just about ready. As soon as Tony prints the last pictures, it will be out of our hands. We're both pleased with the results. Now all we have to do is find a publisher.

"Let's do another one!" he suggested right away. We talked about the possibility of a book about the re-emergence of a burned-out forest, and it would be about the interdependence of life-forms as they appear after a natural disaster. I like the idea, but at the moment, sitting in front of a typewriter charms me not. All I want to do is dance.

April 26

Already, dancing four times a week isn't enough - I want more!

For the first time in my life, I want to give myself over one-hundred- per- cent to what I'm doing. The only other time I knew this confluence of necessity and desire was during childbirth, and that only lasted a few short hours. This state of being used totally is what I have longed for all these years.

Discipline is pure pleasure. Preparing my body to move is

an absorbing adventure - every loosening exercise, every muscle strengthener. It's like being in love, fascinated by every bend and twitch of the lover's body, except the body is my own.

"What's your secret?" a friend asked recently. "You seem ten years younger." I couldn't answer her, because I didn't know whether it was the dancing itself that made the difference, or simply the fact that I'm following my heart's desire.

It's working on a deeper level, too, because there's something about all this movement that is pulling away at protective layers inside, exposing old wounds and bringing up painful memories. I am raw these days, but willing to bleed. It's like scraping scabs off infected sores so they can finally heal properly. Even Kurt can see the difference, although the process, I think, is harder on him than it is on me because I cry a lot in the night.

And wonder of wonders, I'm actually being asked to perform with people! My improvisation teacher wants me to dance in a demonstration performance, and a choreographer from the troupe I saw dance last year wants me to dance in her piece.

"I've been searching all over for someone with your quality of movement," she told me today. She has no idea how many years I have waited to hear someone say that to me.

May 23

I'm in a terrible mood. Everything looks dark, as if life is going by without me, leaving me with an aging body and dashed hopes.

At the age of forty, a woman does not start out to become a dancer, damn it! And if she does, then she had better be prepared to be both an ignorant beginner and a wise old lady at the same time.

I feel frustrated down to my bones after a day full of

rehearsals. They're all so young - adorable, but so immature. I ought to be teaching all of them! I'm like a visitor from another country, where everyone talks baby-talk to me.

Company rehearsals begin with a full modern- dance workout. We stretch and bend and leap all over the place. At the end of the set I'm hot, but not warmed up - inside, I'm cold to the core, like a hot-dog cooked on a kids' campfire.

All this hard pushing can't be good for tendons and ligaments, especially for somebody over thirty. I worry about tearing something. So when the others take a break I do my own warm-up in a corner, rolling softly on the floor to loosen my spine and then shaking out gently. When I feel warm from the inside, then I can dance safely.

I suggested we might all do a softer workout before the fast stretching and bending, but this is not the common wisdom. They smiled indulgently and pulled harder.

With the improvisation crowd, I'm simply puzzled. Something's going on that I'm not privy to. They've got some kind of secret agenda. I even wonder if they aren't part of a cult that lures in unsuspecting new recruits, and that the demonstration performance was just a ruse to hook us in. I feel a bit like a fly caught in a web. I'm curious, though. This may be a cruder version of the ashram - I want to see how it works.

But oh, this is all so beside the point. I want to dance!

June 24

Tonight is my debut as a dancer, and after what has happened today, the last thing I want to do is dance. This is too horrible to imagine.

A young student at the ashram has been killed - murdered in cold blood on the street near the Meditation Hall. They found her lying on the sidewalk with a bullet through her head.

I am weakened down to my bones; my cells are water. No way can I get onto a stage in four hours and dance. I even have the first solo.

June 25

Kurt and the kids all but carried me to the theater and stuck around during the warm-up. I felt like a klutz, and couldn't care less. At the dress rehearsal I lost my balance continuously and misjudged the dimensions of the stage. Stage fright, they said. I didn't explain. I just wanted to get through it so I could go home and cry.

When the lights dimmed, they pushed me out for my solo, telling me to break a leg. The stagelights blinded me, but with the first notes of the music my body began to dance. I took the first plié, shifted from left to right as I was supposed to do, but then something gave way inside me and everything I was feeling surged into my body and danced me. I left the choreographed score and simply did my own dance, totally absorbed by my creation. I danced for the dead student with everything I had.

It was only when the music resolved itself into the final cadence that I registered the fact that I hadn't danced the right dance. When the others joined me onstage, I avoided their eyes and finished the piece as it had been composed. We took our bows and numb, I fled home with Kurt and crawled into bed to mourn.

June 26

When I came in for the pre-performance warm-up, half slinking so I wouldn't be noticed, everyone came rushing over.

"Where'd you disappear to last night?" they demanded. When I started to try and explain, they said, "Half the audience came backstage to see you!"

"What?" I stared at them dumbly. They all hugged me, excited.

"You made the piece! Whatever you did, do it again!"

Will wonders never cease?

July 1

Today was the funeral. Kurt and I went to the service at the ashram along with all the other students.

The Teacher, it seems, only flew in yesterday. Apparently, they had trouble tracking him down with the news, wherever he was. I expect he's good and shaken.

The place was filled with solemn black-robed kids, everyone scared out of their wits. Me too. The girl's parents took part in the ceremony, carrying her ashes suspended from a pot around their necks. They looked lost. Imagine, their first visit to a meditation center, and it's with their kid in a pot around their necks! Kurt and I clasped hands hard. Ice on ice.

It was the whole rigmarole: gongs and bells and incense, processions of senior monks, teachers from other ashrams, chanting, everyone in black or brown or gray. And then, to our collective surprise, comes

THE TEACHER! resplendent in robes of crimson and gold brocade, a stiff wizard's cap of golden threads and ceremonial slippers turned up at the toes.

Not the Teacher, but the potentate, the Grand Dragon, the Lord High Executioner!

The fool.

I was embarrassed for all of us and mortified for the parents of the girl. Has the man gone completely mad? There wasn't a sound in the Hall. I think we were all holding our breaths.

Then he turned and faced the gathering.

"Today is the day of her ordination," he intoned magnificently. "Today, she shall become a priest."

Brilliant move, but theater. The parents looked mystified as their daughter was, in absentia, shaved, sprinkled, dinged over, bowed to. He played it up masterfully - I had to hand it to him. By the time the ceremony was over, he had everyone with him - crimson get-up and all.

"Let us each say our farewells," he announced, properly choked up. He spoke to her intimately - touchingly, I thought - and then opened it up to the community at large.

"Goodbye," choked out one student after another. "Rest in peace," they murmured. Some told stories about her, others couldn't speak at all. I was about to ask for forgiveness for the attacker, but as I drew in a breath to speak, the Teacher said,

"Remember your assailant and have compassion for him. He is the one suffering now."

He spread his arms wide in benediction and everyone gave way to tears. His robes stood out stiffly behind him, but his eyes remained dry and watchful. If ever I saw the lone wolf in him, it was at that moment.

September 21

A new decree has been handed down from on high. Every decision in the ashram must be personally approved by the Teacher. Since he's out of town more often than not, this means everything has ground to an awkward halt. Thus, I still don't have permission to sit the intensive in two weeks.

"Please take my name off the list," I informed the secretary this morning.

"Why?" she asked.

"Because I don't approve of the new regulation," I retorted. (Nor should you, I refrained from adding.)

This is simply the latest of his manipulative strategies and to my astonishment, the students have been accepting one restriction after another. He is at the peak of his power now - I suspect he could get away with murder, if he tried. Someone's got to protest. Maybe that's why I'm still around.

Too bad. I was looking forward to a week of silence, and of observing him close up. And I'm still trying to figure out how he can be such an arrogant bastard, and still give such eloquent talks.

He has not learned how to love came the message this morning. *And you too*, it added, with a hint of humor.

October 5
From the others I learn that the intensive was extraordinary. The Teacher was humble, steady and caring, they said. I expect he was genuinely affected by the student's death.

"He talked mostly about love," they told me. "About how hard it is to learn how to love."

Oh yes.

"He kept reciting one poem over and over - it was like the theme of the retreat."

"Let me guess," I said wryly.

True friendship transcends alienation and intimacy.
Between meeting and not meeting there is no difference.

"How did you know?" they all gasped.

October 22
I am amazed at how popular he has become. People cram

into the Hall to hear his Sunday lectures. The irony is that the less I trust him, the more he appeals to the public. I always have been out of sync...

He sat up there like a benevolent King holding court, his loyal subjects surrounding him and going soft around the eyes at his words of wisdom. Soft in the head too, if you ask me.

He spoke about pledging one's troth - in a voice that could melt butter. I suspect he's got a girlfriend. His wife looked stony-faced and miserable. She and I were perhaps the only scowlers in the room.

He waxed rhapsodic about making the beloved the background of your life, about overcoming hindrances to intimacy. He told how in some languages the word for *'love'* was an ideogram representing a wet sleeve - meaning that you shared your umbrella with someone. Everyone went dewy-eyed.

I wanted to vomit.

October 24

If these improvisers use the word *'power'* to me one more time, I just may haul out and hit them.

My suspicions were correct; they're members of a new age cult which proselytizes for new members by teaching techniques of mind control. They believe they're preparing to save the world, Lord help us.

"We recognize you as a powerful being," they informed me seriously today. "We have tested you and find you ready to help us with our work."

I kept a straight face because I'm not ready to leave yet. I still want to try and understand the method in this madness. If I can figure out what they are about, I might be able to understand why the Teacher has such an irresistible appeal to people.

What I'm seeing is a charismatic male figure who attracts idealistic young followers who get lured into an exciting web of passionate devotion and rigid discipline, and are willing to give up their souls to the cause. Or the man. These young dancers, talking about their leader, sound just like the students at the ashram talking about the Teacher.

I wish I could warn them, somehow. But I know they won't listen.

December 5

Yesterday was the anniversary of the Old Master's death. At the ashram, they rang the gong two hundred times. I sure hope the Old Master was listening.

I did my own ceremony. Whether it was for him or whoever has been guiding me these months, I don't know. But it didn't seem to matter. I used him as a focus of gratitude, in any case. I didn't think he'd mind.

I lit a candle and meditated in front of his portrait for about an hour. Then I silently asked how I ought to proceed in my ongoing saga with the Teacher. For a long time nothing happened. My body grew quieter and quieter and was soon so still I was hardly drawing breath. Every cell felt capable of hearing sound; every molecule capable of seeing light. I was like a fine receiving instrument, sensitive down to the bones.

It was then that the Old Master's face began to change. It got blurry, and then became a young woman's face. Then it re-assembled into the features of a wizened pirate, then flickered into a Chinese boy, an aged woman, a British policeman, an African farmer.

My breaths grew shallow and the pace accelerated.

From an African farmer it became a Thai baby; then a prostitute, an elder statesman, a nun. Then it was a cowboy, a society matron, a drunkard, a sailor, a new mother...

Knobby-kneed girls flashed by, and babies and businessmen and old crones. Everyone in the world was there in the Old Master's portrait.

"Where are you?" I cried, rubbing my eyes. I clutched after the now-familiar signal of my guide, searching behind the hallucinations for that steady, wise presence that I've come to count on. But he remained just out of reach. I felt like a child crying in the crib while her mother watches from the doorway.

The silence in the garage was palpable. The candle burned down to the nub and sputtered. A young girl's face aged by perceptible stages. It could have been me. Then that, too, faded, leaving the outline of a head with nobody in it.

The candle flared and then went out. I was alone in the dark room with nobody to help me. Where my guide had been there was now an empty hole. I shuddered with desolation, a woman without a name, a student without a teacher.

For a long time I trembled in the dark, hearing the phrase repeat itself over and over in my head. A student without a teacher. A student without a teacher...

And then, more gently,
A teacher without a student
A student who is a teacher
A teacher who is her own student
A student and a teacher

Suddenly, as if a bell had rung, it all became clear! I was the student and I was the teacher, both!

I was a student at large in the world - *everyone* out there was my teacher. *There is a teacher behind every bush*, my guide had said. Well, it's true.

That means I have to learn how to be their student. And that makes me my own teacher.

The challenge then is to live up to being my own teacher.

I bowed to the now-empty portrait and thanked my departing guide, or the Old Master, or whoever had given me the sign. I sensed a returning bow, and then the signal faded altogether.

Leaving the garage without looking back, I felt like I was parting from a lover when the time to end had come.

December 16

Yet another decree has come down: students' monthly dues are to be doubled as of the first of the year. I expect there won't be any protests except for mine.

I sent in half my dues, and a note stating that I would pay the full fee when interviews and student lectures were resumed. Then I waited. It only took two days before I got a call for an interview. Money, it seems, speaks.

This time I was not kept waiting - in fact, his bell *dinged* even before my shoes were off my feet.

His study was dimmer than usual, and chilly. In the gloom, he sat there as immobile as rock - or ice. My cushion had been placed so close to his that when I sat down our knees almost touched. He emanated cold, like an ice-giant whose weapon was freezing the enemy's bones. And I was the enemy.

My first instinct was to run away. What was I doing where angels would fear to tread? Why did I think it was up to me to confront this man?

"Good morning," I said in as firm a voice as I could muster.

"You've disobeyed the rules of the ashram," was his response. Now that he had an excuse to force me out, he would do so with dispatch. My chest was freezing up.

When you love him you may leave. That had been the last message received from my guide.

The Teacher's mouth was taut and dark in one corner, and I considered making a bow and getting out of there.

Earn his trust by being completely trustworthy. Was that supposed to be for his benefit, or for mine? I no longer had a guide to ask. I took a deep breath and opted for the truth.

"Our agreement," I began, "was that I would pay monthly dues as a non-residential student, for weekly lectures and monthly interviews." I stopped, out of breath. He waited, not moving a muscle.

"Student lectures have all but stopped and I haven't had an interview in six months." I stopped again. He waited.

"Therefore, I took the initiative to revise my part of the agreement since you revised your part."

He loomed like an iceberg; I was the fragile craft.

"As my student," he said in a frigid voice, "you may not take such initiatives. The teaching is about learning to obey unquestioningly."

This was the man I had to learn to love - this fellow looking like a pompous bureaucrat in a fancy-dress costume? I couldn't stifle a burst of nervous laughter, and I covered my indiscretion with humor.

"Unquestioningly?" I tilted my head coyly and could see that he was momentarily thrown off guard. "Doesn't the tradition demand that we turn questions over and over? What if you were testing us to see who was paying attention?" His face remained rigid. "Then I would have flunked the test, right?"

I gave what I hoped was a winning smile. I think I even tittered. His ice-wall appeared to melt a bit around the edges, and then he grinned back at me like a kid.

"Well done," he admitted. I noticed that his knuckles were white. "The Retreat Hall costs money to rebuild, you know..." He looked scared underneath all that frost, as if he really did connect me and Tony with the accident. Well, let him think so.

"I understand," I murmured, deliberately dropping all guile. The man was literally afraid of me. I looked straight into his eyes and felt a stab of pain in my gut - not my pain, his. Tears sprang unbidden to my eyes. The burden of grief he carried was immense.

"Tell me," I asked softly, "how can we maintain compassion when we're frozen with fear?"

He seemed unready for the change in gears, and he clasped his hands together and closed his eyes. When he opened them again his expression was friendly.

"Hard, isn't it?" he whispered. We sat in cautious silence for awhile. Then he sighed. "When fear takes over, it's hard to stay connected to the truth."

"Yes it is," I agreed. The light softened as the night broke grayly into dawn. A stick of incense sent spirals of fragrant smoke upwards. A gong reverberated from downstairs; all again was still.

"And to each other," he added.

"And to each other," I repeated.

"It's easy to forget that we're all connected. Then when the fear comes on, we don't remember that we're not alone." He glanced towards the window.

"The loneliness is very hard to live with, for me," I said.

"Me too," he admitted after a long pause. Then, "Please don't let go of our connection."

"I won't," I promised. Our eyes met and held; by the time we broke our gaze, dawn had shifted into morning. He uncrossed his legs with a groan, rubbing at his ankles.

"Make yourself comfortable," he chuckled.

"Thank you," I said, not changing my position.

"You are one stubborn lady," he claimed, bowing to me in jest.

"Woman," I corrected him, bowing back.

For the next two hours we talked. It was probably the longest interview on record. We gabbed about everything from politics to the spiritual life. When I finally did uncross my legs, we spoke of the difficulties Westerners had with Eastern postures. I mimed a reclining Vishnu and he did a Ghandara Buddha. He posed as Maitreya, one knee up, and I did an eight-armed Shiva standing on one leg. We laughed uproariously at each other. Finally, I asked him to tell me how he always picked up my themes when he gave his lectures.

"You do know you're doing that, don't you?" I asked.

"Of course," he replied inscrutably.

"How...?" In place of an answer, he said,

"Please trust me."

"How can I?" I asked, exasperated.

"Please," he repeated. I thought hard for awhile.

"If you will trust me, I will trust you," I finally said. We looked at each other, at an impasse. "Let me make a request," I said thoughtfully.

"Go ahead."

"I will sit the next intensive with you, if you agree to sit the whole time with us." He looked surprised.

"Why?" he asked, defended again.

"Because I don't feel safe when your cushion is empty," I half-lied.

"You do feel safe when I'm there?" he asked, suspicious. He had not understood the request.

"Safer..." I said, a bit lamely.

Several times we ended with a mutual bow, but then picked up the conversation again, only to bow again, and again have something to say. At last we bowed, touched fingertips, and even giggled when I got up to leave the room.

Something has changed; perhaps it's possible for me to love the Teacher after all.

January 11, 1980

The Teacher gave his first student lecture for the new year, and the Hall was packed. He looked absolutely radiant.

"We have to learn how to practice warmheartedly in the utter darkness," he said in a tender tone, a whimsical smile on his lips. His eyes were shining, happy. I've never seen him look this way before, and I was touched.

He talked about being willing to trust each other, and being willing to trust the wisdom of the universe at large. He spoke poetically and, I think, sincerely. It was like a love poem to existence and he made us taste, with him, the deliciousness of the life we lived. He wove a kind of spell, bringing in music and color and earthiness, as if he could carry all of us on a magic carpet of his making.

The performance was a spellbinder, and I was won over. He got me. By the end of the lecture, I was madly in love.

Afterwards, he found me in the corridor and came over, beaming.

"Hi," he breathed, resting his hand on my shoulder. Its warmth went right through my blouse.

"Hi," was all I could say. We both must have looked like glowing coals. I still couldn't speak.

"Did you like it?"

"It was gorgeous," I replied, looking down. My heart pounded audibly and I felt like a smitten teenager. "Uh, thanks..." His hand was still on my shoulder.

"Good night," he whispered. We might have been the only two people in the building for all we were carrying on. I had to get out of there.

"Good night," I murmured, forcing myself as far as the outside steps. He followed.

"Well..." he said. I looked up at him and we both gazed, starstruck. Neither of us could move. "Can you come in for an interview tomorrow?"

"Yes...No...Can I call in the morning?"

"Not at the office." He scribbled a number on a slip of paper and thrust it into my hand. On shaking knees I stumbled down the steps to my car and tremblingly revved up the engine. He waited on the steps until I rounded the corner, waving, a delicious smile hovering on his face.

I don't know how I got through the night. I tossed and turned, feverish, my body not big enough to hold my heart. Kurt was solicitous as first, then suspicious and finally, angry.

"What's going on?" he hissed when I turned my back to him. I was too confused to even make up a good lie.

"I don't know," I hissed back.

This morning he watched me with quizzical eyes, hurt, and left for work complaining about the state of the kitchen. I just wanted him gone. The kids' normal morning flurry nearly drove me wild. But when everybody finally left, I stood by the phone for a half-hour before deciding not to make the call.

The only thing I'm good for today is washing the kitchen floor. At least Kurt won't have that to complain about.

January 13

Last night's dream:

I am the keeper of the shrine in the Meditation Hall. My job is to maintain its sanctity by tending the Holy Quilt which the Teacher wears when he enters.

I am standing by the door when he comes and I hand him the Quilt. He wraps it around his body, sinks to his knees and crawls across the Hall to the altar. At the altar, he bows. I hold my palms together to receive his bow next, but he never turns around, does not acknowledge my bow.

I awoke with a start, teeth clenched. How could I have trusted him even for a day? Thank God I didn't call him.

Watch out!

January 18

There is yet another decree to come down. He's reorganizing the community so that there will be an in-group and an out-group. I can hardly believe it. Only students selected personally by him can be in the inner circle and I am told I am one of the chosen.

Oh my prophetic dreams! Does he really think I'd agree to being part of an in-group in a monastery? That's about as inappropriate as holding a diet clinic in a chocolate factory!

"No thanks," I said to the secretary who called, offering her no explanation.

The charade goes on, and it's still not time for me to leave. Friendship has not yet transcended alienation and intimacy. I do not love him enough yet.

February 16

In the dressing room of the dance studio last week I noticed a poster announcing a dance group from Seattle that would be performing here, and last night Eva and I went to see them, deciding at the last minute instead of going to the movies. Someone must be taking care of me.

They are three men and three women, and they did the most inspired improvised dancing I've ever seen. They moved effortlessly, the way the human body ought to move.

"They dance like real people," was Eva's way of putting it. They were strong, agile, soft, supple. They had full range of movement and even better, a full range of expression. They danced for two hours solid and in the end were not even breathing hard.

"What are you doing?" I asked them backstage afterwards. "I've never seen such perfect timing and balance in dancers before. And you're so relaxed."

"That's the trick," they explained. "It's a special technique, and we happen to be teaching a six-week workshop in it this summer in Seattle. Want to come?"

"Yes!" I exclaimed, having no idea how I can manage a summer away. But I will do it, whatever it takes. I think I've finally found my thing.

April 14

Yesterday's public lecture was crammed, people standing ten deep to hear him speak. He's riding a crest of popularity now that's got to eventually end in disaster. He's like a surfer on a high wave, playing to the folks on the beach. But waves crash...

For awhile the lines of communication opened between us, but now they're closed tight. He offered me the role of consort, essentially (or member of harem is probably more like it) if I, in turn, would be one of his adoring devotees. Since I chose not to accept, I am banished like an enemy of the court. He wants me gone. I'm a thorn in his side. But it's still not quite time for me to go.

I wish to God I knew why. I just know that it's not quite yet time.

I wish I had someone to help me through this. Kurt can't understand why I keep hanging on when it's clearly not serving me at all. And he's right - I know he's right. But there's still something important for me to learn here, and I suspect it has to do with love.

May 22
Last night's dream:

I'm at a reception for the Prince of Persia, who is an unassuming man in slacks and a casual shirt. I take to him right away.

The Teacher arrives in his full regalia - silken robes, brocade slippers, beads - and has a fixed, bright red smile on his face. When he arrives, he looks around the room to find the guest of honor. He doesn't seem to be interested in anyone else.

The Prince notices the Teacher trying to find him, and stays unobtrusively in the far corner of the room. The Teacher feels for the Prince's vibration, looks this way and that. Then he cocks one ear against the wall and follows it, listening, his head scraping like porcelain against the plaster.

Everyone is watching. When the Teacher finds the Prince he's confused by his ordinary clothes. The Prince smiles up at him kindly. In frustration, the Teacher tears off his porcelain mask and throws it at the Prince. His real face is gray, depressed, morbid. He glares down with murderous envy and stalks out of the room.

I run after him, calling, but can't find him anywhere.

June 28

I am the mother of children old enough to fly across the ocean without me!

My prayers must have been heard because all three kids were accepted to go to Japan as summer exchange students for eight weeks. The dates coincide almost perfectly with the dance workshop in Seattle, so I'm going!

The group left last night, and all the kids were excited as wrens in a birdbath. Abram was nervous and kept remembering all the things he forgot to tell us: feed the fish; save my stamps; water my plants... Saul, the only student who had learned some Japanese before the trip was giving everyone elementary Japanese lessons and Eva, in her own serene way, stood a little apart from the others, looking elegant. When they marched with their backpacks away from us down the ramp, I broke down. My children! The scene of the three of them leaving at once, going on to their own adventures, got me right in the gut.

The plane lifted - just a thing of steel and rivets - and it trusted the air, holding my flesh and blood inside it. That disappearing dot in the sky had my children in it. And I had turned them over to it! I fell apart.

The other parents left, but Kurt and I stayed a long time, just staring at the tarmac and comforting each other. I never dreamed that the first parting would be so hard.

When we got home, I packed for Seattle and didn't look back.

July 8 - Seattle

I love it here! I love everything - the city, the people, the studio, the work. I'm staying with my old friend Joanna in her cottage on Bainbridge Island and ferrying across to the city every morning with her. By eight a.m. she is at her desk in the financial district, and I am on my way to the studio for a full day of dancing.

First I watch the merchants open up Pike's Place Market on the waterfront, chat with the merchants I'm getting to know, and eat some breakfast. Then I wander along the water to the studios and by nine I'm in my dancing clothes, my hair tied back and my bare feet ready to dance.

There are about thirty of us taking the workshop, both men and women. I am neither the oldest nor the least experienced. The six members of the company are our teachers. So far, I'm in love with everybody.

The technique is a remarkable combination of relaxation

and meditation, but the focus is movement rather than stillness. We visualize ourselves floating, flying, spinning. Lying still, we imagine ourselves weightless and then gradually bring ourselves into motion. It's a brilliant technique. The result is that when you start moving, you move without strain.

"Imagine yourself as seaweed in a tidepool," the teacher will suggest. "The waves wash in gently, moving you. The water is clear, warm, gentle..."

Before I know it, I'm lifted effortlessly out of the floor, and then sink softly back into it. And I never get tired. By the end of the class I'm skimming all over the place, my feet barely touching the ground.

Six hours of classes are not nearly enough for me at this point. I want to dance and dance! Each noon, I skip lunch and stay in the studio, dancing alone. I start to spin, leaning into the air. It cushions me. For an hour I whirl, never tiring, never getting dizzy. When the others return, they join me. Soon the studio is filled with spinning figures.

This is mine!

July 26
Saturday:
Joanna's gone sailing and I've opted for a solitary day of rambling along the shore.

Wading through the water, I examine barnacles on shells, watch a family of ducks waddle down the beach. Mama, followed by seven little balls of fluff, leans into the water and floats. The ducklings scramble and plop. The last one's made it in - Hurrah!

I relish the solitude. Stopping in the shade of an overturned boat, I stretch out. Gulls screech overhead; I toss them bread and they swoop down, greedy. The air is ruffled where their wings have been. Again, stillness.

My cup runneth over. I want nothing more. But even as I lie here, the drifting clouds lift to reveal the snow-capped peak of Mount Rainier. I am doubly, triply blessed.

- Dancing every day like this reminds me of the intensive meditations at the ashram, except that this is consistent pleasure rather than consistent pain. The end result, though, is similar: I am calm, alert, focussed, engaged. Instead of feeling stiff, however, I'm agile as a cat. I could spring into motion in an instant. If I chose to, I expect I could scramble up a vertical wall, or balance on one leg for a day.

Choreographic ideas spring up continuously. I envision solo pieces and large group productions. I'd like to work with screens and shadows, with live singers, with sacred themes.

A suite for four dancers on the theme of *Balance* is taking shape in my mind. Four parts- a solo, duet, trio and quartet will examine all aspects of balance - physical; partnership; emotional; balance of earth, air, fire and water. I'm working on the solo to perform this summer.

The performing class leaves me breathless. Dancing for other people is the most exhilarating thing I've ever done. I become sensuous, totally absorbed and happy. I dance full out, holding nothing back. My body gives me what I ask of it, and what I always ask is - *more!* If delicacy is what I want, then I ask for the subtlety of an indrawn breath; if speed is what I need, I demand flight.

My arms shape embraces and my feet stamp out intricate patterns on the floor. My torso is sinuous as a whip, and I can feel my face smiling the mysterious smile of every temple dancer in the world. With the life-juice of the gods flowing through me, I dance to the rhythms of the world.

I wish Kurt was here to see it. But on the other hand, there are advantages to his not being here...

There's a man in the class who is rather taken with me, and isn't shy about letting me know it. I like him, in fact. He's intelligent and we have good long talks after classes, and he's a pleasure to dance with.

"Damn it!" he complained about two weeks ago over a glass of wine after class. "I wore shorts today so you could see how good my legs were - but did you notice? No!"

I laughed and stroked his, indeed, rather good legs admiringly.

"I'm serious! " he snapped. "What do I have to do to get your attention?" I looked down at my wineglass and took a virginal sip.

"Let's have an affair," he proposed bluntly. I felt like an awkward fourteen year old. "God damn it," he fumed, "Don't you want to share an intense moment with me?"

"But I'm married," I protested, even as a corner of my mind curled up to admit the possibility of a fling in this sweet summer of my freedom.

"So what?" he urged, "haven't you ever...?"

"No."

"Then it's time you were liberated," he claimed.

"But..." I protested lamely, "that's not the kind of marriage we have." My voice must have been weak with ambiguity, because he leaned forward urgently.

"You're here, and he's not...," I couldn't look at him, "and I'm here and my woman's not..."

"You've got a woman?"

"Yes, of course," he said impatiently.

I shook my head slowly and he groaned, holding his forehead. Then he squinted at me appraisingly.

"I'll bet you're the good faculty wife and pour tea for the other ladies," he accused, "and you have a two- car garage, with a Porsche for him and a station wagon for you and the kids..."

"What if I do?" I laughed, imagining the cozy clutter of our funky, wood-frame house.

"...and you have a garbage disposal and a maid who comes once a week to clean..."

"You're absolutely correct," I teased. "Then what?"

"Then," he sighed, swooning theatrically, "Your armpits would still turn me on every time you got up to dance."

For two weeks he has given me every argument in the book on why I am an old fashioned prude if I do not take him to my bed. I've held my ground - not without an internal struggle, I might add - and now he avoids me as if we had never met.

It hurts. In essence he has said,

"No affair, no friendship."

This story is too familiar. I've been here before. Am I doomed to continue replaying this dilemma with people - men, mostly - in which I must follow their rules in order for them to want to know me? But what if their rules are harmful to me? What if I want to help make the rules in the first place?

"Hey!" I want to yell at him. "Let's get this thing straight! We're friends, not lovers - you're throwing out the baby with the bath water!"

But he won't let me get close enough to him to say a word - not even in the dressing room.

- Given a choice of company or solitude, I often choose solitude. Is liking to be alone a sign of weakness, or is it a simple preference?

- The sun is hot on my back. I sink into sand as air, sun and sea seep into me. I am shot through with the essences of the world.

My boundaries seem to fade. The world and I are one - we breathe together, pulse in tandem.

I mingle with the earth and disappear, like a sandcastle melting at high tide. With the wind my substance is held in suspension, and circulates. I dissolve, float and rejoin the elements.

It's as simple as Death.

- Idea for a dance:

Duet for dancer and air. The dancer begins alone, making moving designs with her body. Then her attention shifts to the negative spaces she is forming with her movements. The negative spaces become her partner.

It is a love duet with the air.

- I lie here in the sun like a slug, and dances rush pell-mell into my head. Does that make lying around a choreographic technique?

- Idea for a dance:

Group piece for five dancers and five drummers. One drummer/dancer pair enters at a time and establishes a rhythm.

When the stage is full, there are five different rhythmic patterns going at once, but they add up to a single, rhythmic whole. Like African polyrhythms.

The trick is that each pair maintains its own pattern throughout, but also blends perfectly with the others.

I like the metaphor: How can we maintain individual integrity, and still be comfortable in a group?

- Idea for a dance:

String of haiku for a solo dancer. A reader would recite a haiku poem, which the dancer would repeat in movement. Each piece would take a few seconds and capture the essential mood of the poem, like a brush-stroke painting.

August 15

I don't want to leave! I want to live this way forever, dancing six hours and taking two ferryboat rides a day!

Today was the last day. We all tried to pretend it wasn't, but the air was imminent with change. Nobody could concentrate.

We performed for each other for the last time. I did the solo from my *BALANCE SUITE*, and it knocked me out. The others too, I think.

The piece follows a spiral pattern on the ground, starting very slowly with small shifts of balance and getting faster, wilder and riskier as the spiral gets larger. I took chances I hadn't anticipated - handstands, a tilt towards an open window, balances from leaps. But I always felt in control.

In the middle of the piece I thought of the Teacher.

This is for both of us, I said to him silently. When my body came to rest at the end, I felt the internal motion continuing. Forever, I think.

We ended the day with a free-for-all dance. The studio stayed open til late at night and since emotions were high, nobody wanted to leave. We had our last dance with each other before taking off in separate directions. I didn't stop dancing for a minute.

At one point I felt a familiar back pressed against mine and when the music started, he lifted my arms along with his. For a long while, we danced back to back.

When the music shifted, we turned and faced each other, matching steps, rhythms. In these weeks, even of alienation, we've memorized each others' styles. Merging was easy now.

We danced with caring and regret. We pulled apart and came together; we moved in unison, listening closely to each other. It was the friendship we had started and the love affair we never had. More poignant, perhaps, than a real one might have been.

With the last chord, we were both spent. His smell was pungent. He didn't smile.

I did.

"Goodbye," he said, "you're a beautiful dancer." And then he turned on his heel and left the studio quickly.

August 20 - Home

In the week before the children get back, I've been looking around for classes as good as the ones in Seattle, but they don't seem to exist here. After one short summer, I'm a snob. My limbs are twitching to move and the image of a large, empty studio is like a mirage in the desert. If I don't dance soon, I'll go mad.

August 25

They're back. All talking at once, of course. For twenty-four hours Kurt and I have been their captive and willing audience and the house has again rung with noise and laughter and teenage energy.

They had a wonderful time, all three of them. They seem to have taken on the world and found it theirs. Is this the beginning of the end of my job of mothering?

At the moment they are asleep, surrounded by backpacks, gifts, dirty dishes and dirtier laundry. For twenty-four hours I haven't given a thought to my work, but right now I would give my right arm for an hour alone in a studio.

However, I'm going to clean up, talk to Kurt, make up beds and cook dinner.

September 2

Something's not right. I feel as if I've come back to familiar surroundings and a beloved family - but the wrong life. The fit feels tight. I wrench myself back into a wife and mother role in which my work is irrelevant. I have to adjust to the family's schedules, moods, needs and to expect interruptions. My concentration is shot full of holes.

With wet hands I jot down dance ideas on the backs of stray envelopes. I try out foot patterns while chopping onions; a son entering the kitchen gets a distracted stare.

This is famine after feast. I have gotten hooked on dancing every day - like eating every day - and now I'm starving!

October 7

I am still a poor wayfaring stranger, wandering from class to class, studio to studio to find the place where I belong. Will I, in the end, have to create my own? But I'm not ready yet!

Student and teacher at the same time - that's the trick. The teachers are not so easy to come by, it seems.

At the ashram, the Teacher is again raising the ante. He has bought a thirty-thousand dollar car on ashram funds and raised students' dues at the same time. They apparently have not protested.

Strangely, the whole thing makes me sad rather than angry. He's like a child begging to be stopped from hurting himself, and the community won't take the responsibility of stopping him. If he is bent on self-destruction and the rest of them want to follow him down that path, I finally see that there's not much I can do to help them.

All the more reason to get out. But now I see that he, in his own way, is as much a wayfaring stranger as I am. We're both not where we belong. I can't hate him for being lost, but although it's not easy to love him, that's still what I have to reach for. I wish, just once, I could say all of this honestly to him.

October 8
I have composed my farewell poem:

Leaving, I remain here.
Not meeting, we meet.
On the old plum tree - see -
The fruits continue to ripen
And fall.

When he falls - which is bound to happen sooner or later - I wonder if he'll remember my poem?

October 11
Last night's dream:
I am walking on the sand dunes on Fernandina. The sand is warm and smooth beneath my bare feet and the air is fragrant with brine. Salt bushes arc in the wind.
In the air, two seabirds fly. Another lone figure, coming from afar, walks along the coast. He is wearing the robes of a priest.
We approach each other slowly and upon a sandy rise, meet.
Face to face, we bow. Between us is a peace something like love.

Then I continue walking towards the sea and he continues walking towards the land.

An era has come to an end.

February 21, 1981

In a small shop in Chinatown today I found a green jade figurine of a horse.

"Do you have white jade horses as well?" I asked.

"One," said the shopwoman, "but it has a broken leg."

"May I see it?"

"No. It is broken."

"Please may I see it anyway?" I asked after awhile.

"It is lame," she insisted.

"But that's just what I want - a lame white horse!"

There was a great deal of discussion behind the counter, but finally she handed me the white horse. I held the white horse and the green horse in the palm of my hand, knowing that a circle had just been completed.

"Take it as a gift," the shoplady said with a shrug. "The white horse, after all, is lame."

The white horse and green horse have pointed the way, and the white horse, after all, is lame.

7

FINALE

Crown Chakra - Pineal Gland

Letting in the Light;
awakening to the Spirit;
the transcendent vision;
opening to the totality of all things.

Cobwebs cluttered the corners of the garage like shadow, drooping from mildewed walls and dust-coating the glass panes of the old garage doors. The little light making it through barely illuminated the stacks of trunks and boxes littering the room, the flotsam and jetsam of our family's first eighteen years.

Only my meditation corner was orderly - an oasis of clear space in a desert of debris. My plan was to spend the summer extending this order and with the help of Kurt, Saul, Eva and Abram, clear out the garage down to its bare walls and turn the room into a dancing studio. A room of my own.

Having my own space to work in had become a necessity to me. Ever since my stint in the psychiatric ward I had been thinking about the healing dimensions of dance. I wondered how shamans effected their cures, how trance states worked, what the effects of chanting and drumming were on a community during healing rituals.

Working alone and using my own body as a living laboratory I had discovered that with a simple, guided warm-up followed by movement with focus on specific parts of the body, I could repair wounds, dissolve bad moods and reverse on-coming colds in a matter of hours. Healing appeared to be even more implicit in the simple acts of singing and dancing than I had imagined during my time working at the hospital. There seemed to be a natural connection between health, wholeness and holiness, and I had discovered that all three states of mind and body could be reached simultaneously through the medium of movement.

Now all I needed was a place to systematically try out my ideas. Since Saul was away at College during the school year and Eva and Abram busy with their last years of High School, my time had been freed up considerably. I searched everywhere in town for studio space in which to conduct my research, but one evening as Kurt and I did the dishes, it struck me that the perfect studio, the place where I could work at any hour of the day or night, was right in my own backyard. The old garage!

Abram forced open the garage doors, which creaked protestingly on their rusted hinges, and he held them in place with a pair of heavy andirons gleaned from the junk inside. We all surveyed the scene with dismay, wondering if we were up to the task. Saul, home for the summer, along with Eva and Abram had agreed to help me but the job, exposed to the light, looked daunting. Kurt raised his eyebrows and Saul sneezed from the dust. For a moment I faltered - but only for a moment - and then I marched purposefully into the room, pulling Eva along with me.

"If not now, when?" I quoted dramatically, tugging at a steamer trunk which let loose a cloud of dust. "If not us, then who?"

I dismantled my bits-and-pieces altar, packing stones and shells and pictures into a shoebox while Kurt organized the yard and driveway into working areas.

"Everything we want to keep goes on the grass or the back porch," he directed. "The driveway is the Dump-pile." He marked one spot with a box of books, the other with a mouldy boot. "Trunks we'll pile against the fence - got it?" The kids saluted and disappeared into the garage.

Saul emerged first, a rickity highchair coming apart in his hands. Abram plopped two cartons of books beneath the fig tree and Eva came out with an armload of Halloween costumes which distracted all five of us for the next twenty minutes.

Like a home-movie our life passed before us as tricycles,

driftwood sculptures, old hand puppets and moth-eaten rugs were carted out one by one, and when Eva unearthed a box of family photographs we all crowded around and excitedly snatched at pictures from our past. There we were in the mountains, Saul with his third-grade class, Eva and Abram at a school carnival with painted faces, Kurt in academic robes. Eva held up a photo of me standing by the sea, very pregnant.

"Who were you expecting, Mom?" she asked. I studied the picture, trying to remember. After almost two decades, my three pregnancies merged in my memory. I handed the photo to Kurt.

"That's you, Eva, I think," he mused, sifting through the box for a snapshot to compare it with. "Maybe Abe, though." We were sidetracked by old pictures from New York, then wedding photos, then baby pictures as we dug deeper into the box.

We all waxed nostalgic, telling our family stories. Lying on the grass surrounded by dusty boxes, we reminisced and answered the childrens' questions. We laughed, we grew solemn, we interrupted each other. We got thirsty and made lemonade. We rummaged for more pictures. We did everything but clean out the garage.

"Hey, you guys!" I cried an hour later, jumping to my feet, "This won't do. Get back to work!" I pulled Saul to his feet, leading him back into the garage.

"Yeah, you guys!" we heard echoing from the driveway, "Get back to work!"

Paul and Angie Baker threaded their way through the growing clutter in the driveway and emerged into the garden.

"Garage sale?" Paul asked archly, spearing a loose tricycle wheel with his walking stick. He tried unsuccessfully to set it spinning, and Angie caught the wheel deftly before it ricochetted wildly into the garden. It was a quintessential Baker act: Paul, the maverick, dreaming up renegade schemes while Angie, serene and sensible, quietly maintained order around them. Like a handsome version of tweedledum and tweedledee they came into our garden wearing smiles, walking shoes and matching plaid shirts.

"Hi, you two," we greeted them, dumping a stack of National Geographics before offering them a dusty hug. Abram came forward in a Dracula mask, and they recoiled with satisfying horror.

"Look at this!" said Eva, holding up a snapshot of all of us at a long-ago beach party. Paul and Kurt, leaning against a driftwood log, are reading the Sunday paper while Angie and the kids are digging tunnels in the sand.

"We haven't changed a bit, have we?" teased Kurt, raking his fingers through the silvering hairs of his beard. Angie glanced a bit anxiously at Paul. Her face was composed in a smile however, and she held herself gracefully at his side, her arm linked lightly through his. Her sleek black hair still unstreaked by gray was tied tightly back, showing off her high Grecian cheekbones and flawless olive skin. Angie, at any age, was a classic beauty.

Of the four of us, Paul had perhaps changed the least in the eighteen years we had known him. His hair had thinned somewhat, and the madcap gleam in his blue eyes had softened into a wiser humor, but he still had the intensity and radical intelligence of the doctor who had delivered all my children, had protected me from my father and had first encouraged me, as friend and mentor, in the body-mind research I was continuing to this day.

He looked a bit more tired, perhaps; that was all. Not surprising for a man who still made house-calls at night after seeing patients in his office all day.

"We're not doing too badly, I'd say," he commented as the four of us took stock of each other. For just a moment Angie's expression sagged, but then she caught it, just like the wheel before it fell.

"We apologize for barging in on you like this," she declared, glancing over at Paul who leaned into his walking stick.

"Would you like some tea?" offered Kurt, hauling a picnic bench off the porch.

"Thanks," they murmured as Paul sank sighing onto the bench. Angie watched anxiously, joining him only after he was settled. The gesture was discreet but unmistakable. Kurt shot me a quick look before loping into the kitchen to prepare the tea, and the kids crowded around to greet the people who had been like godparents to them since the day of their births. Angie curved an arm around Eva's waist and gave her a hug.

"What're you guys up to?" Paul asked the boys, nodding towards the mess in the yard.

"Mom's making us," Abram teased, a naughty glance in my direction. Saul balanced a deflated volleyball on his toe and flung it upwards. Paul caught it neatly and then doubled over with an involuntary hiss of pain, clutching at his calf muscle. Eva jumped instinctively out of the way and Angie, in a flash, had dropped to her knees and was pressing her fingers to his calf. She leaned her forehead against his knee, concentrating. Eva's eyes were afraid, and the boys grew very quiet. Finally Paul nodded, his breath escaping in a huge puff, and he sat up slowly. Angie released her hands and regarded him apprehensively.

"Sorry," she murmured, trying to smile reassurance at the children. "He gets these sometimes..." Paul flicked his good-natured grin at them, but his eyes watered slightly and the children were understandably still apprehensive.

"These what?" I asked pointedly.

"These - uh - cramps," Angie replied, trying to shift attention to the tea that Kurt, with his tray of cups and cookies, was handing out.

"How does it feel now?" I asked after they had both sipped some tea. "Better?"

"Better," Paul agreed, but without enthusiasm.

"Not great though?"

"No, not great," he admitted.

"We've been walking around trying to shake it loose," Angie explained, "but it keeps going into spasm."

"Actually Marts," Paul said, "we came by to see if your hands had the magic touch today. Would you mind giving it a try?"

"We hate to do this when you're clearly so busy..." began Angie.

"Don't be silly," I retorted. "Kids! To work!" Paul grinned at Angie and then at me, and I knelt onto the ground in front of him, taking his leg into my hands. Gingerly, I felt the muscles around his calf, gradually drawing my palms over the cramp. He inhaled sharply. Cradling his foot, I pressed lightly on his Achilles tendon and worked my way, gently and slowly, back up to his calf. I could feel the muscles leap and again he drew in a sharp breath. I had never known Paul to be so sensitive to pain.

"Breathe deeply," I suggested, holding my hands softly over the cramp until, gradually, it began to ease. He hauled in a huge breath which hissed out as a sigh, as if he had come up for air from a dive in dark waters. The spasm, with a final twitch, released.

"Whew!" he exclaimed, immediately trying to shift the focus away from himself. "I still want to know exactly what you guys are up to here." The children, subdued, continued carrying loads from the garage. I kept my hand protectively on his leg.

"Are you meaning to say you don't recognize a dance studio when you see one?" chided Kurt, gesturing magnificently towards the chaos of boxes and dust-clouds emerging from the garage. Abram, perhaps not entirely by accident, tripped at that moment over a tangle of old shower curtains, effectively breaking the tension and we all burst into raucous laughter. Taking a bow, he retraced his steps and, for his captive audience, stumbled over the curtains again.

"Well done, m'boy," Kurt congratulated him.

"I want to see this 'dance studio'," Paul said, testing his foot against the ground before placing weight on it. Angie helped him to a stand and he shook out his leg, gave it weight and then stepped, with a deliberately sprightly tread, towards the garage. He and Angie peered in. The air swirled with raised dust; patches of grease-stained cement showed through the haphazard clutter of junk still littering the floor. The last thing it looked like was a dance studio.

"You're to imagine it empty, first of all," I informed them, "and full of light."

"Gotcha."

"How will you light it?" asked Angie.

"There'll be three skylights in the roof," I explained, "and the whole front will be sliding glass doors. And for the nighttime work, two muted overhead lights."

"You guys doing the work?" asked Paul, glancing significantly at Kurt. Kurt, with a grin, pointed at me and Paul raised his eyebrows. Angie raised her fist in salute and I joined her. "I didn't know you knew carpentry," he commented.

"I don't," I admitted, "but I'm learning. I've always wanted to build my own place - this is the perfect project and Kurt and the kids are helping and we've got friends..."

"I think it's great," he assured me, scraping his shoe against the rough cement. "How are you going to do the floor?"

"We're building a sub-floor with plywood and then putting oak parquets over it," I replied.

"She's determined," sighed Kurt, throwing an arm across my shoulders. The two men exchanged a look.

"Male chauvinists...," declared Angie. "If you need extra help, feel free to call on me. I used to help my father when I was a kid."

"Thanks. I will!" I said. Paul gazed thoughtfully into the room.

"How long do you think it'll take you?" he asked ruminatively.

"Probably the summer," I replied.

"And then you're going to use it to work on the dance and healing ideas you've been playing around with?"

"That's the idea."

"Want to try some of it out with me?" he suggested.

"Paul, I'd love it!" I cried.

"Well then," he drawled in a soft voice, "finish it as soon as you can, O.K.?"

Angie phoned the next day to say thank you and to chat about nothing in particular, and the following day the two of them dropped by again during their lunch break. They found me in the garage scrubbing at a stubborn spot of grease on the floor, and held up a bag of sandwiches they'd brought for all of us. Kurt and the boys had gone to the lumberyard and Eva, upstairs in her room, was practicing the viola for an upcoming concert.

"Make us some tea?" suggested Paul. I peeled off my rubber gloves, picked some ripe plums from the tree and put water up to boil.

Paul, from time to time, was in the habit of dropping by during a break in his schedule to rest in the garden or talk over some new idea, but Angie, who worked on the other side of town, rarely did. Without explanation, they spread their sandwiches out on the picnic table and sat down. Eva's etudes drifted down to us through her open window.

"What a tone!" Angie remarked. "She's a real little musician." Eva ended her finger exercises with a flourish, shut off her metronome and launched, rockily at first and then more smoothly into the first movement of the concerto she would be performing in the Fall.

"She's doing a solo with the Youth Orchestra in October," I informed them, pouring tea. Angie's fingers, I noticed, shook when she picked up her cup. "We'll have a big party afterwards, O.K.?" Paul turned his head and stared at the ground, his eyes glistening.

"They grow up so quickly..." he murmured. Paul and Angie, for reasons of their own, had not had children and loved our three dearly. Now, having grown up and becoming poised and gifted adults, Saul, Eva and Abram would soon be leaving. We listened as the music rolled out rich, heartfelt and strong until Eva came to the end of the movement. Paul gripped his knees, looked up and spoke fast.

"I may not make it to the concert."

His words shot out like so many sharp darts. He and Angie both regarded me fixedly, watching for my reaction.

"You're not - breaking up...?" I choked, my mouth suddenly dry. They shook their heads, not taking their eyes off me. "Moving?" I stuttered. Paul had sometimes spoken of going back to school to specialize and I often prayed that he wouldn't leave. They leaned almost imperceptibly towards each other before Paul said,

"My cancer has caught up with me." I was shocked breathless, and for a moment my head went blank.

"Your - *What?*" I finally uttered.

"My cancer," he repeated matter-of-factly. "I've not told you about it." Angie gazed down at the table and drew in a ragged breath.

"*No you haven't!*" I yelled hoarsely, wanting to hit him, to pummel him with both my fists. The music upstairs stopped and Eva leaned out the window at the noise. Seeing the Bakers, she waved cheerily, accepted their compliments on her playing, and went back to practicing.

"No you haven't!" I repeated, spitting it out in an angry whisper. Angie and I reached instinctively for each others' hands, woman comforting woman. My rage was her rage; this was betrayal. This was not possible. I wouldn't accept it. I jumped up, sat down, buried my head in my arms, looked up. Paul waited. "For how long?" I managed to mouth.

"Twenty two years...forgive us for keeping it a secret so long."

"Twenty two years!" I gasped.

"Not bad, huh?" he teased gently. "None of my patients knew - it had to be that way. You can understand, can't you? If we told even one, then the fact would be out." The silence between us, masked by the sounds of the viola, pounded.

"I even tended to forget about it," explained Angie, "as if it was something in our past..."

"I'm sorry..." murmured Paul. "We should have told you and Kurt the other day, but the kids were around and..."

"*You're* sorry? Oh my God, Paul! "

I grasped Angie from across the table and tugged awkwardly at her arms. Then I grabbed for Paul. Then I threw my hands up in the air. Tea went cold in the teapot; the sandwiches went uneaten. Eva's music filled the air like silence. "Tell me," I said at last, my eyes too scratchy to blink. Paul stared for a few moments at his hands. Angie gazed at him.

"You can give it to me straight," I said, not even sure I meant it.

"Thanks," he sighed, glancing at Angie before starting. "My spleen was removed when I was twenty- six . Still in Med school. The chemotherapy worked and I've been in remission ever since. End of story until this year..."

"You mean you went through medical school with cancer?" I breathed. "Paul, you continue to be the most amazing man I've ever met." He smiled, but sadly.

"They found a couple of hot spots a few months ago. I'd been feeling tired, you remember?" I nodded shortly. Angie's jaw was tight. "They're spreading like wildfire, I'm afraid..." He took Angie's hand. "It's in the bone marrow," he said softly. And in a bare whisper, "I'm riddled with it, sweetie."

No! No!

"If chemo worked once..." I tried, after a choking silence.

"Not worth it," he replied shortly. My mind clutched at straws: Mexican herbalists, Hopi shamans, Phillipine healers... Flailing, I blurted out,

"But you look so good!"

"Won't last. Sorry."

"I want him to try more chemotherapy too," Angie

informed me, "but he's adamant." I detected anger. Paul's eyes flickered with impatience.

"Listen," he said, "there's no time to waste. We want to ask you a special favor, which you must feel free to say No to..."

"The answer is Yes, for God's sake!" I declared rashly. "What is it?" We all laughed and all three, I think, started breathing again.

"Well, I meant what I said the other day about working together again. But I don't want to wait until the studio is finished - I want to start right away." He glanced over at Angie, whose head was down. "Maybe you can help both of us through this."

"Of course," I breathed.

"I don't want to beat around the bush... you realize that we'll be working specifically with the dying process..." Angie jerked to her feet and fitfully paced the porch, arms across her chest. He glanced up for only a moment. "Think about it before you agree to it. Talk it over with Kurt..."

"The answer is yes. Of course," I insisted, suddenly very scared. He watched my reaction intently.

"It's an unprecedented opportunity for both of us," he said softly. "You can experiment with me and I can pass on to you a lot of what I've been working with over the years and," he added, "see if I was on the right track. From the inside."

I nodded, numb.

"Not quite what I had in mind..." I told him. He smiled.

"Not what I had in mind, either. Life rarely is. But neither of us will likely get such a chance again, my friend. You get to watch a step by step process that every one of us goes through, and I," he quipped, assuming his familiar, jocular tone, "get free massages for the rest of my life!"

Our agreement was to start in three days, to have our sessions in the late afternoons when Paul's office hours were over, and to meet mostly in Paul's study at home. Our time would be divided between pedagogy, for which I would keep a notebook, and practice, for which I would use only my hands and my intuition.

"It's a project in learning how to listen," Paul had said. "This is a chance to push awareness - mine as well as yours - to its limit." He rubbed his palms together as if we were launching into the most exciting adventure in the world. Angie, thinking her own thoughts, had simply hugged her crossed arms tighter to her chest. My response was a silent prayer.

Meanwhile, Kurt and I scrubbed away at the garage as if, by our very effort, we might cure Paul of cancer. Saul and I patched cracks in the cinderblock walls while Kurt and Abram dragged off loads to the dump. The odor of mildew was replaced by Lysol, and with repeated scrapings the grease in the cement floor was reduced to bleached blotches. By the day of my first session with Paul not a cobweb was left in even the farthest corner, and the garage, stripped down to bare clean walls, was ready for the framing of the sub-floor.

Angie met me at the door, the dog scampering excitedly around us as I entered the house. We gave each other a hard hug.

"He's up in his study," she whispered, tugging at the dog's collar and closing the door behind us. Her eyes scanned my face worriedly, as if I could give her answers to questions she couldn't even ask. I gave her another hug.

"Why is this happening?" she moaned, choking over a held-in sob. We rocked back and forth, the dog muzzling his way in between us.

"I don't know," I choked back. "I don't know why it's happening to him, and I don't know why it's happening to you."

"I can't stand it!" she spit out.

"I can't either," I agreed sadly.

"I know I shouldn't, but I feel you might be able to help him."

" There are always miracles," I said, "but no guarantees. I think he's going to help me more than I'll help him."

"Please do what you can...," she whispered urgently, not letting go of my sleeve.

"I'm bushed," Paul admitted when he led me into his study. Clearing a stack of books from the day-bed, he stretched out flat, tucking a floppy pillow beneath his head.

"Are you in pain?" I asked, seating myself on a cassock at his side. He shook his head and reached for my hand.

"Let's start right in," he said, placing my hand onto his chest. "This is the first session in 'Rapport'." Opening his eyes, he grinned.

"Rapport," I repeated, pretending to write it down in an imaginary notebook. "Lesson One."

"The lesson for today is in learning how to listen for pain in another person's body. Ready?"

"Ready." In fact, I wasn't ready at all. But behind Paul's light humor was a determination of purpose that would not be ignored. "Yes, I'm ready," I repeated.

"Start by getting calm," he said. "While I drift off, you concentrate on becoming very quiet. O.K.?"

"O.K."

"Then listen for what your hands want to do - and do it. Any questions?"

"I'll wait until later for questions," I replied nervously, closing my eyes and sinking, with a pounding heart, into as quiet a state as I could find.

It took some time for my mind to stop its nervous drifting, but when it did my hands, as if of their own volition moved, one to the back of his neck and the other to his abdomen. I felt our pulses beat in tandem. My fingers tingled, and I followed the urge to press lightly into the cords of his neck. In his sleep, he sighed.

Warm rushes seemed to course through me, making my eyelids flicker uncontrollably, and I took in deeper breaths, blowing out what felt like excess air. Paul twitched in his sleep. An itch on my foot distracted me until I wondered if it was his foot alerting me, and I moved my hands from his torso to the soles of his feet. Gently, I massaged his toes and felt the itch creep into my heel. My hands went to his heels and I held them cupped in my palms until my attention was drawn again to his neck. As I changed positions, his eyes fluttered open.

"Tell me," he murmured. "Describe what's happening." At first, I couldn't speak. I closed my eyes again, listening to the feelings in my body.

"I'm feeling like I need more room to breathe - as if my neck needs to be longer." I focussed on the elusive, hard to describe sensations. "My hands want to reach out and pull on your neck."

"Do it," he directed. I felt a yawn coming on, and I stifled it.

"Go ahead and yawn," he advised me through his own yawn. Together we yawned until our jaws cracked, and we laughed. He let his yawning release into bizarre noises, like some kind of wild singing.

The dog, roused by the racket, trotted into the study and leapt into the fray, drooling on both of us with his long wet tongue. Which caused both of us to let loose into real laughter as we fought off his slobbering muzzle. Which brought tears to my eyes, and finally loud, racking sobs. Paul's arm circled my head as I wept into his shoulder.

"Yes...yes," he whispered. "Cry it out."

"I can't...stand it!" I hiccoughed, reaching for a tissue and blowing my nose. "I don't want this to be happening!"

"Me neither," he muttered. "Angie neither. But there it is. Go ahead, cry all you need to..."

He held me like a child, comforting me. He was the strong one; I felt his warmth, his beating heart, heard his voice. His vital, caring presence was right where it had always been. Paul Baker, our doctor, was still here. I clung to him hard as if, by not letting go, I could keep him right where he always had been. I snuggled up closer, practically lying beside him on the bed.

"Do you realize," he observed quietly after my sobs had subsided into wet sniffles, "that if I weren't practically a dead man this would be a compromising position?"

I sat up quickly, shocked. He grinned his old boyish grin, his eyes steadily informing me that the mood had been deliberately broken with humor. My fingers itched, as if with a flash of important information. I picked up his cue and grinned back at him. He pulled a handkerchief out of his pocket and blew his nose loud, handing it over to me to do the same. I honked. We laughed conspiratorially and he sat up and faced me.

"We did a lot of work today," he said quietly after a long while of companionable silence. I nodded. He took both of my hands in his and massaged them gently." Let's give it a day or so to sink in, alright?"

For the next three days, measuring two-by-fours, nailing them to the frame and center beam, testing joists with the level, removing nails and starting over again, I gradually came to accept the necessity for humor. Paul's lightheartedness, I now understood, had been hard-earned. Even while facing the reality of his own death it had been he who, more than any other doctor in the hospital, had soothed harassed nurses and reassured frightened patients with his zany antics. In the context of living with a terminal illness, the details of everyday existence had taken on a different perspective for him than they had for most people. It was from this vantage point that Paul practiced medicine, researched the connections between mind and body, and had been trying to teach me something of what he knew. There was even more to learn from him than I had imagined.

Getting the frame for the sub-floor in place took the efforts of everyone in the family, and making it level all over was a job that took days of painstaking effort. When at last the frame was level, we put down the plywood sub-floor in an orgy of nailing that lasted three days. When the last nail had been hammered in, Eva and I tested our sprung-wood floor with leaps across the diagonal.

"It's three- and- a -half leaps long!" she cried, jumping breathlessly from the garage out into the garden. The boys tested it gingerly, first on one foot and then on both, like on a trampoline. The floor was satisfyingly tight. We showed it off to Kurt, who hammered in a few more nails and we stood back, admiring our handiwork. Although the walls were still raw cinderblock, and skylights still had to be cut out of the roof, and the sliding glass doors had to be installed in the front, still, with the sub-floor laid in and solid, the place was no longer just a garage. It was already a *studio*.

"My studio," I announced proudly to Paul when I saw him the following afternoon, "is three- and- a- half leaps long."

"Three hundred for a grasshopper, I betcha," he quipped back.

"And three thousand for a flea," I retorted.

"Three million for a neutrino! Ha!"

"I'll let you have the last word," I allowed. He held me with his eyes.

"Is that a promise?" he asked softly.

"Yes," I replied after a pause. "As long as you teach me what you know."

"We will begin, no?" He sat in his swivel chair, his legs propped up on his desk and motioned me to the day-bed. The dog lay sprawled at his feet and the windows opened onto the dappled green of the backyard eucalyptus trees. Angie was still at work and the house, except for a grandfather's clock ticking in the hallway, was quiet. For the next hour he answered my questions about cancer cells, describing what was happening in his body and giving a probable prognosis of the progress of the disease. My mental calculations gave him less time than to the end of the summer, and I quickly clamped shut that line of thought.

"You see," he declared as if sensing my sudden cold fear, "we are really talking about a transition, not an ending." For you, I said silently. Not for me.

"The stuff we've been playing around with all these years has to do with the non-material aspects of this body," he pinched a bit of flesh on his arm, "and how we are all connected by an invisible web that has consciousness and can be contacted by our thoughts and feelings."

"Do you think," I asked, " you would have stumbled onto this sort of knowledge if you hadn't gotten cancer when you did?"

"I doubt it," he replied thoughtfully. "It's the sort of notion that crops up when people are older and facing death, and even then our conditioning is so strong that many people can't admit to actually seeing things that aren't supposed to exist. I guess I was young enough," he conjectured, "to still have an open mind."

"So it has influenced your thinking for a long time..." I mused.

"Obsessed it, is more to the point," he admitted. "I'm convinced that the medicine of the future has to include a larger frame of reference than just the physical body. It's got to! That's why it's so important to me that I pass on as much as I can." Swinging his legs down from the desk, he stood up and we changed places, he onto the bed and me to the little stool by his side. He stretched out, got comfortable and closed his eyes.

"We'll work with subtle awareness today. Start as you did the last time, listen closely to every little intuition that comes up, and remember as much as you can so you can report it to me. First anchor yourself to the earth..." Mentally, I sent down roots, like those of the tree outside the window and imagined them grasping the soil mantle firmly, "...and open up to the Light."

I imagined branches covered with leaves and flowers reaching towards sunlight. I breathed deeply and felt myself grow calm. "Good," he murmured. My hands lifted, hovered for a moment above his chest and went to the area of his ribcage and diaphragm. Between his breaths was a pulsing pause. Finding his rhythm, I breathed with him.

"What do your hands feel?" he asked. At his question, the skin on my fingers came alive, sparking with prickles of sensation.

"Your head?" With his words, my scalp tingled and I felt a rush of heat. "Your feet?" They seemed to swell in my shoes. "Your heart?" A flood of love for Paul made me catch my breath. He smiled. "Come back to your hands - what do you feel? Tell me."

"I can barely feel the difference between my body and yours. It's like our skins melted..." I uttered after awhile.

"Stay with that sensation, right at the place where your hands touch me. Concentrate."

Focussing, I kept my attention at the smooth place where my warmth mingled with his. A quiet vibration, like a cushion of air, moved subtly between us. A coolness that melted boundaries. Simple but complex. Comforting. A presence...

"Yes?" he coaxed after a period of time.

"There's a meeting place, where it's neither you nor me, but both of us." I began. "But it's not really us, it's something, uh, more... I don't know how to say it."

"Where do you feel it?"

The sensation, more an emotion than a physical sensation, spread like a radiant heat through my chest. Suddenly recognizing what I was feeling, I bent over and slid my arms around Paul in an embrace.

"Paul, I love you," I whispered, burying my head in his chest. The dog's tail thumped gently against the carpet and he sneezed.

"That's it, my friend," he said softly, hugging me back. "Love. Irresistible. Delicious. No fear, right? And I love you, Marta.

This is what I call the Holy Spirit. Now everything else will be easy."

During the following week we met every day. When Angie was home, she brought up tea at the end of our sessions and we all chatted amiably, speaking little of the work we were doing. In a sense, she didn't seem keen to know; it rang to her of mysticism and hocus-pocus and left her, as well as the technology of Western medicine, out in the cold. It was Paul's purview, not hers. But when I left him sleeping and tiptoed downstairs to greet her in the kitchen, she would prod me in whispers for hints on what was happening and if, in fact, anybody had ever been healed by it.

"If I'm getting so good at this," I challenged Paul one day as he came up out of sleep, my hands on his abdomen sensing a dark knot at the base of his spine, "why couldn't I reverse your condition?" The knot felt deep in the bone. If I focussed on unravelling it and visualized healthy bone and tissue, couldn't I heal him? He closed his eyes again, a pained expression clouding his face.

"I wish the answer was Yes," he confessed after a sigh. "I don't know - but realistically, I think not."

"But can I try?" My mind bashed up against invisible walls.

"Try? Try what - to cure me?" He laughed sadly. "You can't. Nobody cures anybody else. All a healer can do is encourage a person's own healing to take place. That's all..."

"But it's a lot!" I exclaimed hotly, my mind still probing the dark place in his abdomen.

"It is," he agreed, "but in my case, I've already had over twenty years respite. I'm long overdue...I don't really understand why." He said this acceptingly, with a bit of a shrug.

"I'm sorry," I declared stubbornly, "I don't accept that."

"It's taken me fifteen years to be able to say that," he informed me quietly, "but now I can say it - and mean it. Listen," he said urgently, turning and grasping my hands with icy fingers, "this is a big burden to put onto a friend, but I've got to be able to talk openly about what's happening." He took in a shaky breath. "I'm dying and I want to die well, can you understand that?"

"Yes," I breathed.

"And I need to do it consciously, and I want very much to pass on the knowledge that I learn from it."

"I understand."

"This is not something it's fair to put on a wife - and furthermore, Angie's still furious with me for refusing more chemotherapy. Even though both she and I know it wouldn't help."

"This is too awful for Angie...," I murmured. He let go of my hands and let his fall to his sides. His intensity had exhausted him.

"Things aren't so hot at the moment," he confessed after awhile, grimacing wryly. "She's so pissed at me she's scheming with specialists behind my back. Jesus! I called her on it a few days ago, and now she..." His brow furrowed with pain, "...she won't touch me."

"Oh!" I exclaimed, suddenly aware of my position as the 'other woman'. "This is awful, Paul. The two of you have got to go through this together. Would it be better if I weren't around here so much?"

"Maybe. Maybe not. I think she's actually relieved to share some of the responsibility with you. You guys are our family, you know." He reached for my hand and squeezed it. "Sure, she feels a bit left out of what goes on up here, but in a rather substantial way, you realize you're taking me off her hands."

"Paul, that's a stinky way of putting it!"

"Stinky," he mused with a half grin. "This whole business doesn't exactly smell like a rose, but here we are - and what are we going to do about it?"

"The best we can, I suppose," I replied sadly.

"But our best," he teased rakishly, "is damn hot stuff, no?"

Paul slept again. My assignment was to hold my mind

steady, observe when his body entered the dreaming state, try to intuit the images of his dream, and wake him when the dream was over. A tall order.

I held my hands lightly over his torso, letting my eyes close as I felt for a calm internal balance. Grounding my lower body to the earth, I opened my upper body to light, like sediment sinking to the bottom of the sea, leaving clear, sunlit water above.

We settled, Paul and I, our breaths matching easily and a reciprocal flow of energy cycling between us. We shared a space of air. Love was implicit. He and I were known to each other - as all of us must be, I suddenly realized. But by knowing it to be so, we could feel the joy. My chest swelled with gladness. I listened for his dream.

Soft whiteness in motion, like clouds. A cloud stew, bubbling, pouring without heat through space. An aperture, like the lens of a camera, swirling larger, then smaller. It draws me forward, tunnel-like, a cloudy spiral with a tug towards clear light. Cushioned on clouds...

I felt Paul's state change, and with difficulty I opened my eyes. His breathing was rapid, and then snuffled into a few deep sighs. Gently, I tapped him awake.

"Huh?" he started, and then blinked. He closed his eyes briefly, remembering. "O.K.," he said, "what'd you see?"

"Cloudy stuff, like a walkway where people gather, but it's fluffy and insubstantial. It feels soft, and it leads to some kind of opening..." He nodded.

"Here's what I remember," he said. "There's a cloud-like tunnel, and I'm following someone - an old guy with a beard."

"What are the clouds like?" I asked, excited.

"Sort of bubbly - like boiling water, only clouds."

"That's right!"

"And I follow this old guy until he suddenly dives into the clouds and starts swimming. But he's swimming with his butt in the air. I call after him that that's not the way to do it. But he keeps on swimming. I've got no choice but to follow him."

He closed his eyes, looking back into his dream. A tear escaped through one closed eyelid.

"So I dive in after him," he whispered slowly. "I dive...right into the ocean of God."

We had no session the next day. While Paul and Angie took the afternoon off to birdwatch in the hills, Eva and I worked on the studio. With buckets of whitewash we primed and painted the cinderblock walls, sloshing on coat after coat with roller brushes. At the end of the day both of us were as whitewashed as the walls, our arms stiff with paint and our hair speckled with dots. It was foolish, I realized, to whitewash the walls before cutting out the skylights, but we did it anyhow. I couldn't wait any longer to see the place bright.

Sawing through the roof took everyones' efforts and two full days of sawblade noise, flying pebbles and tar dust. Kurt manned the power saw, and the rest of us steadied the incised sections, pulling shattered fragments of old roof out of the blade's path and tossing them over the side.

The volume of debris was staggering. By the end of the first day, Saul and Eva were wheezing and went to bed early. I ran to the drugstore for gauze masks and Kurt, Abram and I carried on, finally opening up three long rectangles in the roof to the sky. By dusk of the second day, after the roof had been swept clear of tar and grit and the floor inside cleaned of scraps and fallen dirt, we all stood inside and gazed up at our hard work. A rich, blue twilight entered the room, letting the world in for the first time. The space was transformed.

The kids cheered. Kurt and I held hands, exhausted. As we stood there, a seagull flying overhead was framed by the first, then the second, then the third skylight opening.

"Did you see that?" I exclaimed.

"A good omen," Kurt declared, sweeping me up in a great bear hug.

"Every muscle in the body attaches to the diaphragm directly or indirectly," Paul informed me at our next session. "That means that any problem in the body eventually shows up in a person's breathing, since the diaphragm is the breathing muscle."

My eyes were immediately attracted to his middle. For several moments I watched his breathing, which appeared to be relatively shallow today. He looked wan, tired. I wondered if today's lesson was expressly chosen to illustrate how low energy manifested in a sick person's body.

"So focus on my breathing," he said as he lay down on the day-bed, letting his eyes close immediately, "and see what you can pick up about where the areas of congestion are." His voice faded out as he fell into a deep sleep.

Looking down the length of his body, I could see how gaunt he had become. The bones of his ribcage quivered against the cotton of his shirt and his thighbones showed through his slacks with no flesh surrounding them. Observing the rise and fall of his breaths, I rested my hands on his chest, feeling the delicate bones expand and contract. His nostrils flared with each inhalation, transparent; his eyebrows, blondish and downy, made him look as vulnerable as a child.

My tears fell, unheeded. I let them fall, not bothering to objectively observe the quality of his exhalations, the congestions in his body. This was Paul and I was losing him! I didn't care that he had accepted his own death - I couldn't! I didn't have his perspective and I didn't have his courage, damn it! And right now, I didn't care if he knew it.

He stirred in his sleep, opening his eyes tentatively and closing them again. Twisting his head to the wall, his eyes again opened and he stared ahead of him, unblinking. After awhile, he spoke.

"I guess cancer cells aren't too courageous," he said. With a sigh he shifted his face towards me. "I'm sorry I'm putting you through all this..."

"Please don't say that," I begged.

"Please let me say what's true," he admonished. "How we act on it is another matter."

"It's true I'm terrified," I confessed.

"Yes..."

"But you can count on me, no matter what."

"Thanks," he smiled, flopping one hand weakly against my knee. "Let me tell you what happened yesterday. I was having a bad day. I didn't go in to work, and Angie stayed home to 'babysit' me..." He chortled wryly, shaking his head. "Giving me the cold shoulder all day long. It wasn't a good scene..."

"I wish I had known."

"Wouldn't have helped," he said. "Anyhow, I decided to pull myself together and bake a few loaves of bread."

"You're incorrigible, Paul."

"Angie and I used to bake together once a week, in the old days," he said wistfully. "I guess I wanted to bring that time back. Anyhow, she wasn't interested, so I did it myself."

"She's hurting so much..."

"I know she is!" he snapped. "I'm not blaming her - but if the only thing that'll make her happy is more radiation, then there's no way I can compromise! I won't do it, and that's final!" He panted with the effort of speaking. This time I really did watch his breathing.

"Anyhow," he whispered when his breath had settled down, "I mixed up the dough and dumped it out onto the board to knead it. There wasn't much strength in my hands, so it took forever to get it springy. I must have been kneading that dough for over an hour. It got so it felt like living flesh under my fingers. I couldn't get enough of it..."

He shut his eyes, breathing hard. His fingers felt for the air and his jaw clenched with longing. I reached for one hand and bent over to kiss his palm. His fingers closed around my cheek, caressing.

"Finally, I shaped the dough and put it into the oven to rise. Angie was upstairs; the dog was out back - and..." He studied my face seriously for a moment, and then suddenly laughed, "...and I knelt down in front of it." His eyes were wide with wonder. "I actually was kneeling in front of the oven."

"This is my body..." I recited softly.

"Take it and eat..." he whispered. We sat in silence, my cheek still in his hand.

"Paul, what about miracles...?"

"The whole show is a miracle, my dear."

"I mean, individual miracles..."

"Like bringing me back from the brink of death?" he asked. I answered only by taking in a deep breath.

"Who knows?" he murmured. "I honestly don't know anything anymore. Fear shadows everything and obstructs my vision despite myself. Unreasonable hope follows me around like a puppy - Angie came close to convincing me to see another oncologist last week. That's how confused I'm becoming."

"No wonder she's so out of sorts."

"Outraged is more like it, Marta." His voice caught and he turned his face into the pillow. "Marta, she's sleeping downstairs now..."

His whispered confession burned like the unexpected sting of a snakebite. I cradled his head in my arms while he shook with sobs. "Believe me," he choked out, "if I thought I had a chance at remission again, I'd go for it. I'd try anything! But it's not in the cards, that's all. Everything in me is preparing for passage - to go against that would be idiocy. Can you, at least, accept that?"

"I can keep trying to," I replied, "but I'm not your wife, Paul."

"Yeah," he allowed after awhile, staring at the ceiling. "I hear you. But all I want is for her to recognize that even *this* is a miracle."

The skylight frames had to be measured precisely because if the boards didn't fit perfectly, the roof would leak. Kurt and I worked together measuring, marking, cutting. I balanced on the top rung of the ladder, holding each board above my head while he, kneeling on the roof, hammered into the skylight opening. My arms, after twenty minutes, ached; so did my heart. I made silent bargains with the universe: if we finish the studio in time, Paul will live; if the skylights are in place by Monday, Paul will have an unexpected remission. Kurt may not have known it, but we were hammering in a race.

As we worked, we discussed nail-sizes and board feet. We mumbled about what to make for lunch; whether Abram could take off to go swimming. We never mentioned Paul, but he was there with every nail we hammered in, every lined-up corner.

By late afternoon the job was done and Kurt and I went our separate ways, he to his office to do some work and me into a hot bath for a soak. Every muscle in my upper body was stiff from holding heavy boards above my head and my mood in general, was grim.

I was about to step into the steaming water when the phone rang; it was Angie.

"Paul hasn't gotten out of bed today," she informed me, not attempting to conceal the edge of anger in her voice. "He's sleeping. You don't have to come if you don't want to."

"You don't sound so good..." I responded, lowering one leg into the hot water.

"You can bet I ain't so good!" she retorted, her words snapping across the wires like firecrackers. "I don't like this one bit, and I don't know how the two of you can be so damned mystical when what he needs is medical attention, and I'm so furious I could spit and God damn it, this is driving me crazy!" She broke down into sobs. There went my bath. I pulled my leg reluctantly out of the water.

"Want to come over?" I suggested.

"I can't leave the damn house!" she shouted into the phone.

"Want me to come to you?"

"Yes..ss," she wailed, letting the receiver fall with a clatter before she hung it up.

The teapot shrieked on their stove while Angie and I, hugging by the sink, ignored it. The dog shoved his muzzle between us and we let him in.

"Oh, shut up!" she yelled at the teapot, leaning over to shut off the stove. Flinging first one cup and then another onto the table, she stomped from one end of the kitchen to the other, fetching napkins, sugar, teaspoons. If she could have thrown plates against the wall, she would have.

"*God Damn!!*" she cried finally, "*I can't stand this!*"

"I can't either," I admitted ruefully.

"But you - *both* of you, God damn it,- wander around with these calm smiles as if everything were just hunky-dory. *And it's not!!* Everything is awful. All this spiritual crap is a swift pain in the you-know-where! I don't want to hear about it anymore! He keeps getting sicker and sicker, won't go to the hospital, and keeps smiling like some imbecilic angel - God, I could brain him! And you don't make it easier, Marta. You're playing right into his hands!"

"I know how you feel," I admitted after awhile. "Except I don't think he's making a mistake..."

"Not one thing you guys have done has made him any better, and you know it!" she spit out between clenched teeth. "You know what I think? I'll tell you what I think - I think he wants to die!"

Her face crumpled with misery, and she bent over the kitchen table, racked with sobs. I put my arms around her and the dog again pressed his body against her chair. When her tears had quieted down, I said,

"Maybe he's just had a long time to get used to the idea."

"Too long," she sniffled wearily.

"And I think he's made some kind of peace with it."

"Built his life on it," she corrected me bitterly. "You'd think he could have just let it go once it was clear he was in remission. I've thought of it as something from our past - for at least sixteen years. But not him - it's as if he was in love with it." She broke down again into tears.

"This must be horrible for you...it's not fair, is it?"

"No!" She softened after a moment and said, "But it's even worse for him. He's had to live with it in his own body all these years. Cancer with a capital 'C' was always with us, lurking around in every corner. I would keep things smooth and pleasant, but I knew he was always in some kind of race against time. Every single minute counted. He was always *on*."

"There are worse ways to live," I commented. "He's had a full life, done a million things, made a big difference to an awful lot of people...everyone loves Paul, you know that..."

"Everyone loves Paul...," she repeated mockingly. "Sure everyone loves Paul. And who kept Paul together? Who had to keep the secret? Who got to worry at night? Angie, that's who! He wouldn't even let me tell you guys all these years!"

"Why, I wonder?"

"Why, indeed. I think he liked having a tragic secret - it added pizzaz to his life. Not to mine, though..."

I put my arms around her and held her a long time. She didn't cry. At last, with a shuddering sigh, she disengaged herself and gazed at me sadly. "I'm sorry for all the histrionics," she said.

"Nothing to apologize for, believe me."

"I don't want you to hate him, Marta."

"Hate Paul? I couldn't hate Paul if I tried. I love him with all my heart."

"I do too," she murmured, her head down.

"But I love you too. I wish there was something I could do to help."

"You can," she replied. "Tell me something I can do that

will make us not so angry with each other."

"Bathe him," I said with sudden inspiration, not looking up. For a moment she stared at me and then, lowering her head, she nodded.

Saul and I worked on the torn-up roof around the skylights, spreading layers of waterproofing, letting them dry, and covering the whole with flashing. The skylight windows arrived by truck in the early evening, and most of the neighborhood was out to watch us carry them off the truck and hoist them up onto the roof.

The next day Saul, Abram and I nailed them in place and then I scrambled down the ladder to see how they looked from inside. The mid-day light was warm, muted and towards evening, softly bluish.

I came down again in my nightgown at the first light of dawn, dew and sawdust sticking to my bare feet. The light was gentle, cool. I stood inside the half-finished studio looking up, and smiled.

Little by little, my studio was taking shape.

Paul's condition, meanwhile, deteriorated slowly. He lost more weight and his face, shrunken, bony and gray, was taken over by piercing blue eyes. Like beacons, they stared as if illuminating what they saw, watching hugely, saying little.

I found him one afternoon half asleep in the living room, stock still in his armchair. Angie was out, the dog was sprawled on the floor by his side and a late Beethoven String Quartet played on the stereo. A shaft of sunlight coming through a window above the mantle lit Paul's shrinking figure and pooled into the colors of the Oriental carpet on which the dog lay. Neither Paul nor the dog made a move until the last chords of the Quartet died away. Then the dog pumped his tail lazily and Paul said feebly,

"I'm cramming." His grin was like a familiar landmark on his strangely skeletal body.

"Cramming?"

"Memorizing all my favorite music. At least if there's no music there, I can hum my own."

"Haven't you ever heard of the music of the spheres?" I countered, fondling the dog between his ears.

"Oh, I forgot about that," he admitted. "But do they have Beethoven? Do they have Schubert?"

"Where do you think those guys are anyway?" I shot back, grateful for every last bit of silliness we could have.

Our sessions were quieter now. Paul slept and I concentrated. Occasionally he would interject a directive - often only a word or two - and later I would tell him what I had experienced. When I was on the right track, he just nodded. When I was lost, he corrected me, often with a lesson given in halting shorthand.

"Transitions," he murmured. "No boundaries - don't get stuck."

I closed my eyes, one hand on his bony brow, the other on his stomach. Immediately I got an image of flesh, a carcass on a beach being devoured by maggots. Repulsed, I began to pull my hands away but Paul muttered for me to stay with it.

The maggots bored into the muscle, into the bone, waxing fat. Fat, fat until they burst into flies which buzzed about the carcass eating, pushing, mating, laying eggs. Which lay embedded in moldering flesh until the pupae hatched maggots. Which bored into muscle growing fat, fat...

"Where is the bug?" he whispered at length. "Only movement. Change. All at same time, no?"

"Are you saying that everything is in motion, nothing stays as it is?" He nodded, a small smile on his lips. "It's like a continuous dance, right?"

"Yah... *Shiva*..."

"*Shiva's* dance?" He nodded.

"Everything moves at the same time and the whole thing looks like its staying the same?" I asked. He nodded.

"No endings...," he rasped.

"No death?" I asked.

"No death...," he whispered, and then, "and yes, death. Both."

At home I worked like fury on the studio. Kurt went with me to select a pair of sliding glass doors at Sears and we brought them home in a neighbor's truck. To frame the front of the studio, we enlisted the help of a carpenter and installed an old railroad tie as a header where the old garage doors had been. Then we lay down runners, measuring with the level at every step since the garage was not plumb. It took two days to construct the frame, and then another day to set the glass doors in place.

Right next to the doors, in the corner of the room, I set aside a space for my shrine. Then at night, after the family was asleep, I came down to the studio and by the light of a bare lightbulb, fashioned an alcove of redwood for my bits-and-pieces altar. It took most of the night, but when it was in place and ready to receive all my little talismans, I felt reassured. Once I had a space to dance in, I would have the power to heal. With only the oak parquet floor to go, then it was almost ready.

For what - for Paul? It didn't matter. I just knew I had to get the job done.

"Marta, this is Angie."

Her voice was urgent on the phone. Or exasperated. "Listen, Paul wants to talk to you." Strange. Paul hadn't been out of bed for awhile, and rarely spoke anymore.

"Paul?" My heart pounded at the bottom of my chest.

"Will you...take me...," his voice rasped feebly through the wires, "up to the...birds?"

"You want to go up to the hills to see the birds?" I asked, incredulous.

"Yah."

"Uh...let me talk to Angie." He put Angie back on and I asked her what was going on. She sounded at the end of her tether.

"He's adamant," she claimed. "He wants to go up to the birds and he wants you to take him. Not me, you."

"Do you know why?" I asked, trying not to hear bitterness in her voice.

"He just says it should be you. You don't have to say yes, you know. I don't know what he's up to now."

"I can do it," I breathed, not sure I could at all.

"I think he just wants to be able to see the hills - you don't need to even get out of the car," she offered.

"It's alright with you?"

"Look, it's alright with me. What can I say?" For several minutes both of us just breathed into the phone.

"I can be there in fifteen minutes," I said at last.

I hadn't seen Paul on his feet for weeks. He was more scarecrow than man, a thing of sticks and tatters - and huge blue eyes burning either with fever or some species of mischief, I couldn't tell which. They stared with intent as Angie and I maneuvered him into the front seat of my car, strapping him in like a baby and surrounding him with pillows. I regarded him half-scared, half-suspicious. He avoided my eyes.

"Do you want me to follow you?" Angie whispered anxiously.

"No. Take a break," I returned with false bravado. "You could use one."

"You don't have to keep him out long..."

"Give us about three hours," I said. "If we're not back by then, then come up. You know where we'll be."

"That's what scares me," she muttered, imagining the long

hike to the ridge where they normally went to watch birds.

"Don't worry. We'll stay close to the parking lot. I think I can handle it."

"In two hours, if you're not back..."

"Make it three," I said again, knowing somehow that whatever peace Paul had to make with the hills would take three hours and not less.

When we rounded the corner from their house, he turned his head to me with difficulty, and winked. Laughing uneasily, I winked back.

"Hah," he said weakly.

"Paul," I began aloud, continuing my thought silently. *I love you dearly, but if this is a scheme to get up to the hills so you can die amongst your beloved birds — with me in attendance — I'll never forgive you.*

I turned my head to catch his expression as I accelerated on the road up towards the hills. He gazed straight ahead of him, his eyes thirstily taking in every tree and house we passed, his face a vivid study of beatitudes.

Ours was the only car in the parking lot. The sky was clear except for an occasional wisp of cloud above the trees, and the midsummer hills were tawny with dry grasses. In the heat of the afternoon few birds flew, and I scanned the sky fruitlessly as I opened Paul's door to help him out.

"Haaaahh...," he breathed, sucking in great gulps of the earth-fragrant air. "Haaaahhh..." He scrambled feebly to get his legs out over the side.

"Why don't we watch from here?" I suggested. He gazed up at the ridge as if calculating his strength to make the trek.

"No," he insisted hoarsely. "Help me." Holding out his arms like a baby, he let me lift him from the seat and set him down unsteadily on the tarmac. Pointing a bony finger towards a cedar

atop a small knoll not far from the car, he commanded,
"T-tree."

Then he all but toppled into my arms, dragging me as we stumbled, aching step by aching step, towards the tree.

We were both panting by the time we reached the base of the cedar, and when I lowered him towards the ground he collapsed, unconscious, onto his back.

He was doing it, the devil!

For a moment I was too panicked to think. I couldn't leave him and run for help; I couldn't call - nobody would hear me. There was nothing I could do but sink to the ground beside him and hold him desperately in my arms and pray.

Why had Angie agreed to this excursion in the first place? Why had I? Did I think I was some kind of heroine or something? Why hadn't I even called Kurt and told him?

I felt my hands grow hot and still. Deliberately, I pressed them against his back, grounded myself to the earth and opened to whatever forces were watching us now.

"Please," I begged. "Help us. Please don't let him die. He *can't* die yet - please!"

My whole body, like a lasar beam directing current, focussed on my unconscious friend. I felt my boundaries melt away and fuse with his, spreading dense, thick, coursing heat through the two of us.

"Keep him alive," I prayed between my teeth. "Don't take him yet, please. He knows so much and can teach so well - please, we need him here. Spare him now. Give him a few more years - please, please..."

I rocked him in my arms, singing in a monotonous undertone. My eyes were shut tight, and I swayed back and forth repeating the same words over and over.

"Spare him please...give him time...spare him please...let him teach...spare him now...give him time...spare him please..." Still unconscious, his lips parted slightly and his breath wheezed shallowly in and out. I sensed a spark of communication between us and I listened hard. I felt a struggle going on inside him, a hand reaching out for help. With my mind, I grasped hold and pulled.

"You can stay," I intoned, addressing my prayer directly to Paul. "You don't have to go yet...There's still work to do...Stay with us, here...Paul, you can stay...You don't have to leave so soon...You've got work to do here...Please, Paul...please, Paul..." My song went on and on as the sun made its transit in the sky.

I rocked back and forth, my eyes closed and my face lifted to the sky. The words faded out to a silent prayer, stilling my body at the same time.

Like a rock - dense, immobile, only its molecules dancing their slow, imperceptible dance - I sat beneath the tree with the unconscious Paul in my arms. The earth carried us on its rounds, the galaxy spun us about our sun, and we sat still as stones, our hearts beating, our lungs breathing.

The sun shifted more, casting cool shadow. Still we did not move. Then my shell cracked open, letting in unimpeded light. It flooded through me, around me, became me. My eyes flicked wide and the world reached me, its outlines ordinary, gorgeous. My arms lowered Paul to the ground, my hands lifted away from him and came back into my lap.

Simply that.

Paul quivered, rubbed his cheek with the back of his hand and grinned up at me.

"Was I sleeping?" he asked in a normal voice, blinking. "Hey, look!" he cried before I could answer. Fumbling for the binoculars in his jacket pocket, he held them to his eyes and followed the flight of a red-tailed hawk swooping out from the branches of our cedar tree. With strong, flapping strokes it gained height above us, sailing on wind currents and circling the knoll three times. Paul handed me the glasses.

The hawk was joined by another, and then a third. All three

circled above our heads, playing with the air. I gave Paul back the binoculars and gaped at him.

Color had returned to his skin, and his eyes followed the movements of the birds, alert.

"Lookit that!" he cried as a pair of doves skittered out from under the cedar and took to the air, tumbling about as they chased each other around the small meadow. "Bingo!" he rasped happily, reaching for the canteen of orange juice we had brought along with us. "Aren't you glad we saw that?"

"Yeah..." I choked, unable to take my eyes from him. Paul was back. And he appeared to be quite unaware that he ever had been gone - or that something quite extraordinary had taken place in the course of the last two hours.

"I'll have to take you to Coyote Point one day soon," he said between swigs of juice. "If we get there early in the morning, we can see the seabirds come out by the millions - murres, cormorants, gulls - it's an amazing sight. I'm surprised we haven't dragged you and Kurt out there before this."

"Sure..." I breathed, trying not to stare.

"Soon as I feel a bit stronger...," he said, following the flight of the hawks as they circled one last time and headed out over the trees on top of the ridge. Then he raised the canteen to his mouth with shaking hands, threw back his head and guzzled the last of the orange juice.

Soon as he feels a bit stronger...as if he were recovering from the flu. I shook my head, disbelieving. Then he wiped his stubbly chin off with his fist, turned to me with a grin, and burped.

We sat in calm beneath the cedar tree until the air grew chill. The breeze ruffled what was left of his scraggly hair and he lifted his face to the wind, sniffing ecstatically. The sun, as it sank, seemed to glow right through his transparent skin. He sucked in sun like food.

"I think we ought to get back," I said finally. "Angie's

waiting." He nodded, but didn't make a move. Then he took in a deep breath and turned to me.

"Thanks for bringing me up here," he said softly.

"You're welcome, I'm sure," I replied a bit shakily.

"And I'd like to apologize..." he began, his head lowered with mock contrition, one of his old, teasing grins playing about his lips, "for being such a pig and drinking up all the orange juice myself..."

All I told Kurt was that it had been lovely up in the hills and that we had seen birds. When he asked about Paul, I just shrugged.

By the next morning, I was convinced that in my imagination I had made a mountain out of a molehill, that Paul had simply been invigorated by the fresh air, had had a good long rest and so of course had felt better for it. As for the hawks, they lived there; flying in circles above the meadows was what hawks did. So what?

But I remained restless all day. Leaving the boys to sand the plywood sub-floor, I went into the house to phone Angie. Then I thought better of it; I would just drop by unannounced. Standing undecided by the car I changed my mind and started back towards the porch and nearly stepped on a small, gray feather lying on the path.

It lay all by itself, perfectly centered on a flagstone, like a sign. I looked up; not a bird flew in the sky. I bent down and glancing about to make sure nobody was watching, I picked up the feather and brushed it against my cheek.

"Thanks," I whispered. Perhaps it hadn't been my imagination; maybe something had indeed transpired in the hills. Perhaps everything was going to be alright after all. Placing the feather carefully in my shirt pocket, I walked slowly back to the car, got in and drove over to the Bakers' house.

"What did you do yesterday?" Angie asked urgently when

she met me at the door. The dog jumped all over me, whining with impatience.

"Why - is he...better?

"He's working!" she exclaimed in a high-pitched voice. "And he ate like a truck driver this morning! I can't believe what I'm seeing."

"What's he working on?" I asked stupidly, leaning against the hallway wall for support.

"The endocrine paper he's been working on for years. He's determined to finish it, now. What happened yesterday?" She pulled me through the hallway into the kitchen and sat me down at the table. "Tell me everything!" she demanded.

"I don't know what to tell," I declared honestly. "He walked all the way to that cedar tree near the parking lot, collapsed with exhaustion, had a long rest and got up feeling much better." She eyed me suspiciously. "Oh, and there were three hawks that came out just as he woke up..."

"He was mumbling something about hawks last night..."

"And, I guess I got sort of scared and did a bit of mumbo-jumbo," I confessed with a little laugh. Folding her arms across her chest she stepped back and said,

"*What* mumbo-jumbo?"

"I guess," I finally told her with my heart in my mouth, "what I did was pray." Against my chest, inside my pocket, I felt the gray feather breathe in and out with me.

I left without disturbing Paul, and hurried home to place the feather on my new altar. The sub-floor was smooth after its sanding, and the insulation and panelling for the ceiling were piled up in the far corner with the ladders.

The feather sat right in the center of the alcove, my first offering to the shrine. I stepped back, said a little prayer for all of us, and bowed deeply - the first bow in my new studio.

FINALE

For days we cut strips of insulation and stapled them onto the old ceiling, taking turns holding and stapling. Our arms all ached and we were crosshatched with tiny fiberglass burns, but once the insulation was in the pine panels went up quickly.

Paul, meanwhile, gained weight and strength. Angie had moved back upstairs, the daily bath had apparently become a ritual, and by the radiant looks of both of them, they were back on track.

We suspended our sessions together until Paul completed his endocrine paper and Kurt and I got further on the studio. As soon as the floor was in, Paul and I would be able to add the dimension of movement to our work together.

I wanted to try dance warm-ups before the laying on of hands; I wanted to try focussing on affected body parts while actually dancing; I wanted to experiment with talking and moving at the same time. He was intrigued.

"Finish it," he said over the phone, "and when I've gotten this paper out of the way, we've got a date."

The floor went in last, after we put up shelves and hung the light fixtures, tacked molding over every raw edge in the room and removed all the tools and lumber scraps from the plywood sub-floor.

I opened the sliding glass doors, letting in the mist and green-gold light of early morning. The sub-floor, newly sanded, felt soft to the touch and cartons of square oak parquets, along with buckets of glue to affix them to the plywood, sat stacked on the grass right by the doorway, waiting. I knelt down to read the instructions on the glue-pots, and on the grass my hand grazed a long narrow feather, edged with yellow.

For a moment my heart stopped in my chest. I picked up the feather and examined it closely, wonderingly. A cat could account for it, but there were no other signs of a birdhunt. The feather sat by itself on the grass just where I might find it. I held it to my lips and kissed it, hastily bringing it into the studio and placing it next to the gray feather, before Kurt, Saul, Eva and Abram emerged from the house. Then I turned my attention to glue spreaders, rubber gloves and oaken squares.

Eva and I worked as spreaders, Abram and Saul as parquet-setters and Kurt made the necessary cuts, banging each line tightly in place before we started on the next row.

We worked bent over like planters in a rice- paddy, but instead of putting in rice shoots we were planting a floor - with glue so noxious and thick that our fingers were cramped and our stomachs nauseated after only five rows.

"Why did I ever eat breakfast...," moaned Abram, staggering out into the garden to flop onto the grass. We all groaned with him and went out to pant in the air and peel stiffened rubber gloves off our hands.

"It's revolting," I agreed, "but we can't stop. This stuff is drying hard in the buckets as we talk."

"Two at a time," directed Kurt, plunging back into the stinking studio and motioning for Saul to follow.

All day we worked in pairs - two laying tiles and three gasping in the garden. When the two could no longer work, they were replaced by two others. Lunch, in the circumstances, was out of the question.

"How about a break for a swim?" Abram suggested. Kurt regarded the room appraisingly and said,

"We won't get it done in one day if we go swimming. I don't want to still be doing this tomorrow, do you? Let's keep at it; just rest when you need to."

It was during my time to rest that Paul phoned.

"Hi," he said cheerily, in a voice that was muted, but clear. "The paper's finished. I want to send it out to *Scientific American* and want your and Kurt's reaction to it - do you have time to read it?"

"As soon as the floor's all down," I replied. "It's about halfway there, and we're all retching with the fumes."

"You're that close to finished? Well, that calls for a celebration!" he exclaimed. "I can't wait to see this. Can we start working in it by next week?"

"You bet," I returned. "In fact, why don't we plan on a little housewarming party this Sunday for the whole crowd, and then you and I can have an inaugurating session in it on Monday. O.K.?"

"Sounds good to me. Angie and I'll bring the wine - and balloons!" he said before hanging up.

By nightfall, the plywood had been covered with honey-hued oak parquets. The floor gleamed gold in the light of the newly-risen moon, and against my bare feet it felt as smooth as skin. By mid-night the fumes had dissipated and I came in, after the others were abed, carrying my shoebox filled with talismans for the shrine.

First, to the two feathers in the alcove, I bowed. Then I carefully hung up Tony's portrait of the Old Master, and beneath him tacked Joanie's drawing of Verona.

Eva's riverrock came next, and alongside it I lined up the green jade horse and its broken white jade twin.

For a long while I held the spiral shell in my hand, remembering, and next to it on the altar I lay the blue-glass chips of mosaic from Ravenna. The chalky knob of bone from Fernandina went alongside the lame white horse, as if to make up for the missing limb.

Then I lit incense, held my palms in front of my face and bowed. My talismans were in place; the studio was finished; the space was ready to be danced in.

"Thank you," I said aloud to whoever might be listening in the night. "Thank you."

The studio-warming on Sunday never took place.

Angie phoned just after lunch, her voice rigid with panic, saying that Paul had taken a fall and cracked his pelvis.

"He just bent over to pat the dog - he seems to be sinking quickly, Marta. The doctor just left and wants to move him to the hospital, but he's putting up a fuss. Could you...come?"

My mind dragged me backwards while my legs propelled me towards their house. While Kurt told the kids, I climbed the steps of the Bakers' porch, my feet heavy as lead. I nearly walked over the feather that lay right in the middle of the next-to-last stair. It was white, long and pointed. For a moment I didn't register what I saw. Then I bent over to pick it up, clutching it in my fist. Everything would still be alright.

The dog greeted me first, pressing against my legs and trembling hard. I wrapped my arms around him, but he didn't stop shivering. Angie came down from upstairs, her eyes apprehensive and we met in a strong embrace.

"It's going to be alright," I wanted to tell her and show her the white feather. But I couldn't. The dog, frantic, whimpered to come in on our hug, and still holding the feather tightly in my hand, we opened the circle and let him in.

Paul's bedroom smelled stale. The shades had been drawn against the bright sun and a bouquet of wildflowers wilted in a vase. On the bed, covered by only a sheet, Paul was nothing but a long, narrow mound topped by his bony head half lost in the shadows of the pillow.

"Hi," he said in a muffled voice. "Here we are again." The pin of the white feather dug into my palm.

"Hi. I brought you something." I held up the feather for him to see, and placed it into his upturned hand. He rubbed it tentatively with his thumb. "It was in the middle of your porch," I informed him quietly. "It's the third one I've found since we saw the hawks."

"No shit..." he declared after awhile.

"No shit," I sighed. "I've interpreted them to mean that everything's going to be alright." He closed his eyes, nodding. "This one's for you."

"Thanks," he whispered, his face resigned, but peaceful.

"How're you feeling?"

"Interesting," he replied. "Everything's going to be alright. Just the way you say. Just the way it is. Right?"

"I'm...I'm not sure what that means," I protested. "The hawks seemed to indicate something different, no?"

"The hawks can be trusted...," he whispered. The creases in his face seemed to deepen perceptibly, as if he were aging before my eyes. Spittle gathered in the corners of his mouth and he licked his dry lips with his tongue. I held his head and put a glass of water to his lips. He took a small sip.

"Sit by me," he murmured, reaching for my hand. "Listen..."

Placing my hands lightly above him, I listened. At the level of his pelvis pain stung like dark needles against my palms, but throughout his upper torso I felt a warm effulgence, like lemony-yellow light.

"Listen..." he repeated faintly.

I seemed to fall right into his dream, watching it from above. There was a stage crowded with actors, as at the final curtain of a Shakespearean play. Paul, in costume, was surrounded by men and women, children and animals, all of whom danced hand over hand, their colors weaving in and out of one another. The dance was courtly and the colors wove themselves into a gorgeous fabric which rose and fell, curved and straightened. They chanted to the audience loudly and the audience roared with applause, roared and roared...

Paul was coughing. I came to with a start and eased up his arms to relieve the strain on his pelvis. The fit brought up phlegm, and I wiped his lips. He sank back exhausted, his eyes spurting tears.

"Wha'dyou see?" he mouthed after awhile. I told him. He confirmed the vision with a smile that was half a wince. "Almost..." he whispered finally. "Remember the...fabric. Weave..." One finger made a snake-like motion and dropped again onto the sheet. "Moving...always moving. But, look - whole cloth!"

"How do I learn to see the whole cloth?" I asked, bending over him urgently. He smiled and with effort, whispered,

"Let go."

"Let go? How?"

"Watch...hawks..."

"I'll learn how to let go by watching the hawks?" He nodded. "Is that what the feathers were really saying?" His eyes, rheumy and blurred, glistened.

"Let go." The room was silent except for his labored wheezes.

"You want to let go?" I asked in an undertone after a long while.

"Yah." A finger plucked at my sleeve, and his face gathered intention. Pulling together his strength, he laboriously formed a sentence. "Watch - after...for breath!"

"What?" I bent over again, concentrating.

"After death...watch for my breath."

"You mean...you won't really be gone?" His eyes flickered, impatient.

"Subtle breath. You'll see it. They...won't. Watch...watch..."

"What does it mean?"

"Means...I'm still there. Listen...still listen..."

Exhausted, he fell into an open-mouthed sleep, his hand still light on my arm. I sat and watched him sleep until Angie came up.

"I'm scared," she shivered, gazing at her sleeping husband.

"Would you like Kurt and me to stay with you?" She nodded mournfully. "Let me go call him and get the kids squared away. I'll be back in less than an hour."

"Come back," she begged.

By the time Kurt and I returned, Angie had called Paul's brother in Boston, neighbors had begun dropping off food and offering help and Paul's doctor had been by to see him. Kurt sat by the telephone and Angie and I took turns in the sickroom. Paul lay comatose, his body seeming to shrink beneath the sheet.

We stayed through the night, dozing and waking fitfully each time Paul made a move. He seemed to float in and out of consciousness; from time to time a disconnected phrase would be uttered, often too mumbled to be understood, and one time he opened his eyes, scrutinizing us intently before drifting back into sleep.

In the morning, when Kurt went to pick up Paul's brother Jed at the airport and Angie had gone downstairs, I leaned over and boldly whispered in Paul's ear,

"Where are you?" He spread his fingers on the bedsheet, unable to coordinate speech. A sound emerged from his lips, not quite language. With two fingers he formed a V, like a stylized bird in flight.

"Flying?" I asked. His nostrils dilated slightly in assent. "With the birds?" I added. He almost smiled.

When Angie came in to take over, I stumbled into Paul's study and fell into a deep sleep. Kurt had left to spend some time with the children and Jed, now sharing the vigil, sat with Angie by Paul's side. Downstairs, friends and neighbors gathered, bringing food and waiting for news. They held tense, whispered conversations, like family around an expectant mother after labor has begun.

After my nap, I slipped back into Paul's room, hovering beside him with his wife and brother.

"Paul," I said to him silently, gazing down at his unconscious face, "it's just like you were giving birth - everyone's downstairs waiting for the baby." In my mind's ear I heard him chuckle.

"At last," I thought I heard him say. "It's about time I got to be a mother."

By that night, Paul heaved with the effort of drawing breath in and out. Angie, Jed, Kurt and I stood around his bed, our attention fixed on the man disintegrating beneath the sheets. Once, he opened his mouth unexpectedly and cried,

"Empty pockets!" and fell back into his coma again. We gathered more tightly around him, watching.

"He wants us to hold hands," exclaimed Angie, reaching for mine on one side and Jed's on the other. The four of us formed a circle around Paul, breathing with him as he sucked in huge breaths and wheezed them out with body-shaking shudders. It seemed more than his fragile frame could stand. I sensed his ascent, the impression of light swelling inside and around him. A slow, warm joy, it built up like the pleasure that precedes orgasm. Sexy. It rose, growing sweeter and sweeter, shimmering as it gathered fullness.

"*That's it!*" I seemed to hear him crow. He brimmed, triumphant ,towards his climax.

"*That's it! That's it!*
Life is the foreplay!
Death is the climax!"

Panting, his breaths surged towards his new shore, faster and yet faster.

"*Love it!*" he seemed to be crying. "*Love your life! Don't lose a second! And when it's over, LET GO!*"

"*I'm flying, dear ones, I'm flying!*

LET'S...GET...ON...WITH...THIS!"

FINALE

Angie's grip suddenly tightened.

"He's....flying with the hawks!" she exclaimed, sobbing.

I clung to her hand, transfixed by Paul's leavetaking. His body continued to take in gasps of air, but Paul had left. He had flown the coop and was up there, soaring with the birds. Even Angie had witnessed it.

We were held upright around his worn-out shell as if strung there by invisible guy-wires. Paul's body still sucked hard on the air of the world, spitting it out again by force of habit. It was going to take more than mere Death to stop Paul Baker.

Another gasp and the engine broke its own rhythm. The last breath escaped with a rattle that shook the room.

He was gone.

For a long time we wept in each others' arms, Paul lying at peace amongst us. His death bonded us, as the birth of my children had initially bonded Kurt and me with him.

"You saw it happen, didn't you?" Angie cried over and over. "He flew right up to be with his beloved birds! I saw him go! I saw him fly!"

We sobbed into each others' shoulders, then held onto each other as we gazed down at Paul's body.

"Watch for the subtle breath," he had admonished me. I saw no motion, only the strangely still figure of my friend. Angie, with shaking hands, lifted the top of the sheet, preparing to draw it over his face.

"Wait!" I cried.

"Why?"

"I'm not ready yet," I mumbled lamely. Pulling over a chair I sat down and tried to focus my attention. I stared, watching for something, but could see nothing. Angie began to grow restless, and whispered to Jed that someone should go downstairs to let people know. The sheet clung to the shrunken contours of Paul's wasted body, outlining his figure.

"Paul, I can't see it," I complained silently, concentrating with all my might.

"Let go," I heard. Of course.

I took a deep breath and relaxed, closing my eyes for a moment of centering, and then opened them more passively. Easy concentration. As he had been trying to teach me all along. I listened as I looked - and yes, I saw it. A minute expansion and contraction breathed his body, like an angel's breath. The breath after death. Paul had indeed given birth.

"Go well on your way, my friend," I prayed silently as Angie lifted the sheet and draped it over his face. "I will miss thee powerfully much."

"Listen...." was the last thing I heard as we left the room, Kurt and me first, then Jed, then Angie.

I looked back one last time before Angie closed the door and it was clear as the nose on my face - Paul was still breathing.

My studio, in the early morning light, glowed like honey and amber shot through with sun. The air, fragrant with dew and flowers, hung with dappled green mist. Only birdsong broke the dawn's stillness.

Still dressed in my nightgown, I stepped onto the oaken floor and looked around. The floor took my weight and gave it back to me, alive. If only Paul could have lived to see it.

In the center, a leaf had fallen, probably blown in by the wind. I stooped to pick it up, but close-to I saw that it was not a leaf at all, but a curling brown feather. Downy. Still warm.

Bursting into sobs, I held it to my lips, wetting it with my tears.

Paul. Paul. The sun sent a shaft of sunlight through the open skylight, which pooled yellow on the golden floor. It lit the whitewashed walls and spread onto the objects on the altar.

Cupping the new feather in my palm, I carried it reverently

FINALE

to my shrine and bowing, placed it alongside the others beneath the portrait of the Old Master.

I breathed in the fragrance of fresh wood and morning light. Facing the East I bowed, and facing the South, I bowed.

Turning West towards the garden, I bowed, and to the North, I bowed again. In every direction of the compass my studio rang true.

I lifted my arms to my sides, my chest still heavy with weeping, and brought them slowly above my head.

With one foot I beat out a rhythm, and twisted my hips to the side. Leaning into one leg, I tilted until the momentum caught me into a wide, swooping circle around the space.

It grew faster, tighter.

Within it I twirled around and around until, with a dizzying leap I broke out of its confines and spun in the other direction. The air swirled like wind around me, flowing in eddies about my arms, my legs, my torso.

There was nothing that could stop me - not even Death.

I breathed in the world, lifted my whole being towards the Light, reached out with my arms and I danced.